4/14

$26.95
B/CLAIBORNE
McNamee, Thomas, 1947-
The man who changed
the way we eat

*f*P

The Man
Who Changed
the Way We Eat

◆

CRAIG CLAIBORNE AND
THE AMERICAN FOOD RENAISSANCE

THOMAS McNAMEE

FREE PRESS
New York   London   Toronto   Sydney   New Delhi

B
CLAIBORNE

FREE PRESS
A Division of Simon & Schuster, Inc.
1230 Avenue of the Americas
New York, NY 10020

First Free Press hardcover edition May 2012

FREE PRESS and colophon are trademarks of Simon & Schuster, Inc.

For information about special discounts for bulk purchases,
please contact Simon & Schuster Special Sales at 1-866-506-1949
or business@simonandschuster.com.

The Simon & Schuster Speakers Bureau can bring authors to your live event.
For more information or to book an event, contact the Simon & Schuster Speakers Bureau
at 1-866-248-3049 or visit our website at www.simonspeakers.com.

Manufactured in the United States of America

1   3   5   7   9   10   8   6   4   2

Library of Congress Cataloging-in-Publication Data
McNamee, Thomas.
The man who changed the way we eat: Craig Claiborne and the American food renaissance /
by Thomas McNamee.
p. cm.
1. Claiborne, Craig. 2. Food writers—United States—Biography. I. Title.
TX649.C55M38 2012
641.5092—dc23
[B]
2011049125

ISBN 978-1-4391-9150-7
ISBN 978-1-4391-9151-4 (ebook)

This book is dedicated to
The Stomach Club—
in particular
Miles Chapin,
Roger Sherman and Dorothy Kalins,
and Michael Anderson.

CONTENTS

The Man
Who Changed
the Way We Eat

A Sensation

Putting a piece about food on the front page of the *New York Times* was unheard of, but on April 13, 1959, they did it.

ELEGANCE OF CUISINE IS ON WANE IN U.S.

Two time-honored symbols of the good life—great cuisine in the French tradition and elegant table service—are passing from the American scene. . . . Cost control cramps the enthusiasm and inventiveness of master chefs. . . . Training facilities for cooks and waiters are virtually nonexistent. Management and union officials are apathetic. . . . Menus soon will be as stereotyped as those of a hamburger haven. . . . Americans seem always to be in a hurry. . . .

Humbert Gatti, executive chef of the Plaza Hotel, predicts: "Within five years kitchens à la minute will replace haute cuisine in America's major cities. The public will be offered broiled steak, broiled chicken or broiled fish. Or only sautéed dishes. No more sauce Champagne. No more sauce Robert, no more filet of beef Wellington. Even today, you walk into kitchens that don't have a stockpot. . . . I know places with a big business where they don't use ten pounds of butter a day."

The New York restaurant world was stunned. You didn't come right out and say things like this. It wasn't just New York, either. Restaurateurs across the country were outraged. There was no such thing as food criticism in those days, no such thing as a restaurant critic. Newspaper pieces about restaurants were written to please the advertisers. Food articles usually relied on recipes sent in by readers or on corporate press releases. And food writers? A few did exist, but M. F. K. Fisher, good as she was, never complained, and James Beard's judgment was for hire.

This was something entirely new. The writer, Craig Claiborne, had been the food editor of the *New York Times* for a year and a half, but until this moment he had been largely ignored by the brass. Their concerns were more serious than the decorators and couturiers and casseroles touted in the small section headed "Food Fashions Family Furnishings," commonly known as the women's page, where Craig's work had till now always rather obscurely appeared.

What nobody realized was that Craig Claiborne was going to become the most powerful force American food had ever known.

§

The editor of the women's page had always been a woman, and it had always been the custom at the *Times* to speak only sparingly of restaurants, and always politely. What had been noticed, vaguely, of the new, male editor was that he was a somewhat foppish Southerner with a distinctly literary style and an air of scholarly authority, but nobody high up had paid much attention to him till he pressed forward quite aggressively with his idea for this piece.

This was Craig Claiborne's dream job. New York was where he was meant to be; his element, he'd felt it from his first moment; the glamour and the gaiety, so many chic women, so many such good-looking men, the dark hum of power unceasing under it all. The voice of the *New York Times,* the ultimate voice of authority, was now his. And he had more than a dream; he had a plan. He was going to teach America what good food was, and bad. With his intelligent and sympathetic criticism, a new excellence would arise.

He had looked forward to an exploration of fine dining in America's leading fine-dining city, but New York's supposedly best restaurants were proving quite a disappointment. Craig had been classically trained in cooking and in service at the best hotel school in the world, in Lausanne, Switzerland, and he had learned there just how fine the degrees of excellence were that could be discerned by a well-trained palate and a discriminating sense of taste. He expected to find in the serious restaurants of New York a more than ample arena in which to exercise his critical faculties. The city had, after all, attracted a plethora of French and other European chefs brought up in the rigorous traditions of their homelands. The farms of northeastern America were capable of growing fruits and vegetables as good as those of Europe. The region's pastures were rich and abundant. The Atlantic and its bays, sounds, and estuaries teemed with fish and shellfish. Jet planes could now bring to these shores fresh European wild mushrooms, truffles, Normandy butter, sole fresh from the Strait of Dover, even the matchless fishes of the Mediterranean—turbot, Saint-Pierre, *loup de mer*. Money was no constraint in the postwar boom years, and the topmost restaurants of New York charged accordingly.

By the end of his first year and a half at the *Times,* however, Craig was fed up. His experience of the city's restaurants—with one exception—had ranged from dispiriting down. Though he longed to celebrate the greatness that he knew a serious restaurant could achieve, time and again he found himself stymied. He really believed in his mother's old Southern maxim that if you can't say something nice, you shouldn't say anything. If a place displeased him extremely, his preference was not to write about it at all. When pressed by his editors, he would comment only with his native strained reticence. Of Maud Chez Elle his faint praise was that "It is to this establishment's special credit that the beans were cooked properly."[1] One can picture him blinking in prim dismay at Trader Vic's "Scorpion, a gardenia-bedecked potion served to four persons from one container equipped with four straws." It seemed to pain him even to mention the Trader's "Queen's Park Swizzle and the Doctor Funk of Tahiti."[2] One easily deduces his thrill at covering the opening of a new branch of the Stouffer's chain in Garden City, Long Island, of which he managed to observe that it had "a capacity for 586,"[3] or the Continental Restaurant, in a shopping center in Paramus, New Jersey, where the closest he could come to saying anything nice was that "Opulence and a long menu are very much in evidence."[4]

The great exception was Le Pavillon, a grand French restaurant in Midtown Manhattan descended from the French government pavilion at the 1939 World's Fair in Queens and now ruled by the tyrannical Henri Soulé. Soulé was a snob to the public and a despot to his staff, but when it came to the classic *haute cuisine* of France he was an exacting perfectionist, and the food that emerged from his kitchen was superb. Le Pavillon was not only the best restaurant in New York; it was considered among the best in the world. Craig loved everything about the place.

In early 1959, he had persuaded his editors that the extreme contrast between his standards, as embodied in Le Pavillon, and the reality of dining in New York anywhere else was a story he ought to spend some time on. Once he got the go-ahead, his reporting for the piece was exhaustive. Interviewing classically trained chefs, he found nearly all of them institutionally thwarted. They were bitterly angry over union rules, cheapskate owners, arrogant waiters. Some of the restaurateurs, chefs, and dining room staff he talked to were long since hardened to sloth and corruption. But at Le Pavillon he found precision, excellence, devotion, and cooking nothing short of sublime.

Having had so many bad experiences as a diner, and so sharing the anger of the willing but frustrated workers behind the scenes, he concluded that the only proper course for his piece was to indict New York's restaurants across the board, to identify the non-inevitable causes of their mediocrity, and to show in the example of Le Pavillon that excellence was possible. Back in the newsroom he couldn't stop typing. The piece got longer and longer. Craig might have expected his editors to tell him to throttle back—this was only a piece about food, after all—but they didn't. He also wanted a big photo spread, mainly of the kitchen at Le Pavillon, and they agreed to that, too.

This was a quite surprising request to make of a restaurant. One did not look into restaurant kitchens, and one did not photograph chefs. Too many kitchens were greasy, grimy workplaces, too many chefs growly old bloody-aproned laborers. The legendarily intractable Henri Soulé, however, told Craig that the *New York Times* would be most welcome in the kitchen of Le Pavillon.

The kitchen was spotless, and the chef, Pierre Franey, in his starched white apron and tall toque blanche, was startlingly young for a chef of such prestige—thirty-eight, Craig's own age—and strikingly good-looking. The distance between the excellence of Le Pavillon and the absence of it in all the rest would be illustrated by a step-by-step series of photographs, adjacent to Craig's piece, showing Franey preparing a

4

whole fish stuffed with a mousse of sole and then covered with a Champagne sauce and garnished with a skewer of fluted mushrooms and black truffles. In another photograph, obviously of another restaurant, trays of tired, preheated food populate a steam table.

The headline type was small, and below the fold, but still it was on Page One, and the continuation inside took up most of a page: The piece was twenty-four hundred words long, a length the *Times* granted only to articles the editors deemed to be of real significance. It was a public sensation, but it would prove significant for Craig in another, entirely unanticipated, and personal way: He and Pierre Franey would become friends, and then professional partners; and they would work together for the next almost thirty years.

As for Craig's criticism, "Elegance of Cuisine Is on Wane in U.S." was just the beginning. It wasn't just New York restaurants that he had it in for, and it wasn't just high-end restaurants. It was nearly everything about food in America.

What Craig Claiborne saw when he looked out across the vast expanse of the United States was a gastronomic landscape blighted by ignorance and apathy, a drearily insular domain of overdone roast beef and canned green beans. The more he learned of it, the bleaker it looked. American food was terrible, and it was getting worse.

Household after household was losing its connection to the past. Old family recipes were consigned to attics, even tossed out with the trash. Canned-soup casseroles, Reddi-Wip, Swanson's TV Dinners, instant coffee, Cheez Whiz, and a host of other abominations—reinforced by relentless advertising of unprecedented effectiveness via the suddenly ubiquitous medium of television—were freeing the American housewife from drudgery, and lulling American households into culinary torpor.

World War II had given American women a taste for employment and the sense of autonomy that it engendered, so much so that the prospect of "going to work"—out of the house, and collecting a paycheck of one's own—had become a powerful social force. Making fresh coconut cake with vanilla boiled frosting and braising a mushroom-stuffed shoulder of lamb all afternoon really didn't fit the picture anymore. Slapping together some dehydrated onion soup, a can of tuna, and some Miracle Whip, however, with a layer of nice crunchy Fritos on top and half an hour in a hot oven, while you, exhausted, and your equally worn-out husband put your feet up and watched the news (and the commercials)—well, that was not too bad. Add in some kids, and it wasn't only not too bad, it was, or soon came to seem, indispensable.

Peg Bracken's *I Hate to Cook Book* was widely popular, and genuinely funny, in part because it was so embarrassingly true to the psychological reality of the home cook of the day:

Just shut your eyes and go on opening those cans.[5]

When you hate to cook, you owe it to yourself never to pass the canned Welsh Rabbit shelf in your supermarket without adding a few cans to your collection.[6]

Speaking of this, recipe books are always telling you to get a can of a ready-prepared dish and spike it with something, as though the product isn't quite good enough for you as is. . . . But my own feeling is that you should give the prepared thing the benefit of the doubt and *taste* it before you start spiking. After all, those manufacturers have worked themselves loop-legged in their sunny test kitchens perfecting a formula that a lot of people like.[7]

The people of the United States had little connection to the great cuisines of the world. With the exception of the isolated pockets of recent immigrant groups who had maintained their cultural traditions, Americans just didn't know what was possible. Chinese food was chop suey and chow mein, and did not even remotely resemble what real Chinese people ate. Italian food was pizza (Chef Boy-Ar-Dee from a box!) or spaghetti and meatballs. French? Something that called itself *cuisine française* could be had only in the biggest cities, and even there it was bastardized beyond anything anyone French could have recognized.

The United States had no equivalent of the great hotel schools of Europe, or of the rigorous apprenticeship system of Europe's restaurants. Most restaurant cooks learned their trade from existing restaurant cooks who themselves were barely competent. In his front-page jeremiad Craig had pointed with some relief to the "one person making a valiant effort to perpetuate classic cookery in this country . . . Mrs. Frances Roth . . . administrative director of the nonprofit Culinary Institute of America."[8] The CIA was literally the only fully developed professional cooking school in the nation, and, at the time, frankly not a very good one.

In many parts of the country, there were few restaurants of any kind. In others, there might be a diner here or there, or a simple town café, or a boarding house, or a hotel dining room. When Craig was growing up in the Mississippi Delta, the nearest decent restaurant to his home was hundreds of miles away, in New Orleans (and it would have been pretty good, too). His mother served delicious Southern and Creole food in her boarding house—which meant that young Craig's exposure to good food was truly exceptional.

Now at last from his high promontory at the *New York Times*, looking out across the whole dreary landscape of American food, he knew his challenge, and his great opportunity. If, bringing all his skill and all his knowledge to bear, he could elevate food, cooking, and dining to the level of significance he believed they should occupy in American life, he could be a cultural critic on a par with the paper's critics of art, music, books, and the theater. He could change the way Americans ate, the way they thought about food, the way they lived. He could bring a realm of pleasure into their lives of whose existence they had previously not even known.

2

Beyond
the Delta Horizon

Craig Claiborne spent much of his childhood in fear. Any child in the Mississippi Delta had good reason to be afraid. There were poisonous snakes everywhere, wasps that stung like fire, hookworms that bored in through the soles of your bare feet and ate up your insides, dogs on short chains that when they howled their masters beat them and when they got loose might bite a child just for smelling of fear. Ordinary punishment at school could be a paddling mean enough to raise blisters.

Craig had more reason for fear than the other children did. His junior high athletics coach was also a teacher, and on the first day of the term he asked everybody in arithmetic class to write down the sport they'd be playing. Craig wrote his name but no sport. "I see we've got a sissy in the class," said the coach.

In his memoir, *A Feast Made for Laughter,* Craig wrote: "From that day on in junior high and high school, I became the victim of a bunch of childish thugs who took delight in tormenting me."[1]

The disparity between Craig's mother's airs of aristocracy and the family's all too apparent poverty didn't help. They tormented him often enough that his terror of the next ambush was constant.

No adults came to Craig's defense, no teacher, no friend, neither his mother nor his father. But there was nothing notable in this situation. The Delta was hard country. Since the time when Andrew Jackson brutally cleansed the forests of Chickasaw and Choctaw Indians and set them on the Trail of Tears to Oklahoma in the middle 1830s and on into the present day, agriculture has been the only way of life the Delta has known. That life has always been very rich for some and very poor for others, and rich and poor in violent fluctuations—violent, and hard.

The Mississippi Delta is not to be confused with the estuary at the great river's mouth, three hundred miles to the south. A flood plain bounded by the Yazoo and Mississippi rivers, the Delta stretches from its northern extremity just below Memphis, Tennessee, two hundred miles to its southernmost reach. It is seventy miles wide at its widest and roughly a pointed oval in shape. It is virtually all dead flat, and when the rain comes—and rain there is frequent and heavy—it is mostly either mud or under water. For tens of thousands of years, the Mississippi's silt-laden floodwaters had poured across the Delta every spring, leaving behind layer on layer of the powder-fine soil known as loess. Then came revetments and levees, measures of heroic ambition and magnificent expense, the twentieth century's concrete dreams of containing the river's feral course. They will without question be defeated someday, as so many other of the Delta's illusory dreams already have been.

In the first years of settlement and for generations thereafter, before the advent of modern engineering and hydrology, human attempts to convert the Delta's swamps to agriculture were a never-ending nightmare. The Delta's forests were mephitic jungles. The mud sucked down whole mule trains. Malaria and yellow fever struck again and again. By the turn of the twentieth century, only a third of the land had been cleared.[2] But what soil! All topsoil, all the way down, the richest soil in the world—capable of sustaining astounding yields of one of the world's most demanding and most lucrative crops: cotton.

Cotton made the people of the Delta hard—black and white, slave and free, sharecropper and planter, janitor and banker, housemaid and housewife—for the economy of cotton required cheap, abundant labor, not only in the fields but in sweeping your floors and fixing your dinner. Slavery, the War, Reconstruction, yellow fever, depressions in 1873 and 1893, the merciless racism of the Jim Crow laws, the World War—each of these, too, had made the people of the Delta harder. Big fortunes came to the hard and lucky.

Lewis Edmond "Luke" Claiborne came to the Delta from Tennessee in

Lewis Edmond "Luke" Claiborne,
Craig's father.

1892 in search of one of these fortunes. Three brothers, William, Samuel, and Augustus Craig, along with their sister, Mary Kathleen Craig, arrived from Alabama the same year with the same idea. In 1898 Luke Claiborne and Augustus Craig joined forces to establish the firm of Craig and Claiborne. Three generations later, Mary Kathleen would write:

> The county was undeveloped, no roads as there was no drainage so most of the year the few roads were impassable. One small railroad known as the "Yellow Dawg" ran in the morning from Yazoo City to Clarksdale & back at night. You had to grasp the seat in front of you every little while to keep from being jostled into the aisle . . . as the road bed was so rough.
>
> There were only three white families in the town, many negroes, no school, no church. Rev. Stevenson Archer held services every few months here coming from Greenville on the train when possible or in a canoe if the train couldn't run. . . . Malaria was quite prevalent, having no doctor they would send a hand car nine miles to Moorhead Miss. for Dr. J. W. Lucas. . . .

Over the next thirty-odd years Craig and Claiborne acquired interests in a mercantile business, a construction company, a grist mill, a cotton gin, and—always most important in the Delta—land, farm land, a great deal thereof. In 1907, Luke Claiborne married Mary Kathleen Craig. He was thirty-two years old, she seventeen. Luke and Augustus built new houses across the street from each other in the hamlet of Sunflower, Mississippi. By 1919 Luke was president of the bank of Sunflower.

The people of the Delta did not see far beyond its hazy horizons. Luke Claiborne believed that he was growing rich during and after the Great War. Cotton prices, indeed all crop prices, were rising spectacularly, first as the farms of Europe were soaked in blood and their farmers died in the millions, and then, in the postwar recovery, as mills were built and demand grew still greater. Cotton doubled in price between 1916 and 1919, with prices outrunning demand in a quintessential bubble. When agricultural markets collapsed worldwide in 1920, the price of cotton fell by half, and Luke Claiborne was ruined. He was not a hard man. For the rest of his life, he remained quiet, prayerful, and withdrawn: stunned to immobility.

The poverty that ensued for his family was therefore ineradicable, and it was into that fixed position that Raymond Craig Claiborne was born on September 4, 1920.

Against all the evidence, the baby's mother deemed the family to be aristocrats only temporarily indisposed and herself an unbowed grande dame. Reduced to keeping a boardinghouse, Miss Kathleen, as she was known to all, maintained her illusion with long white dresses, monogrammed silver, fine china, and crystal. The family may have been harried from house to rented house by debt, but she set the most formal and immaculate of tables, and the elegance of the service was known throughout the Delta. She, like her mother, had gone to college, Judson College, in Judson, Alabama. What was more, she had studied music at the conservatory in Birmingham.

Craig's father could not bring himself to play along with his wife's great-lady act, and so kept to the shadows. "There was a sadness about him in my early childhood," Craig wrote, "that I believe transmitted itself to me,"[3] while Craig's sister, Augusta, eight years older than he, and his brother, a second Luke, four years older than Craig, both "seemed to have been in emotional control, unfazed and undaunted by the Depression."[4]

"I suffered in silence in my family's poverty," Craig remembered. "I had an extremely delicate nature and I was often on the verge of tears. . . . engulfed with childhood feelings of self-doubt and inadequacy."[5]

Craig's mother apparently reinforced his sense of delicacy. When the boy had been diagnosed with "a slight heart murmur," "she started to treat me with excessive concern, reminding me relentlessly that I was 'fragile.'"[6] He sought warmth in the arms of his nurse, "Aunt Catherine," but when the family moved from Sunflower to the larger town of Indianola, Aunt Catherine was left behind forever.

Craig remembered his father with a certain dark sexual strangeness, a subject to which this narrative will return. In *A Feast Made for Laughter,* the language of his memory is so opaque as to seem at times to fuse with dream—a danger to which he was attentive: "There is a condition that is known as childhood amnesia," he wrote, "that stems from feelings

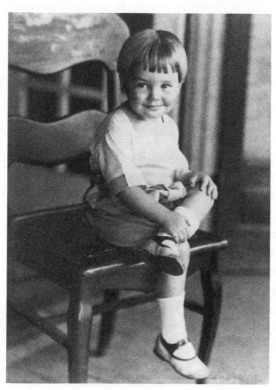

Craig Claiborne, 1923.

13

of desolation, loneliness, and deprivation in the formative years of life, and . . . I am confused as to the precise dates of certain acts that caused uneradicable scars on my spirit and well-being."[7] To find the shape of the actual events of his childhood in the mists that shrouded them would be the largely fruitless work of years of psychotherapy, a source of bitter frustration for the rest of his life.

Miss Kathleen was a species of grande dame who might have been expected to keep her distance from the kitchen, but Craig's mother did know food and was proud of it. At the boarding house she served her gentlemen a fare of considerable refinement—not only old-time Southern dishes like cornbread, hushpuppies, greens, sweet potatoes, hominy, okra, field peas, fried chicken, country ham, Brunswick stew, fruit pies, layer cakes, ambrosia, and homemade ice cream, all executed with finesse, but also Creole cuisine, which she had learned in New Orleans and had taught to her cooks: jambalaya, grillades and grits, gumbos of every sort, oysters Rockefeller, shrimp rémoulade, crawfish étouffée, red snapper *en papillote*. It took some doing to get that fresh seafood to Indianola, Mississippi, but she did it.

Working in a kitchen like this was one of the best jobs an uneducated black person could find in the Delta. It didn't pay well, but then nothing did. You got plenty to eat, however, and there were always people around to talk and laugh with, and once you got the cooking and the serving to suit the lady of the house, the white folks pretty much left you alone. Miss Kathleen was a battle axe, no question about it, but she didn't holler and scream, she didn't dock people's pay, she didn't fire people unless they rightly deserved it, and when she said such a dish needed such and such, she was nearly always right. Mr. Luke never stuck his head in the door, nor the two older children either. Just that sweet little sissy boy Craig.

The kitchen was where Craig found refuge. He would sit in the lap of the head cook, Blanche, and lean into her soft bosom as they waited for something baking in the oven, and together they would flip through the pages of a picture book (Blanche was probably illiterate). Just for him she made coconut cake, ambrosia, fried chicken gizzards. Sometime she would let him stir a gravy or baste a roast. In the kitchen he could be quiet and calm.

Craig also finally managed to find friends—two. David Sanders was a poetic, erudite, not-of-this-world young man of such perfect self-

Craig on the lap of "Aunt Catherine,"
with his sister, Augusta, and brother, Luke Jr.

assurance that none of the sort of eccentricity-phobic opprobrium that rained down on young Craig and himself meant the slightest to him. From David, Craig learned that simply ignoring contempt could be a sufficiently effective defense against it.

Gordon Lyon was Craig's other close friend in their teenage years. He was a bluff and hearty regular guy who, Craig would write, "liked girls and comic books. . . . On Saturday nights, we would sometimes go to nearby roadhouses with a couple of girls and dance to a jukebox." Craig also wrote that his "great joy was spending weekends in his home, innocently sharing his bed." Though Craig's mother found Gordon's mother "a bit common, a good deal beneath her"—quite the opposite of the actual case—Gordon's father was wealthy and also the mayor. His mother played golf and smoked cigarettes, "then a far-out thing for a woman to do."[8] Gordon's friendship showed Craig that he needn't be nearly the misfit he had felt himself to be.

By fits and starts—often compelled by his interest in food—Craig widened his sphere of acquaintance, and his sense of the larger world. Through Mr. Colotta, the fish dealer, Craig discovered that in little Indianola there was a real Italian community. Craig came to idolize a Jewish girl and, invited to her family's seder, was initiated into the mysteries of matzoh ball soup, matzoh brei, and gefilte fish. A Mexican pushed a cart through the town hawking hot tamales. Craig's father's sister Elizabeth Claiborne came home from years of service at a Methodist mission in China with dragon-figured porcelain bowls, ivory carvings, and fascinating stories of delicate children, the classification of Chinese flora, and the massacre of missionaries. Aunt Elizabeth taught him to use chopsticks, which "to this day I prefer . . . to knives and forks."[9]

As Craig's interest in the world beyond Mississippi made him a rare child, it was a rare inhabitant of that wider world who took an interest in Mississippi. So when Professor John Dollard, of Yale University, came to Indianola to conduct the sociological field work that would lead to his epochal *Caste and Class in a Southern Town,* he arrived with more local knowledge than the natives expected. Such was the renown of Kathleen Claiborne's board, said Dollard, that there was no question of where he should lodge.

The book vividly portrays Dollard's discomfort in the exotic, isolated, rigidly stratified, and racist society of the Delta. He lived, he wrote, with an unceasing "sense of torsion, willing but unable to conform to the conflicting elements in the social pattern."[10] But in the Claiborne house he also lived comfortably, and ate well.

Craig by then was in high school, and he still sought refuge in the kitchen, where he drew comfort not only from the staff's kindness but also, now, from his unambiguously higher social rank. His father had fallen from a foothold in what Dollard called the lower upper class, and although Miss Kathleen fancied herself entitled to membership in the Mississippi aristocracy, her values and behavior showed her to be firmly anchored in the upper middle class, where church, respectability, dignity, order, and rules were paramount. The upper class of the Delta—

Miss Kathleen: Mary Kathleen Craig Claiborne,
Craig's mother.

and they were few—got drunk, raised hell, and had affairs. Church was for weddings, funerals, and Easter, and that was all. They lived in houses with names, their farms had names too, they were all kin to one another, and they knew who they were and who wasn't them, and though the Claibornes on both sides had the ancestry, they didn't have the wealth or at least a sphere of wealthy acquaintance, and even if their ancestors may have known how to behave, they didn't. Which is to say, badly.

Another Yale researcher, Hortense Powdermaker, also studied social class in Indianola, and her guide was the indubitably upper-upper-class writer William Alexander Percy. If he had happened to befall Miss Kathleen Claiborne and her aristocratic airs, the best he might have

17

accorded her would have been a sniff. According to Percy's standards, Indianola was

> a town where [Powdermaker] found no genuine members of the white upper class. After she reported on an initial meeting with an edgy and suspicious group of Indianola's leading white citizens, Percy responded with scornful laughter and told her, "Now you have just seen the flower of our Southland." Powdermaker was struck by the openness of Percy's contempt for the status-conscious middle-class whites in that community and by the way in which they deferred to Percy in spite of his obvious disdain for them.[11]

One of John Dollard's findings was that the members of the upper class tended to get along very well with their servants, or at least believed that they did. The families, black and white, had often been together for generations. When one of "your people" was broke, you lent him money. When the sheriff threw one in jail, you got him out, and for good measure left the redneck cop with a flea in his ear. *His mama raised me,* was all you had to say to your friends, and they all understood. You and that boy—a "boy" who might be fifty years old—y'all could count on each other.

Drop down a notch on the social scale, however, and a wariness set in on both sides. A maid in a middle-class house could be out on the street in two shakes, and in Mississippi that could mean starving, and her children, too. Once, "a Negro friend" came to call on Dollard at the Claibornes' and "knocked on the *front* door," which caused "strain in the social atmosphere of the house thereafter."[12] Race relations in the Claiborne home, as in nearly every other *respectable*—which is to say middle-class—white household in the Delta, kept a tight grip on an uneasy peace.

But in the Claiborne kitchen, because Master Craig had grown up there and was such a sweet child, and mostly didn't put on bossy airs, the comfort seems to have been genuinely shared. That paradox—of unexpressed hierarchy underlying overt classlessness—would forever be characteristic of Craig Claiborne's sense of social comfort. And the fragrances of old-fashioned Southern cooking would always evoke it.

§

Craig started at Mississippi State College, in Starkville, and even was tapped for the properly prestigious Pi Kappa Alpha fraternity. The raucous, back-slapping, football-rabid sheer testosteronality of the place was such anathema to him, however, that, as he had done when a child, he withdrew inside himself. His fraternity brothers, as was to be expected, abused him, and he would not react. His mother had persuaded Craig that he wanted to become a doctor, but his premedical science courses baffled him. "I got the vapors at the scent of formaldehyde, fainted at the sight of blood, and at the midpoint of my sophomore year, I did not, to my recollection, have a passing mark in any of my studies."[13]

Craig insisted on remembering his time at Mississippi State as uniformly miserable, but he kept a poem for many years among his effects that reveals that he seems to have fallen in love there, with a woman at the nearby Mississippi State College for Women. The poem is dated November 16, 1943, four years after the scene it describes. The object of his affection is probably older and probably married, at least at the time of writing, and the poem also posits a formal distance between them—which might be courtly, or might be kidding—for he addresses her as

My dear Mrs. Wood,

September, September!
Pack the bag and grab the C.&G.—God, it's hot,
But the nights, the Sunday nights at M.S.C.W. will be cool—
And well lit,
Good evening, Miss Kearn,
Sure, we'll be back. Soon as the Golden Goose closes.
(The Blue Goose don't close.)

. . . It smells of gardenias (cape jasmine),
And carnations. Gardenias
And carnations. Then reverse.
"Time on my hands, you in my—." Oops! Dropped
Your program.
Your beautiful white program that says
"Pi Kappa Alpha Autumn Prom, __ September 193_."
Oh, pardon me,

I didn't mean to bump into—into—
. . . Are those eyes really yours,
Or have I suddenly stumbled eternity's length
Toward heaven?

[The poem goes on at considerable length, liberally quoting, misquoting,
and paraphrasing several popular songs of the day.]

. . . You're drunk.
Drank too many beers
Gardenias and carnations.

But I gotta. Goodnight.
No, not another second.
I've got a ten minute quiz tomorrow,
Besides,
I'm sleepy—.
Besides,
we've got the rest of our life for this.[14]

Craig never said that his romance with Mrs. Wood, or its ending,
had anything to do with the fact that by the midpoint of his sophomore
year at State he had applied to transfer to the highly regarded journalism school of the University of Missouri. While there, he would recall,
he tried to take a girl to a dance but split his borrowed formal pants right
beforehand (and then "Chances are I got drunk"); wrote a musical comedy called *Much Ado About Mary,* which won a prize; and "Other than
that, the days I spent at the University of Missouri seem highly forget-
table and insignificant."[15]

The Japanese attacked Pearl Harbor on December 7, 1941—the
December of Craig's senior year—and when a United States Navy
recruiter came to the campus that spring in quest of volunteers for officer candidate school, Craig applied. He was turned down, however,
owing to "a malocclusion of the upper and lower teeth."[16]

Well, he was accustomed to embarrassment by now, more or less, and
it was his custom to swallow hard and press on.

3

War and Love

Somehow Craig had managed to graduate from journalism school without having mastered the typewriter. It was June of 1942, and he was determined to defend his country in war, and perhaps also to get away from yet another place he did not care for, but the navy evidently didn't want any even slightly buck-toothed officers. Now he found himself prohibited from enlisting even at the lowest rank, as a yeoman third class—essentially, a secretary—by his inability to type. Undaunted, he threw himself into a six-week crash course at the keyboard and was thereby enabled to join the navy's intelligence division in July. His first posting was to Chicago, where his duties consisted primarily of sorting mail, stuffing envelopes, and—typing.

The boredom didn't last long. It was followed, at first, by total confusion. He found himself well belowdecks of the heavy cruiser U.S.S. *Augusta,* steaming across the Atlantic, mission unstated (at least to yeomen third class). His baffling assignment was to write up random lists of nouns.

The *Augusta* was a legendary ship: She had until recently served as President Roosevelt's flagship in his early war-planning meetings at sea with Winston Churchill; the president of the United States had also enjoyed fishing from the *Augusta*'s forecastle. General George S. Patton and Rear Admiral John L. Hall Jr. were now aboard, to oversee the imminent invasion of North Africa.[1] Craig had not the slightest idea of any of this.

His random nouns turned out to be prospective names for various operations within the invasion, and when the moment came, Craig would be on deck, engaged in a bloody and terrifying battle. The *Augusta* anchored off Casablanca. From her bridge Patton commanded some thirty-five thousand ground troops. More than a hundred Allied ships moved in on Casablanca, including five American aircraft carriers. Vichy French submarines, German U-boats, and massive artillery defended the harbor.[2] From November 8 through November 12, 1942, there was seldom a doubt that the American forces would prevail, but the shelling and extreme danger were constant. The *Augusta* came under heavy fire in five separate engagements, yet somehow the ship remained undamaged, and not one member of the crew was so much as wounded. Through it all Craig maintained an eerie detachment: "I was witness to an awful lot of bombardment and more than a little carnage . . . I watched ships sink, bodies fall overboard, and the gunfire was deafening . . . [but] the entire show . . . seemed more like a celluloid spectacle. . . ."[3]

What Craig chose to remember, and vividly, was the blissful aftermath. On the Atlantic crossing, he had forged a special friendship with his lieutenant, "which had gone beyond the ordinary course of an officer–enlisted man relationship."[4] After the battle, the lieutenant was going to go ashore with Admiral Hall himself, chief of staff of the whole naval task force, who was now going to be stationed in Casablanca. Craig asked if he could come along. The next thing he knew, he was offering himself up as the admiral's personal secretary, and being smilingly accepted.

One of the many things Craig had not known when he joined the navy was that over centuries, on those long, long voyages far from home and mother, the navies of the world had evolved a whole subculture of men who loved men. If you knew what to look for, the evidence was all around you. The naval uniform spoke a language not difficult to understand. The swabbies' white bell-bottoms, with their placketless crotches and bun-hugging seats, couldn't have sent a more stylish signal of welcome to those who wished to see it as such. (One misread it at one's peril, of course.) The officers' dress uniforms—the buttons, the cutlasses, the aiguillettes, the symmetry, the neatness, the *just-so*-ness— and, oh, add a pair of MacArthurian dark glasses—and a tall, handsome *admiral*——

The fact was that Craig was barely getting around to admitting to himself that he was—well, this narrative will employ the term "gay," though its usage in the contemporary sense was all but unknown then.[5] It is difficult for many people now to imagine the clandestinity, the lies, and, for not a few, the shame imposed, in those years, on gay men. There was not even a word for what they were that was not either a clinical diagnosis or a term of abuse. The love that dare not speak its name? It was the love that *had no name*.

But the navy was a fairly safe place to be gay, as long as you avoided disastrous misidentifications. And Casablanca was famously a dandy place to be gay. Craig was "fascinated by the many soldiers and sailors who would come out of those half-dark doorways, some still buttoning their trouser fronts."

Moreover, the food of Casablanca was like nothing he had ever tasted. He found himself invited into the home of Moroccan strangers, friends of his friends, to sit cross-legged on their fine carpets and dine on "magnificent lamb couscous with sweet dried fruits and that best of all hot sauces, harissa."[6] The admiral, the lieutenant, Craig, and their friends all ate—messily, voluptuously—with their fingers.

As death and horror continued their rampage across Europe, Craig and his officers spent the next eight months sampling the tagines, the bsteeya, the countless varieties of olives, dates, oranges, lemons, and spices of Casablanca. Craig discovered a Parisian *pâtisserie* and fell in love with *barquettes, tartelettes,* fruit pastries of every description. He found a little French restaurant in Casablanca called La Comédie, where he learned to love the simple classics of Parisian bistro cuisine— grilled chicken, roast chicken, omelettes. He could not dine there with his lieutenant, however, because "it would not have been proper, I believe, for him to have been seen dining with an enlisted man."[7] (He and the lieutenant traveled into the Moroccan hinterlands on weekends, but the subculture also knew when to lie low.) Craig's friendship with the couple who owned La Comédie grew so close that he began to visit them at home, and to call them *Maman* and *Papa*. And at long last, it was with his commander that he had sex for the first time in his life.[8]

§

Craig's naval life was not, however, all *crème pâtissière* and trysts in the souk. Admiral Hall and his staff were now to be headquartered at Oran, Algeria, and on the rough drive overland from Casablanca, Craig was obliged to make use of an army latrine, the stench of which caused him to vomit violently. In the navy, afloat or ashore, one had proper toilets, showers, hot and cold running water. But there was still a real war on, and Craig saw plenty of it, serving under Admiral Hall in the monthlong Allied invasion of Sicily from July to August of 1943, as well as the harrowing landings at Salerno in September.

At the admiral's office in Oran, Craig intercepted a naval directive asking superior officers to make recommendations of enlisted men for officer training back in the States. He promptly took out a clean sheet of stationery bearing the letterhead of Admiral John L. Hall Jr. and on it typed up a recommendation of Yeoman Raymond Craig Claiborne for said training. He then inserted the letter in a tall stack of correspondence which he knew the harried admiral would sign his way through without a glance.

Thus it was that in February of 1944 Yeoman Claiborne found himself back on American soil, at the University of Notre Dame. Three months later—the program produced what were known as "ninety-day wonders"—he emerged an officer.

Ensign Claiborne was promptly made executive officer of a submarine chaser, patrolling the English Channel. He did not chase any submarines, nor, fortunately, was the converse ever the case. He was sent to Okinawa for the last, horrific battle of the Pacific, and there served on another sub chaser. This was a very, very dangerous job, but the main thing Craig remembered of it was watching mildly from his deck as Japanese kamikazes howled out of the sky to smash into American aircraft carriers and explode in flame and gore. As at Casablanca, the violence seemed less than real to him: "It looked like something theatrical and somehow removed from my very own uniformed existence." With equal sangfroid he recalled that "there were mines everywhere . . . [but] every time we launched our mine-sweeping gear, it sank."[9]

Like many another veteran of World War II, Craig Claiborne chose to favor remembering the sentimental or the comical over the horrible. Wrestling a jeep across the Sahara evoked in him a "sweet surge of masculinity."[10] Nursing his leaky and understaffed sub chaser back to Hawaii after the Japanese surrender—with an uncalibrated compass, a corroded sextant, a non-transmitting radio, and no radar—he recalled not the terror of being basically lost at sea but that "old navy saying, 'When in danger or in doubt, run in circles, scream, and shout.'"[11]

Somehow, in the midst of his sub chasing, mine sweeping, and staying alive, Craig had received and signed a most curious document. Apparently the flame had continued to burn between him at sea and Mrs. Wood in Mississippi—the same to whom he had written the poem in 1943—for after he had received the document, written in her hand and already signed by her, he added his own signature, thereby making it a sworn statement. He kept it for many years.

MARRIAGE INSURANCE

Within 6 months after September 15, 1944 the undersigned do solemnly swear to be joined in holy matrimony, with the provision that neither of the aforesaid has been theretofore married.

> Signed
> *Mary Frances Wood*
> *Raymond Craig Claiborne*[12]

This was obviously serious, and it makes nearly certain that even though Craig had addressed her as "Mrs." less than a year before, if she had been married then she certainly wasn't now. Perhaps her husband had been killed in the war? Perhaps she was long since divorced. Impossible to know. And what happened after this solemn vow? Again, it is impossible to know.

Was he genuinely ambivalent even now about his sexual identity? Could he have been—both now and in the poem—just messing with Mary Frances Wood's mind? That seems like more cruelty than he could have been capable of. Occam's razor tells us to take him at his word, but on this subject Craig never said another one.

§

After the war, Craig was quite sure that returning to Mississippi would be unbearable, and he was intimidated by the very thought of New York.

I went to Chicago because I had met a guy who was gay in the navy. And I didn't realize it, that there were other people who were gay besides me. He introduced me to this whole crowd of gay people. And I was wild. It was that time, when everybody was coming home from the war, from World War II. And every night there'd be another party for somebody who was gay and coming out of the navy or the army. . . .

[My friend] encouraged me to join the publicity department at ABC. . . . After I'd been there about a year, I told [my boss], I said, "[Boss], you know, I'm gay." And he shrugged his shoulders. So the next day I told [my friend], "You know, I told [my boss] I was gay last night." And he said, "What did he do, give you a raise?"

I decided I was going to bed with somebody at one of those parties. I said, "I'm going to take [this guy] home." And I said, "What if you get that stuff in your mouth? What do you do, swallow it?" And [my friend] said, "Get out, girl, leave me alone." He couldn't believe the innocence.[13]

Chicago was not all high jinks. Craig worked hard at his public relations job, though he didn't like it much. With a gift from his sister of *The Joy of Cooking,* he was making himself a popular dinner party host. He even managed to sell two short pieces on food to the Chicago *Tribune.* And for the first time in his life, Craig fell in love.

Somehow, however—he never did say how—his mother "fouled that affair."[14] Elsewhere he explained the end differently: "Those fires of a first passion [had] cooled to the point of extinction and no amount of heavy breathing could rekindle them."[15] Craig's memories of stressful events involving his mother sometimes came in multiple versions, and sometimes failed altogether.

Although Miss Kathleen was not physically present in Chicago, she maintained a constant and irritating presence in Craig's consciousness. In 1945 she had attended the Antoinette and François Pope School of Fancy Cooking there,[16] and in 1948, when Craig was learning to love to cook and earning praise for it, *Liberty* magazine published a glowing account of Kathleen Claiborne's boarding house cuisine—her sweet potato biscuits, her three-layer party salad, her coconut cake. She was haunting him. By 1949 he was ready to clear out of Chicago, and the United States too.

§

Craig Claiborne's Paris in 1949 and 1950 was pretty much like every other young American's Paris, a swirl of foggy streetlights and ancient beauty, arias and trolley clatter, late-night cigarette smoke and early-morning bakeries. A drafty walkup. An orange-haired landlady out of Toulouse-Lautrec.

Thanks to the G.I. bill and a modicum of frugality, he had arrived with the minor fortune of a thousand dollars in savings at his disposal, which went a long way in those days. His visits to good restaurants were few nonetheless. Those few, however, left vivid impressions. Of scrambled eggs with tarragon he remembered, "I had never tasted such heavenly food." Of *choucroûte à l'alsacienne* at the Brasserie Lipp: "[I] ached with the glory of knowing for the first time the grand heights to which sauerkraut could be elevated." His first taste of *sauce béarnaise* produced an "ecstatic trancelike state." *Pommes de terre soufflées* "were almost more joy than one body could contain."[17]

After a brandy-soaked trip to Italy with a reckless American girl, in the course of which he was robbed of his remaining fortune, Craig set sail for home aboard the grand old liner *Île de France,* where he tasted what a column of his in the *Times* years later would headline as "The Fish Dish That Changed His Life"—*turbotin à l'infante,* which translates, awkwardly enough, as small turbot in the style of the princess of Spain. He asked for the recipe and found it next morning—in French, of course—slipped under his cabin door. It was nothing more than fish baked in white wine and fish stock, sauced with a reduction of the cooking liquid enriched with egg yolk and butter, but it dazzled his young palate as nothing had before. The recipe referred to that cooking liquid as a *fumet de poisson au vin blanc,* which confused him, because he hadn't tasted anything smoky in it. It was years before he learned that a *fumet* has nothing to do with smoke.[18] It is a stock made with fish bones or flesh, white wine, and seasonings.

When Craig returned to Chicago and the doldrums of public relations, his life once again felt aimless and stale. Then in the summer of 1950 the Korean conflict broke out. He was still a member of the U.S. Naval Reserve, and he quickly volunteered for active duty. He was assigned to serve on the destroyer escort U.S.S. *Alfred Naifeh* as operations officer. "To this day I would be hard put to describe what an operations officer was, except it had to do vaguely with communicating from one vessel to another, plotting maneuvers, and so on and so on to the point of total ennui."[19]

Craig's recollections of this war seem almost entirely to omit that it *was* a war. The fact was that the *Naifeh* shelled holy hell out of North Korean coastal batteries, railroads, and factories, and she dodged plenty of artillery bombardment in return. Betweentimes, the *Naifeh* escorted an aircraft carrier, cleared floating mines, ran cover for South Korean torpedo boats and minesweepers, hunted down submarines, and blasted away with her guns as required,[20] but the closest Craig came to describing all this was "maneuvers."

He did have a lot on his mind. Foremost was the fact that he fell in love with the *Naifeh*'s skipper, Captain John Cornelius Smits. And in the midst of all these maneuvers, bombardments, mine-clearing, submarine-hunting, ennui, and romance, Craig began for the first time in his life to think seriously about his future. When his two-year enlistment expired, in the summer of 1952, he was going to be facing his thirty-second birthday.

So. He liked to cook. He loved good food. He believed he wrote well. Could he make a living writing about food?

It seemed unlikely. The little food columns in newspapers were just that: little. And they were always down in the middle of the women's page. And they were always written by women. They were dumb, too—mostly dumb recipes that some reader sent in, for pound cake or tuna casserole or some damned congealed salad based on Jell-O.

What if he were to do it differently? Better, and bigger? Much better and much bigger?

First, he would have to know a lot more. He could no more prepare a *turbotin à l'enfante* than swim from Pyongyang to Paris. He still didn't know why the fish *fumet* hadn't made it taste like smoke. Paris, then: That was where the knowledge was. He would study at the Cordon Bleu, the most famous cooking school in the world.

He wrote to his mother to tell her what he was going to do with his life.

Of the fateful subsequent event he told two stories.

The one he wrote in *A Feast Made for Laughter*, published in 1982, is, "She wrote to tell me that only the night before she had met the banquet manager of the Peabody Hotel in Memphis, Tennessee . . . [who] had spoken in enthusiastic terms of . . . L'École Professionelle de la Société Suisse des Hôteliers. Or, in English, the Professional School of the Swiss Hotel Keepers Association."

In 1992, however—ten years after that book's publication, and, as will be seen, a long ten years—in a graduation talk at the Culinary Institute of America, he remembered it this way: "I met a fellow seaman who said, If you want to learn to cook, why don't you go to the finest hotel school in the world? It is called the Professional School of the Swiss Hotel Keepers Association and it is [in] Lausanne, Switzerland. . . . His brother had attended the school and he was then manager of one of the largest hotels in the South, the Peabody Hotel in Memphis, Tennessee."

The essential datum here is surely the presence of Craig's mother in the one version and her absence in the other. "Over the years, in times of stress, my memory pulls a disappearing act,"[21] he wrote—and behind the stress, very often, lay the shadow of Miss Kathleen.

Craig applied to the hotel school at Lausanne only to find it already fully enrolled for the next twelve months. The school did say, however, that it would be happy to accommodate him thereafter.

He re-upped, therefore, for another year in the navy and obtained an assignment as "chief port director" on a small Pacific island by the name of Kwajalein, in the Marshall Islands chain, which is about as far from anywhere as it is possible to be on this earth—twenty-five hundred miles of open ocean southwest of Honolulu, twenty-five hundred miles of open ocean southeast of Japan.[22] In San Francisco he equipped himself with the latest in audio technology: a long-playing record player and some of the new 33⅓-rpm records (Verdi and Puccini) that it required. He also bought a Bible and the complete works of Shakespeare, and was ready for war in the South Seas.

Craig assigned himself quarters with a terrace that opened directly onto the beach. On the terrace he installed a refrigerator and a small stove, where he turned out simple dishes—poached eggs in Mornay sauce, fish fresh from the lagoon. Gin was sixty-five cents a bottle. It was as quiet and contemplative a life as he could have dreamed of. As for his duties as port director, "I doubt that ten ships a year put into that magnificent harbor. . . . Each day that followed another on Kwajalein was as much like the day just past as the waves that lapped the shore. . . . "[23]

§

Between 1946 and 1958, sixty-seven American nuclear weapons were tested in the immediate region—high in the blue air, balls of blinding flame, burgeoning mushroom clouds, howling winds of anonymous poison—including, in 1954, a hydrogen bomb that was the most powerful weapon of any kind to have been detonated in the history of the planet. In 1956 the Marshall Islands were declared by the U.S. Atomic Energy Commission as "by far the most contaminated place in the world."[24] The people of Kwajalein were forcibly relocated to a shantytown on the islet of Ebeye, popularly known as "the slum of the Pacific," where they continue to this day to live in poverty. Kwajalein Island remains under lease to the United States government as part of the Ronald Reagan Ballistic Missile Defense Test Site. Its only inhabitants today are American military personnel.[25]

Good at Something

His fingernails were clean and neat. His fingertips were not trembling. This being Switzerland, he had learned not to smile so readily. He was not calm, he had never been calm, but he was resolute and that was new. At the age of thirty-three, Craig Claiborne believed that he had found a means to end his adolescence: two years of study at the École Professionnelle de la Société Suisse des Hôteliers—the Professional School of the Swiss Association of Hotel Keepers—in an atmosphere of uncompromising steadfastness and devotion.

On the shore of glittering Lake Geneva, in the ancient, cosmopolitan city of Lausanne, the school was founded in 1893, when Swiss tourism and hospitality were at their most glorious—the time when young English aristocrats commonly traveled to Switzerland on their Grand Tour, often staying for weeks or even months. Mountaineering and skiing were newly popular. Artists and writers came from all over the world for the mountains' beauty and tranquility. Swiss banking's tradition of secrecy made the country a natural attraction to the very wealthy. Between the early nineteenth century and the outbreak of the first world war, about a hundred grand hotels were built in Switzerland, and it was to serve their needs for peerless excellence in management, cuisine, and service that the school had been founded. It was the oldest hotel school in the world, and when Craig arrived, it had long been regarded as the finest.

Nearly all other hotel schools were private, profit-making ventures; this one had always been pure of purpose and strictly nonprofit. It was housed in the Hôtel d'Angleterre, with the French-speaking and very

Swiss city surrounding it and very much determining its culture, conjoining the gentility of old-fashioned French service and the punctilious discipline of Switzerland.

Study was organized into three courses, each a year long, all of which were mandatory: cuisine, service, and management. In each, you would spend six months in house, in study and practice, and six months in the field, working as an intern in hotels and restaurants chosen by the faculty for having the most exacting standards. Craig's first interest was in cuisine, and he had no interest whatever in management. He was greatly surprised to find himself fascinated by service in all its forms—from folding bed linens to waiting at table to understanding the organization of the service corps of a hotel or restaurant.

Craig and fifty of his classmates in the *cours de service* stood at rigid attention in a long straight line, trying not to shiver in the freezing alpine dawn. Each wore a starched white jacket, a black bow tie, and creased black trousers. When Monsieur Michel stopped in front of him, Craig presented his clean pink hands and well-shaven pink cheeks for inspection, and huffed a little cloud of impeccably fresh breath into the professor's face. Bad breath would have been a severe infraction.

The boys and the few girls of the service course were required to serve those of the *cours de cuisine*. Craig loved the precise disposition of the flatware and china on the table. He kept a notebook of meticulously geometric drawings of all the proper settings. He loved the crispness of the linen napkin that he had learned to carry just so over his left forearm. He had always loved things neat and well ordered. His fellow students struggled to get things right that were all but instinctive to him—they were so young. His years in the navy had given him many advantages, not least a sense of discipline and order so thoroughly inculcated as to be unconscious.

From a chafing dish on a bright-polished brass wagon he served *escalopes de veau à la viennoise*, moistening each veal cutlet with lemon juice and brown butter, ranging around it three separate little arcs of chopped hard-boiled egg whites, egg yolks, and parsley, then centering a slice of lemon on the cutlet and on that an anchovy rolled into a ring around a single fat caper. He did it all without dropping a crumb. Bending at the waist, back straight, napkin and left forearm remaining horizontal, he placed beside the veal a large, smooth dome of *purée de pommes de terre*.

Behind him, he heard a sharp intake of breath from Monsieur Conrad Tuor, the most distinguished professor of the school, whom Craig both feared and worshiped. "Mr. Claiborne," he said—in French; no other language was spoken here—"nothing is more vulgar than an excess of food on the plate."[1] Monsieur Claiborne's carefully shaped serving of mashed potatoes was too large, too much; it was *gross*. For the rest of his life Craig would abhor immoderate servings.

§

In those long, slow days on Kwajalein, Craig's full intention for himself had gradually taken clearer form. By the time he arrived in Switzerland he was happy to accept a truly exacting discipline—something he must have expected from the military but had seen hardly a whit of in it. He was also ready to work hard. From the moment he arrived in Lausanne, he believed he knew where he was going to go when he left, and that was New York, and he believed he knew what he was going to do, and that was to write about food. In his last, languid months in the South Pacific his aim had narrowed further yet: He was going to write about food for the *New York Times*. It was an impossibly narrow (not to mention hubristic) goal.

For the first time in his life, Craig's attention was fully engaged at Lausanne. His fellow students were certainly serious. Half of them were Swiss, with that particular Swiss seriousness about dedication to one's profession; many of them were members of families that already owned old, well-known, and beautifully kept hotels in Switzerland. The other half of the student body were from countries around the world, and they also had come with a single aim in mind, either to run or to own a grand hotel, or else to climb a corporate ladder. Some of these were the ones who would turn out to be the stiff-backed Old World hôteliers mocked in Hollywood comedies but, alas, real enough. Some would be well prepared to evolve into blandly competent executives in the coming age of hotel chains.

The students who came from hotel-owning families, especially the Swiss—too often misunderstood as cold because they were so reserved—tended to have hospitality in their blood, a natural warmth, an affection for service, a graciousness, an almost unconscious sense that making an extra effort for a guest, no matter how trivial or absurd the request, or even when there had been no request, could contribute to the person's happiness, and therefore to the hotel's own happiness and therefore to one's own. This was the quality that Conrad Tuor and his colleagues most admired, and which they sometimes found it difficult to impart to the students who did not arrive with it already in their blood.

Greatly to their dismay, M. Tuor and the general director, Paul Barraud, found that economic ambition and a drive for prestige seemed to be the primary motivations of a growing proportion of the students. It was necessary, certainly, for any good hôtelier to understand budgeting, efficiency, personnel management, and accounting. But there were more and more students to whom this represented the *real* world, to whom cuisine and service were what in the real world one hired others to do—or, in a company sufficiently large, hired others to hire others to do.

Today, in fact, the École Hôtelière de Lausanne, its name newly simplified, also known as the Lausanne Hotel School because it is resolutely bilingual, matriculates some eighteen hundred students of eighty-eight nationalities, with a faculty of about a hundred and a staff of four hundred drawn from more than thirty countries. In 1975 the school left the Hôtel d'Angleterre behind for a gleaming high-tech campus surrounded by lawn and forest at Le Chalet-à-Gobet in the mountains outside Lausanne. And while there are still students from little family-owned hotels up in the Alps, there aren't so many little Swiss hotels like that anymore. What EHL, as it calls itself now, mostly does these days is prepare its graduates for the world that had been rather cynically foreseen by Craig's management-minded classmates, the corporation-dominated world that has become the real one.

The school now grants a four-year bachelor of science degree in "international hospitality management," "in response to the increasing complexity and diversity of the hospitality industry and the need to make decisions which are informed and far-sighted at both operational and strategic level" and a master's in "hospitality administration," equivalent to an American MBA, for people already in the business but seeking advancement or those in other fields looking for a change of career. Graduates may end up in the hotel industry, but many find jobs in banks or other corporations in which hospitality is a growing aspect of their business. EHL also consults with start-ups, develops accreditation systems for other countries, and assists in designing market research projects.[2] In short, fifty-five years after Craig Claiborne's day, nearly everything about the school has changed.

§

Craig had not imagined that in Switzerland he would discover inside himself a great advantage and a well of inspiration in his childhood hours in the kitchen and dining room in Indianola. The memory of those aromas, and of those countless meals at his mother's boarding house table, where lonely men found such pleasure and comfort in delicious food and one another's society, still quickened his heart. Surely that deep memory and its association with kindness and good company were the source of the instinct for hospitality that M. Tuor recognized in Craig.

Conrad Tuor's formality was the structure that held in place a generous heart. What the best students learned at Lausanne was not only warmth but empathy: In the courses of cuisine and service you were not learning to *be* chefs and dishwashers and waiters and busboys, you were learning what it was *like* to be them, and by the time you were finished you would be able to do nearly any job in any hotel. You would have felt the blast of the pastry ovens, known the mortification of spilling hot soup down a lady's neck, and scrubbed floors till your knuckles bled. You would also have played the part of the guest, cosseted when lucky, soup down your neck when not.

For the rest of his life Craig would know in his bones both the drudgery and the exhilaration of restaurant cooking of the highest order. Craig's bible was written by none other than Conrad Tuor. It was titled *L'Aide-Mémoire du Sommelier*—"The Sommelier's Handbook"—an odd name, for it was an encyclopedia not only of everything a wine steward must know but also of everything a fine waiter must know, or a true chef, and, if he expected to graduate, every student at the École Professionnelle de la Société Suisse des Hôteliers. The range and precision of knowledge M. Tuor demanded seemed almost inconceivable.

> The waiter should be quiet, quick, and never intrude on the customer. . . .
> When serving soup, take great care to avoid dipping one's thumb in it. . . .

Never give a dishonest reply to any question. Never lean one's hand on the table or on the chair back.[3]

White wine is poured from a greater height than red wine, that is to say from 5–10 cm above the glass. If the wine is of the sparkling type, it can be poured from quite high up, so that the bubbles of carbon dioxide are freed as it enters the glass and rise to the surface of the wine in the famous "star" form.[4]

You had to memorize and memorize—drinks, sauces, preparations of every imaginable foodstuff. Cocktails: Angel Face, Baby's Special, Big Boy, Blue Lady, Breakfast, Caruso, Charlie Chaplin, Dixie, Doctor, First Love, Gypsy, Pink Rose, Pluie d'Or, White Nun. . . . There were eighty-one of these, plus four kinds of Flip, six Fizzes . . . Cobblers, Egg-nogs, Grogs, Sours, Coolers, Daisies, Collinses . . . sixty-two specific consommés, including *Andalouse, Bouquetière, Brunoise, Célestine, Crécy, Diablotins* . . . ninety-nine veloutés, crèmes, purées, soups, potages . . . one hundred sauces . . . forty-nine recipes for tournedos of beef alone—never forgetting, to take one example, in which fashion the artichokes were to be incorporated in which garnishes (*Clamart,* artichoke hearts filled with peas; *Cussy,* artichoke hearts filled with mushroom purée; *Givry,* diced artichoke hearts, slices of fried onion, and parmentier potatoes; *Masséna,* artichoke hearts filled with bone marrow) . . . kidneys, livers, sweetbreads, brains . . . woodcock and snipe, *à la crème, Financière, flambée, grillée, Hongroise, Souvaroff.* . . .

Scores of dishes, hundreds, and all to be committed to memory. In the *cours de cuisine* you had to learn not only how to cook and serve each dish but also the provenance of its name: *Agnès Sorel,* mistress of King Charles VII, 1422–1450; *Bragance,* Portuguese royal family removed from the throne in 1910; *Chantilly,* a commune in the department of the Oise; *Cyrano (de Bergerac),* French poet, 1619–1655. . . .

Craig kept scrupulous notes, all recorded in French in a hand far neater than he would ever write in again. He kept those notebooks all his life. Twenty-five years later, he would write a single phrase in the center of an otherwise blank sheet of paper: "an obsession with order and arrangement."[5]

School life consisted almost entirely of work. There were no sports, no games, no songs, no clubs, no outings, no band, no gym. Craig had one close friend, a young American named James Nassikas, who would go on to manage a number of the best hotels in the United States, and to own the Stanford Court in San Francisco. "When I was an undergraduate at the University of New Hampshire," Nassikas recalls, "I was supposedly studying hotel management, but it was all theory. From the moment you started at Lausanne, though, they were handing you pots and pans. It was hands-on. On a typical day in the *cours de service* you were at your station at seven a.m. You'd serve breakfast to the other two-thirds of the student body."

—Faculty prowling the floor for false moves?

"Exactly. Then for the rest of the morning you'd have classes."

—A lot of memorization?

"Oh, my God. The memorization. Then you'd serve luncheon. Classes all afternoon. We got a one-hour break in the afternoon. Every day, all day, we're wearing starched white shirts, black ties, white jackets—to class, everywhere. Shoes perfectly polished. *Une place pour chaque chose, chaque chose à sa place*—that was the motto. One place for each thing, each thing in its place. Then dinner service. After dinner we had cleanup. That was till eight-thirty or nine o'clock."

Craig's social life was close to nil. His sex life was absolutely nil—the slightest hint of his kind of sex life would have meant immediate expulsion, no questions asked, no appeal. After dinner cleanup he might have time for a short game of bridge with Helen Nassikas, Jim's wife and a fellow Southerner, while Jim slipped away to the movies—"to learn French," Nassikas recalls, which was something Craig never did get very good at. There would be more work waiting at home: washing, pressing. "You took care of your own uniform," says Nassikas, "and it had to be perfect. Some of the kids would try to make their shirts last two days, and they'd be downgraded for that. Haircuts also. All this would go to a category on your report card, under *ordre*. Oh, yes, and *ponctualité*. God help you if you were late for anything."

They had every third weekend off, and then Craig and Jim and Helen might treat themselves to dinner at Chez Max in Lausanne. "Entrecôte and pommes frites! Very reasonably priced, but we still had to scrape. Craig hated it when there were candles on the table, because they interfered with your sightlines of one another."[6]

In summer also you worked. Craig spent his first summer at a little family hotel on a lake in the Alps. The family Reinhard embodied all the sweetness, and the plainness, of old-fashioned Swiss hospitality. The Hôtel Reinhard was so high in the mountains it could be reached only by aerial cable car. Craig cooked, he made beds, he mopped floors, he scrubbed toilets. Yet he was never tired. It was the happiest summer of his life so far.

To serve, to serve well, far from impugning his dignity, could be an act of grace; and to cook well was to nourish, to nurture, and could be an act of love. Combine them, and you had what would suffuse Craig Claiborne's writing about food: his love of beauty, his insistence on it.

§

Craig's second year at Lausanne, his *cours de cuisine,* could not have begun more auspiciously. He loved to cook, and he loved the exactitude and grace of the formal presentations of the *haute cuisine*. He also loved the feeling of being very good at something, which he had not often been. He was "starting to feel like an adult for the first time in my life."[7]

At Christmastime he made his way back through the snows to the Hôtel Reinhard, and with the family's encouragement, and despite his lifelong aversion to exercise and sport of all kinds, he undertook to learn to ski. It was a disaster. Half-frozen and gasping at the foot of his first non-beginner's slope, he found himself coughing up blood. Pneumonia followed.

What to anyone else would have seemed an expression of kindness and concern—a phone call from his mother to one of the chief instructors of the school, inquiring after her son's health—was to Craig Claiborne "an insupportable humiliation. Here she was, her whole presence filling that room and smothering me, her infant son, her thirty-odd-year-old babe in the cradle."[8]

Craig survived his mother's astral projection—though the hospital stay did cost him the period of instruction in ice sculpture and the working of spun sugar—and he graduated a quite respectable eighth in his class.

He was ready now: to shed the skins of infant, adolescent, sailor boy, party boy, student dependent, and to take on the life of a man.

5

Spring Like a Cat

It was, legendarily and in fact, a city of dreams: So many New Yorkers, especially the ones on high, had dreamed themselves there from somewhere else. The Mississippi boulevardier felt right at home, felt no need to swallow his accent; yet he was also so nervous that on his pale pink cheeks there appeared, for the first time since half his life ago, a spattering of pimples. As his mother would have done, he carried himself as though the blemishes did not exist, and within the first month of his arrival that happy spring he had telephoned the food editor of the *New York Times,* Jane Nickerson, and asked her if she would like to interview "a young man who knows all about French cooking and a lot about wine."[1]

On May 10, 1954, the name of Craig Claiborne made its first appearance in the *Times*: "Graduate of Swiss Hotel School Tells of Study of French Cooking," by Jane Nickerson. The "fresh-faced young man . . . was eating a lunch that included, among other things, a Martini and a shrimp cocktail," she wrote. "One put down Mr. Claiborne's choice of such Americanisms to his gladness at being back in the United States, where he plans to write about food professionally.

"Mr. Claiborne showed a modest pride in his fish in white wine, as well he might, we thought, after he had showed us the recipe. For it was so elaborate and long as to fill a column of newsprint. . . . He advised American home cooks to become familiar with the savory flavor created by white wine."

This was where Americans' knowledge of the culinary arts stood in 1954: Cooking with wine was a novelty.

Craig could easily picture himself in Miss Nickerson's position, face-to-face with a wilderness of gastronomic and culinary ignorance, and far more capable than she of conquering it. He could bring scholarship, his prodigious technical skills, and European panache to a perspective on American food; and he would not be buffaloed by pretension. "I knew that my professional credentials were beyond dispute," he would write years later. "There wasn't a poorly made sauce that could be palmed off on me. . . . I knew the names of the *répertoire de la cuisine* from *américaine* and *andalouse* and *anglaise* through *viennoise* and *zingara* by heart and taste. . . . I could not be traduced by an uppity waiter or *maître d'hôtel* or a second-rate *chef de cuisine*."[2]

But he knew also that the job he had in mind did not much resemble the job that existed, and he knew how slim his chances were of getting it. The food editor of the *New York Times* had always been a woman, immured in the section that was officially headed "Food Fashions Family Furnishings" but known by all as merely "the women's page." The headlines of Miss Nickerson's columns spoke eloquently of everything Craig relished the thought of undoing, and of how far his vision was from American reality:

FRUIT AND EGG FLUFF

PACKAGED FRESH JUICE SALES GAIN

A THRIFTY FRUIT TO ENLIVEN WINTER MEALS

HAM AND EGGS TOP LIST OF WEEK-END BARGAINS

ZESTFUL TRICKS FOR CANNED FOOD

Craig bivouacked with some kindly distant cousins on Staten Island, and started pounding the pavement. He landed a job making phone calls to prospective customers of the banquet department of the Waldorf-Astoria Hotel; five days of cruelty from his boss did him in. He went from magazine to magazine with his two little nine-year-old clippings from the Chicago *Tribune*—his entire published oeuvre—and Jane Nickerson's piece about him from the *Times,* making as much as he could of his training at Lausanne and his journalism degree. The editors were kind, but they had no work for him. And then that fall, Ann Seranne, the editor of *Gourmet,* suggested he try a piece for her on tea.

It was a Friday afternoon. Craig walked directly to the New York Public Library at Forty-second Street and Fifth Avenue and frantically scribbled a hundred-plus pages of notes. He worked all weekend, and on Monday morning at nine o'clock he showed Miss Seranne his article. She liked it. She would pay him three hundred and fifty dollars for it, she said, and she'd like him to try another, on the subject of vodka. She liked that one, too.

Craig Claiborne, professional food writer, was launched. He decamped from Staten Island and took up residence in the heart of Manhattan, at the West Side YMCA. "Steeped in History" was published in the January 1955 issue of *Gourmet*, "Blithe Spirits" in March. Three hundred and fifty dollars was very good money—the equivalent of $2,800 today.

Craig spent the summer of 1955 tending bar at an upstate rat hole called the Do Drop Inn, and then that fall, with great relief, he accepted from Ann Seranne the position of receptionist at *Gourmet*, at a salary of five thousand dollars per annum. Soon he was also anonymously writing a column, editing recipes, and contributing articles that—painfully—lacked his byline.

It was a nice part of Craig's job that he dined out often on the magazine's account, usually in the company of Seranne or other *fins becs*. At first it was thrilling: New York's serious restaurants, most of them French, tended toward the grand, with elaborate décor, formal service, gleaming surfaces everywhere, and all the flourishes he had come to love at the École. But then he began to notice a stuffiness, a coldness, an *hauteur* that were lacking in the true hospitality he had been taught at Lausanne. In too many French restaurants in New York you got the feeling that the customer was being asked to live up to some unstated standard, was perhaps even held in a certain contempt—for being what? American?

Closer attention revealed shortcuts, little cheats, even outright deceptions—reheated roasts, vegetables limp from freezing, fish a day too old over-sauced to conceal its off aroma, specks of black olive in place of truffle. Dishes came late and to the wrong person, empty wine glasses languished, the check came too soon. Complaints were met with frost.

Like nearly every other member of the educated class of New York—including the editorial staff of the *New York Times* and most of its readers—Craig Claiborne saw the sad state of American food from two quite limited perspectives. When he thought of restaurants, he thought almost entirely of the expensive and formal ones, and his point of reference was the European style of grande luxe. And when he thought of the food of the common people, he dreamed of the farm, an innocent Eden where everything was fresh, home-grown, homemade, and the women of the house—and their servants—had all the time in the world.

(It should be remembered that the New York of which Craig and his peers-to-be were the élite comprised only one of the city's five boroughs, Manhattan, and only certain parts of it at that. A select few suburbs would come to be accepted as extensions of their New York, but in the 1950s, Greenwich, Princeton, and Oyster Bay were still referred to as "the country"—a region to which one repaired on weekends and for the beastly summer.)

The restaurants of New York in 1956 were a pallid shadow of the best of half a century before. The Claremont, on Riverside Drive in Morningside Heights—and this is only one example among a number of grand New York restaurants in the early 1900s—operated its own shad nets in the Hudson offshore and hauled in fresh roe shad twice a day in season. It had a fountain stocked with live brook trout shipped in weekly from Pennsylvania and could serve them *au bleu* in fifteen minutes from demise to plate. The Claremont had daily shipments of whitefish from Lake Superior, Malpeque oysters from the St. Lawrence, Montreal melons, English mutton and game. The wine list was rich in Champagnes, Bordeaux, Burgundies, and German rieslings; there was even California zinfandel.[3]

In the early and middle nineteenth century, European visitors to the United States—Anthony Trollope and Charles Dickens among the best known—had been appalled by the squalor and crudity of Americans' feeding habits. But refinement has always taken money, and in 1840 there were fewer than twenty millionaires in the nation. By 1880 there were more than a hundred, and then came the explosion of robber-baron wealth: A mere decade later, in 1890, the country was home to four thousand millionaires, and by 1916 forty thousand.[4]

The Claremont existed to satisfy these steamship-traveling sybarites' every whim. If they had dined on sweetbreads *jardinière* in Europe's grand hotels, or Dover sole, or Malossol caviar, or boned squab stuffed with foie gras, well, they could have them here, as fresh and as perfectly cooked and served as in Paris, or close enough to it to believe in. The Claremont offered plentiful American provender as well, presented with equal pride: green turtle soup, Virginia ham, wild strawberries and raspberries, the riches of local waters—Long Island bluefish, Ches-

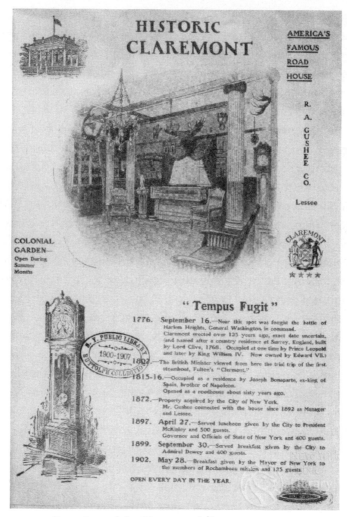

Page four of the Claremont's four-page menu,
August 13, 1907.

apeake softshell crabs, Maine lobsters, Rockaway oysters, Little Neck
clams, whitebait from the Atlantic surf.

This kind of splendor wasn't limited to New York, or even to restaurants. The Subsistence Department of the United States Army offered
to the passengers of its transport ship *Thomas* on September 11, 1908,
consommé *à la printanière,* fried Spanish mackerel with *sauce tartare,*

cucumbers, and *pommes pailles,* ox tongue with *sauce piquante,* shoulder of veal with Allemande caper sauce, oyster patties with *sauce suprême,* pigeon sauté "au Madeira," and quite a bit else, all the way down to plum pudding; vanilla-sauced chocolate fritters; dried fruit including raisins, dates, and Smyrna figs; and mixed nuts[5]—in short, soup to nuts.

A dining car on the Chesapeake & Ohio Railway, on May 1, 1900, offered, among many other choices, duckling *au chasseur,* shad roe, fresh asparagus, Georgia yams, pickled mangoes, and imported cheeses—for lunch.[6] A Cunard liner's typical dinner menu—this for February 23, 1900—consisted of seventy-two dishes, from *pâté de foie gras* to calf's head with bacon-and-brain sauce to roast pheasant to diplomat pudding with sherry sauce, and a wine list too long to print—one had to consult the sommelier.[7] On September 23, 1900, the Grandon Hotel, of faraway Helena, Montana, offered (somehow) filet of sole in white wine sauce, deviled crab, spring lamb, calf's feet and head Turkish style, Roman Punch, and an intriguing dessert called Peach Moonshine, with whipped cream.[8] This kind of thing took money—lots of it. Even that army dinner, presumably, came at the behest, and perhaps out of the pockets, of wealthy generals.

The massive concentration of wealth at the top of the American social scale was not sustainable. Theodore Roosevelt's attempt to address the spiraling inequities of American society—the Square Deal, as he called his campaign—came to little, but there would be plenty else to rip apart the smiling comfort that those restaurants, dining cars, and ocean liners seemed to predicate as permanent. Soon enough there would come war, immigration, the temperance movement, labor unrest, and the global agricultural economy's collapse (the same which ruined Craig Claiborne's father);[9] and the Claremont and all its ilk would crumble.[10]

In New York the very wealthy became fewer, but those who remained still expected to dine in the grand old style, and could. In 1972 Eleanore Carruth described one of their refuges: "There were not many in New York before [World War II] who could afford to pay $3.50 to revel in the splendor of dinner at the old Ritz Carlton, where chef Louis Diat presided over a kitchen staff of sixty—including five *sauciers*—with a waiter (and assistant) for every two tables and a captain for every four to ensure that service was nothing less than perfection."[11] But even the Ritz and the way of life that sustained it could not, in the end, survive.

Craig cited "two great catastrophes" in particular as the agents of destruction of that era: the "national disgrace" of Prohibition, which lasted from the year of his birth, 1920, until 1933, and World War II, which "clobbered . . . a fledgling restaurant industry."[12]

All of this was entirely invisible to the world of Craig Claiborne's youth. The stock market boom of Craig's early childhood, which thrilled New York with the illusion of a return to fabulous wealth and debonair decadence, hardly touched Mississippi. Despair in the Delta came to desperation in 1927 when the Mississippi River surged across the land as it had a thousand thousand times before in its primeval and monstrous past; but the people of the Delta had no memory of time as deep as that and so were taken by astonishment and then by horror. The water was thirty feet deep. It flooded twenty-seven thousand square miles. Below Memphis the river was sixty miles wide.[13]

And then—there was no mercy—came the Depression. The arcadian little farms of New Yorkers' romantic imaginings, if ever a few had existed, lay buried in mud, or dried up and blew away, or died of debt. A Union Pacific dining car menu of 1958 was a sad shadow of what had been a half century before: tomato juice, today's soup, pot roast of beef with noodles, Boston baked beans with frankfurter, ham sandwich, cheese sandwich, fruit salad, head lettuce ind. portion, toast dry or buttered, cold bread, ice cream, cookies pkg., pie, doughnuts, sweet roll, coffee, tea (pot), decaffeinated coffee, non-caloric sweetener available on request.[14]

In the same gastronomically depauperate era—the 1950s—Craig was beginning to realize what a miracle it had been that his mother had put such fine food on the table when her boarders began to fail in their payments, she was plunged into debt, and the Claiborne household's distress was not just gastronomic but economic, and severe. By Mr. Colotta's mysterious means she had gotten twenty-pound red snappers from the Gulf, baskets of crabs to devil or to make into gumbo. Craig remembered his father's home-smoked hams and sausages, and his mother's—well, his mother's and her cooks'—"fantastic caramels, divinity fudge, a luscious coconut cake with meringue and fresh coconut topping, the best, richest pecan pie in the world, incredible fried chicken, great shrimp rémoulade, chicken turnovers in an awesomely rich pastry served with a cream sauce. . . ."[15]

The labor demanded by authentic old-fashioned American food could be prodigious, though it wasn't as rough as it used to be. A typical recipe for fried chicken—from *Housekeeping in Old Virginia,* published in 1879—began, "Kill the chicken the night before, if you can."[16] Liver pudding required, as a first step, "Take two hog's heads, clean nicely; two livers, two lights [lungs], and cull all the good part of half a dozen milts [spleens]; half a dozen sweetbreads; half a dozen kidneys, split open."[17] The rest of the dish took a couple of days longer. "There is no reason," the editor writes, "why the poor man should not have as well prepared and palatable food as the wealthy, for, by care and pains, the finest bread may be made of the simplest materials."[18] Care and pains indeed.

Only a few kitchens persisted that produced a cuisine of true grandeur, comparable to that of the Gilded Age: in the great hotels of Europe, where the exacting *anciens* of Lausanne upheld those traditions and the very rich of the world were willing to pay accordingly, and on the few remaining intercontinental ocean liners. At lunch on the S.S. *United States* on August 6, 1960, among the offerings were cold dishes of eel in jelly, smoked Irish salmon, prime rib, chicken, duck, turkey, fresh ham, leg of lamb, veal *fricandeau,* pork loin, capon, partridge, and thirteen other meats; twelve salads on the buffet and six more to order; six soups; five egg dishes; frog's legs, halibut, pompano, and gefilte fish; four other hot entrées plus three grills; eight vegetables, five potato preparations, six fruit compotes, twelve desserts, six cheeses, and fresh fruit. "Special dishes" could be ordered a day in advance.

Dinner tended toward even fancier delicacies, such as caviar, *foie gras aux truffes,* fresh crabmeat cocktail—frozen crabmeat is ghastly, so they must have kept live crabs!—and kangaroo tail soup *en tasse.*[19]

The wine lists, their prices adjusted for inflation, can break a modern heart. On the Holland America Line in 1961 a bottle of Château Margaux 1953 or 1949 could be had for the equivalent of $36. Lafite '53 was the same. Château Latour 1947 was *cheaper.* Richebourg, Le Chambertin, Corton-Charlemagne, Le Montrachet—not one of them a penny more than five 1961 dollars, not even the most lusciously Lucullan wine in the world, Château d'Yquem.

Because Craig associated gastronomic excellence with luxury, there was much that he was blind to. He believed that America, now deprived of European tradition and standards of excellence, had become a gastronomic wasteland. There was much to justify his belief—the creeping industrialization of agriculture, the blandness of the postwar diet, the dullness of so-called convenience foods, the widespread sense that "showing off" was to be avoided, that mediocrity was what was safe. The hedonism of la cuisine française was sort of *embarrassing*. These were all salient characteristics of the white middle class who dominated the world's idea of America, and most of America's idea of itself.

But of course there was much more to the country than that; and in time Craig's eyes would open to wonders in the myriad traditional cuisines of poverty, which were, after all, all around him—and still all but invisible to the privileged of Manhattan, including the women's page of the *New York Times*. In Little Italy and East Harlem, thousands of Italian immigrants were making extraordinary cheeses, pasta dishes, sausages, pastries. In Chinatown, a dozen Asian cuisines crowded the tenements and narrow, pungent streets. The non-Chinese might come to dine, but what they were served was something the Chinese themselves never ate. Puerto Ricans, Dominicans, Southern American blacks, Jamaicans, Trinidadians, Brazilians, Poles, Czechs, Ashkenazi Jews from a dozen old countries and traditions, Sephardim from North Africa—these and almost limitless others were all right here in New York.

The great supposedly empty American foodscape that Craig had dreamed of conquering was a good deal less bleak than his simplistic fantasy had held it to be. Good farm cooking did still exist: Thousands of small farms were still thriving. And there were plenty of just plain good home cooks in the cities and suburbs. Some of them preserved recently foreign heritages, but long-established American regional traditions were still going strong as well—Pennsylvania Dutch, Tidewater, Low Country, Cajun, New Orleans Creole, Southwestern Spanish, New England.

And among them all were good cooks, both at home and in restaurants. If you did some digging, you could find out where they were. This was all gold.

What they all had in common was that their food took hard work—often as hard as the classics Craig had learned at Lausanne. What the declining fancy French joints of Midtown had in common with the junk that more and more of the American middle class were shoving down their gullets at home was laziness.

If, somehow, he could ever get that job, if he could really be food editor of the *New York Times,* could he hope to persuade his readers to do the hard work necessary to make good food? He took some comfort in remembering that at Lausanne, you learned even the most complex of tasks in small, simple steps. The greatest cooks could explain things that way. They could teach you what at first seemed impossibly difficult techniques without intimidating you. It was because they understood everything so thoroughly that they could make it simple. Craig knew then that he had to understand everything about food equally thoroughly.

§

But Craig had not counted on the fluidity, the unpredictability, the vast unknowability of life in the infinitely complex city of New York. All of a sudden Ann Seranne had quit as editor of *Gourmet*. She was starting a public relations firm, and she wanted him to come with her. Should he? It was the very field that had given him the creeping jeebies in Chicago back in the forties. For a real writer—and that's what he was, wasn't he?—public relations was, well, it was prostitution. But this was different, this was going to be about food, and he did love Ann. So okay. What choice did he have anyway.

Their primary client was an oleomargarine called Fluffo, which was dyed yellow to make it look somewhat like butter. Craig's job was to take New York's food editors—the ladies of the press, Ann called them—out to lunch and dinner, and persuade them to run in their pages recipes in which Fluffo was substituted for butter, on "the awful pretense that the shortening was all but the equal of the more expensive spread. Shameless. The mind reels."[20] He even pushed a recipe employing Fluffo in a mock buttercream icing for a wedding cake.

At such temples of snootery as the Colony restaurant, Craig, "not dressed in what might remotely be thought of as sartorial splendor," and the ladies on his arm, who "certainly did not look as though they had stepped out of the pages of *Vogue*,"[21] were seated in obscurity and treated with the disdain which had become virtually reflexive when the unknown or non-chic crossed their lordly thresholds. Once, when he had ordered a bottle of Puligny-Montrachet, he informed the Colony's arrogant sommelier that it rather tasted, to him, like not Puligny- but *Chassagne*-Montrachet. These two great white Burgundies come from vineyards separated only by a narrow country road, and even the most masterful of wine tasters is lucky to tell the difference; Craig's trick was having sneaked a look at the label of the erroneously delivered bottle. His status rose accordingly.

But he wasn't getting any closer to the *Times*. Fluffo be damned. The world of Fluffo and these dreary ladies of the *other* press was decidedly not what he had had in mind on the beach at Kwajalein, when emulsifying sauces at Lausanne, or when moving from Staten Island to the Midtown Y with stars in his eyes. The *New York Times* was a world unto itself, and a world away.

At night sometimes he would stay up late in his crappy little apartment in Yorkville drinking himself "into a stupor, [then] touring the streets, dangerously roaming in search of sexual gratification." As was often the habit of gay men haunted in those days by the larger society's identification of their very nature as evil, sometimes he sought danger as much as gratification: "Some of my uniformed objects of desire would have been capable of arresting me on the spot."[22] He was trying to pick up *cops*.

(Sodomy would remain a felony in all of the fifty United States until 1962.[23] In New York City one was unlikely to be prosecuted for homosexual behavior in private, but if you hit on the wrong policeman—and nearly every man on the force was the wrong policeman—it could surely happen.)

By the sober light of day, however, and without talking much about it, he continued to take himself and his future seriously. When not promoting the dubious virtues of Fluffo, Craig had been giving demonstrations at Bloomingdale's department store, and these had culminated in what must be called his first book—more of a pamphlet, really—called *Au Gourmet Cookbook,* bearing the byline "R. Craig Claiborne" and published by Bloomingdale's. It featured such then exotic dishes as quiche Lorraine, eggs Florentine, beef Stroganoff, sole Marguery, and babas au rhum. More usefully, he had begun preparing formidably sumptuous dinners at home for a widening circle of friends. They may have had to eat from plates on their laps and sit on the floor, but the food was dazzling. One New Year's Eve, he roasted a whole suckling pig.

Craig still had the copy of *The Joy of Cooking* that his sister had given him after World War II, and it offered nearly infinite variety to the ambitious cook, no matter how deep his formal training. After the uses he put it to, "there [was] no longer a spine on the volume and the pages [were] well stained with the juices of one roast, one sauce, or another."[24] The recipes in *Joy* were nothing like the exquisite creations he had learned at Lausanne, but they were serious cooking. The authors did not abhor canned soups—"a boon to any housekeeper"—but they also affirmed that "It would be a mistake, and false economy, to eliminate homemade." Here Craig found food that was not terribly difficult or time-consuming to make, instructions that were logical and clear, outcomes that satisfied taste, belly, and budget. He more than learned from *The Joy of Cooking*: He absorbed it.

Satisfaction, then, yes. But never the sublime, and the sublime was, after all, what he had been trained in Switzerland to seek, and what his heart and palate yearned for. In his experience so far, there was only one place where simplicity and sublimity met, and it wasn't, yet, in anything he himself had been able to cook.

Once in a while, if a prospect seemed very promising, the firm would spring for dinner at Le Pavillon, and then Craig Claiborne was in heaven.

Ruled over by the tyrannical Henri Soulé since its birth as the French Pavilion at the 1939 World's Fair and its reinvention in Manhattan thereafter, Le Pavillon upheld standards of near-perfection—the most impeccable ingredients, the most elegant presentations, balletic service, sublime cuisine. Le Pavillon was also guilty of ruthless snobbery. A man in brown shoes was beneath Soulé's contempt, unless he was a movie star or a duke. A woman insufficiently chic would be exiled instantly to the nether regions that Le Pavillon's favored habitués had christened Siberia. And the prices were stupefying. Craig adored the place.

On these rare occasions he would ask to keep its splendid menus, which were calligraphed daily on thick, luxurious watercolor paper. Most of them he would keep till the day he died. One,[25] with a whimsical print of dancing, half-naked *putti* on the cover, reads as follows:

Perrier-Jouët "cuvée Pavillon"

~

Menu

Caviar de Beluga

Mousse de Sole Pavillon

Caneton à l'Orange

Pommes Soufflées

Salade de Laitue

Crêpes Soufflées

Café

Henri Soulé at Le Pavillon.

§

Craig by now felt himself worthy of the *Times,* sufficiently knowledgeable, fully capable. When Jane Nickerson announced her resignation as food editor in 1957, he was ready to spring like a cat.

Ann Seranne shared his confidence that he would make a bang-up food editor for the paper. She called Nickerson and invited her to lunch with herself and Craig at the suitably imperious and expensive "21"

Club. They plied the editor with Chassagne-Montrachet, a wine Craig had, no surprise (after his victory over the Colony's sommelier), come to like particularly. They toasted her departure with Cognac. Craig, brimful of Dutch courage, wrote to Nickerson that afternoon, offering his services as her replacement. She did not reply.

But weeks later, when Craig was out on Fire Island with Henry Creel, his on-again off-again companion[26] since navy days,[27] a phone rang in their little rented cottage, and Henry came running down the sand, yelling, "Dobey"—he always called Craig Dobey, which Craig never explained—"Dobey, it's the *Times!*"

His first interview was with the very proper Elizabeth Penrose Howkins, editor of the women's page, in pearls, white gloves, and black Chanel. Howkins was known as an editor who "hired unseasoned but hungry writers who were to achieve notice on a wider scene."[28] She scanned Craig's few *Gourmet* articles and Nickerson's piece about him and his fish with white wine sauce, looked him up and down, and, having passed over a number of more experienced writers, decided, on a whim, or intuition, to take the chance. She passed Craig along to Turner Catledge, the managing editor of the *Times,* who just happened to be an old Mississippi boy.

Moments like this are when lives are made. Craig's year and a half at Mississippi State College had been the quintessence of misery, but State was Mr. Catledge's alma mater and Craig now suddenly remembered it with saccharine nostalgia. *Missippi* State, they both called it, drawls thick as river mud. On learning that Mr. Catledge—the Mississippi boy in Craig would never dissever the Mister from the editor's surname— had lived in the dormitory known as Polecat Alley, Craig, face alight with amazement, said, Why, damned if he didn't, too. Which was a lie.[29]

6

Becoming
Craig Claiborne

"Although their reputation was blighted by that episode in the Garden of Eden, apples have long since ceased to be regarded as the scourge of creation," ran the first sentence of Craig Claiborne's first piece in the *New York Times*. "Without them the law of gravity might never have been formulated and we would lack a particularly appetizing fruit filling for a pastry fantasy."

It was September 26, 1957, and he was already in full command of his voice: genial, magisterial, casually knowing, and sort of funny-peculiar. Much of Craig's future self-in-print was foreshadowed in this début—for example, his happy acceptance and praise of someone else's idea:

> The pastry shape in question is the invention of an amateur chef and an inveterate collector of Venetian glass. This gentleman devised an ingenious method for turning out pastry shells that resemble—down to the last ripple and marble striation—the free-form glass from the Adriatic shores.

The "ripple and marble striation" was vividly displayed in the accompanying photographs. Three of the apple pastries surmount a Venetian glass cake stand; two more are arranged on a plate with Swiss hotel school geometry. Fruit swells opulently from a Venetian glass vase.

Three filter cigarettes sprout from a little parrot-tulipesque cup while a pair of Venetian candlesticks in the form of dolphins stand guard.

The recipe itself was a model of precision and clarity, and something of a dare. This was not for the Jell-O salad and tuna casserole set. Unless you had a lot of experience in pastry, in fact, it was not far from impossible. You had to form a very breakable dough into deep, softly curving flowers "to resemble the shape of Venetian glass bowls," and then, to give them that special Venetian striping, "for marbled effect, rotate a toothpick dipped in food color from center of pastry to edge."

It is much to be wondered how many readers accepted Craig's dare and actually tried to make the crazy thing. At any rate the new food editor had planted his flag, and on terra nova. Jane Nickerson's world of canned fish and weekend bargains had been left far behind. Craig Claiborne was going to take you where you'd never been before.

And who was the gentleman collector? Craig didn't say. That was unlike his future self, who would credit and often make famous those with whom he shared his spotlight.

As for the particular variety of apple he preferred, he did not dictate one, just made a mild recommendation:

> Though the number of known and named varieties of apples runs well into the thousands, the current sovereigns of the season are the aromatic, broad-shouldered Delicious varieties and the crisp-textured, tart McIntosh. Both these apples are delectable for eating out of hand and the McIntosh, unlike the Delicious, is tender and rich for cooking.

What he didn't say was that the Delicious and the McIntosh were pretty much the only kinds of apple his readers could lay hands on, unless they had an ancient and faithfully tended tree in the yard. That also was unlike his future self, whose enthusiasm for unusual and hard-to-find foods could set off a flood of demand overnight. In his earliest columns—despite his occasional flourish or fussiness—Craig tried to remain the modest, mannerly Mississippian, deferential to the vast American gastronomic reality that may have saddened him but nevertheless encompassed not only him but the *Times* and all its readers too.

Soon, however, he would begin to exert a little pressure. After less than three months on the job—in the issue of December 8, 1957, writing in the *Times*'s prestigious Sunday magazine, with a much wider circulation than the daily paper—he tried a rather bold experiment, to find out if he could persuade his readers to push against their habitual boundaries.

> There is a strong possibility that Beau Brummell was not only the greatest dandy the world ever produced but also the gentleman with the least enthusiasm for vegetables. When asked if he'd ever sampled a vegetable, he reputedly replied that he once ate a pea. He was fond of meats.
>
> Americans by and large have a healthy yen for garden greenery, but they generally fall into the Beau's category when it comes to viands. Last year the American diet included, on a per capita basis, 167 pounds of meat—an average of half a pound a day a person.
>
> But there's more to meat than steak. The unusual meats, sometimes disregarded in this country, are delicacies abroad. Americans have never heartily endorsed variety meats such as brains, sweetbreads, tongue and tripe. . . .

He presented recipes for brains in black butter, veal kidneys Bordelaise (requiring shallots, hardly known to most of his readers and nearly impossible to find), *tripes à la mode de Caën* (requiring also chopped calf's feet), and, with a tip of the hat to his native region, broiled sweetbreads Virginia (with ham). This was the sort of food the very thought of which made most Americans' hair stand on end, or their gorges rise.

The Claiborne style was taking shape. There would often be history, or legend, breezily invoked—Newton, Brummell. There would be scholarship, or statistics—nearly always something he'd had to learn from research—as in this piece, 110 million barrels of apples harvested per year, $18 million' worth of American offal sold annually to foreign countries. He delighted in hidden poem-rhythms— "ripple and marble striation," "free-form glass from the Adriatic shore." There was always a foundation of practicality, typically delivered in a delicate formal tone—"It might be added that most variety meats have a high nutritive value and are relatively inexpensive." From the beginning he had a flair for apposite attribution and quotation, often with a wink—(this from *The Wise Encyclopedia of Cookery*) "Tripe, like certain alluring vices, is enjoyed by society's two extremes, the topmost and lowermost strata."

In his fourth published piece, the little boy in him seemed breathless over an upcoming dinner at the Waldorf-Astoria for Queen Elizabeth II and Prince Philip: "Four thousand persons will attend . . . and 150 cooks, 500 waiters, 25 bartenders and 400 captains will be employed for the occasion." He proceeded to recount the menu with American pride, and also his Lausanne tongue hanging out: South Carolina green turtle soup, Long Island striped bass, filet of beef with truffles, and a *savarin au rhum* with a *sabayon* sauce. For the savarin and sabayon he provided an elaborate and dramatic home recipe ("may be served blazing").

Craig then pulled himself, and the royals, up short, with a comparison to an earlier dinner—one given for Elizabeth's eighteen-year-old great-grandfather at Delmonico's restaurant in 1860. The honoree was the Prince of Wales at the time, later to become Edward VII. New York had fêted the young prince, Craig wrote, with soup, oysters, salmon, trout, beef, game pâté, turkey galantine, suckling pig, ham, tongue, chicken salad, lobster salad, grouse, pheasant, snipe, and four desserts.[1] (The boy had an appetite, and was father to the man: As a grown-up, King Edward not only continued eating on an Edwardian scale but smoked twenty cigarettes and a dozen cigars a day[2]—no doubt how he got his name on the band and his face on the box of King Edward Cigars.)

While having the time of his life, Craig was also working very hard. After that first piece on September 26, 1957, he published another on October 3rd ("There are millions of Americans who have never known the delicate flavor of a fresh mushroom"), another on October 6th (Albert Stockli, "Swiss-born titan with the toque blanche"). More followed on October 14th (the royal dinner), 15th (opening of Café Argenteuil), 17th ("Spicy Fruit Cake Should Be Baked Now to Begin Aging"), 20th (winter soups), 21st ("Julian Salmon of London, England"), 23rd ("Authority Says Chablis Is 'Dying Out'"), and 27th ("If one may borrow a prefix from the Greeks—*turos,* meaning cheese—it can be said that America is becoming a nation of turophiles"). And that was only his first month.

And so it continued through the year—cornucopian variety, breakneck pace.

AMERICAN PORT DRINKERS ARE DESPAIR OF EXPERT

ASPIC KNOWS NO SEASON; LOBSTER EN BELLEVUE PARISIENNE

WHITE HOUSE PRESS-AIDE ENTERTAINS

NOW A POLYNESIAN TREND IN FOOD

SETTING A TRADITIONAL TABLE FOR FESTIVAL OF HANUKKAH;
ROAST GOOSE AND PANCAKES OF GRATED POTATO ARE USUAL

AND HUMMINGBIRDS' TONGUES

The story Craig liked to tell of his miraculous hiring by the *Times*—his larky Mississippi badinage with Turner Catledge—was the dinner-party version. Craig did not walk into the office of the managing editor of the *New York Times cold,* are you kidding? He had studied up on the man. He knew perfectly well that Turner Catledge had roomed in the Mississippi State College dorm nicknamed Polecat Alley. He had learned in advance that Mr. Catledge loved to play on his ol'-boy persona in the newsroom. Craig sensed also that Mr. Catledge would see through his act to the seriousness beneath. Neither of them would have to wink—the wink would be implicit in their first quick volley of Delta palaver. Did Mr. Catledge know he was lying about Polecat Alley? Probably not, but it wouldn't have mattered.

Craig had also had to pass through the fires of Lester Markel, the editor of the Sunday paper, "a despotic and highly temperamental one-man show . . . who ruled his kingdom with ruthless brilliance," known for "incapacitating breakdowns and frequent tirades."[3] Markel took "sadistic relish in bullying [his staff], belittling them in public,"[4] and had "broken the spirit of more than one gentle soul who had worked on the Sunday magazine."[5] The way Craig told it, in his memoir and to his friends, he, the gentle-spirited supplicant, had merely presented his pink-cheeked cherub's smile to this dragon, informed him that he spoke French (without saying how badly), casually spun off some bits of his erudition, and flustered the monster—a fine tale, and one that flew in the face of everything anybody had ever known about Lester Markel.

Craig liked to say what a fraidy-cat he was, and sometimes he himself seemed to believe it. But he believed, or said he believed, a lot of things that weren't true—palmistry, extrasensory perception, and mind reading, for example.[6] He seldom let the facts stand in the way of a good story. It was only in his old age—and when he was no longer employed by the *New York Times*—that Craig finally admitted how painstakingly prepared he had been for those first interviews. He had "done all sorts of research"[7] on the backgrounds and careers of Howkins, Catledge, and Markel.

§

No question, the job was fun. He loved food and wine, and now his job was—food and wine. He wasn't traveling far and wide, yet, but he could eat pretty much wherever he wanted, and spend pretty much whatever it cost to do so, and nobody was telling him what he could or couldn't write about. The *New York Times* was a highly structured, fiercely hierarchical company—its executives, editors, and reporters fought for scraps of advantage like street dogs—but somehow Craig never got caught up in the factions or fracas. Maybe it was the mildness of his manner or the survival instinct of the born sissy. There was a look about him of fragile porcelain.

It probably didn't hurt that when he dined out on assignment—that would be on *self*-assignment most of the time—he often chose as his companions senior editors of the *Times,* the company's high executives, and their wives. He had put himself in a position where, subtly, or perhaps even unconsciously, his superiors courted *him.* Another of the rather wondrous things about this job Craig Claiborne had fashioned for himself was that the distinction between research and indulgence was always going to be a soft one.

He was nonetheless careful to maintain a solemn, *Times*ian mien both at work and in his columns, for he aspired to the status of the *Times*'s critics of art, literature, music, and drama, and he was determined to bring to his work a rigor and gravity equal to theirs. Those classical allusions of his were surely part of his effort to be accepted as Serious, though it seems open to question whether the august likes of Orville Prescott, Dore Ashton, Harold C. Schonberg, and Brooks Atkinson would have been exactly electrified by Craig's grandiloquence. Certainly, however, his voice of formal authority was something new in American writing about food (the French had been doing it for centuries). "The same rules apply to the preparation of food," he wrote, "that apply to the designing of textiles or the writing of a symphony."[8]

Craig's realism obliged him to understand also that for all his dreams—not so long ago—of conquering an empty landscape, the field he had entered on was hardly an open one. His ventures into the exotic were not unprecedented. His predecessor, Jane Nickerson, had not been all fruit and egg fluff and zestful tricks for canned food. While it was true that on one day she'd be writing encomiums to "that ubiquitous domestic tool, the can-opener,"[9] on another she'd be finding spicy olives in the Greek markets of Ninth Avenue,[10] or tasting "one of the most interesting wines available in New York"—zinfandel[11]—or exploring recipes for feijoada, paella, or authentic Indian dishes.

Craig's future rival James Beard was also already very much on the scene, and as a widely known writer about food, even something of a celebrity, he was standing directly in Craig's way. Beard had published five cookbooks, the most recent one French. In the *New York Times Book Review* of August 22, 1954, Charlotte Turgeon—who herself had been popularizing French cooking in America since the 1940s—wrote that "Jim Beard is considered by most to be the Dean of American Cookery," and that sobriquet would follow Beard down through the years. Beard had come into food journalism at a time when gifts from manufacturers, luxurious free junkets, spectacular free meals, and endless varieties of what Craig considered bribery were more or less the norm; and Beard, a man of stupendous appetites—for food, sex, money, you name it—stunned his subtler colleagues. In his biography of Beard, Robert Clark writes that he was "adept at extracting hospitality from [film] producers and at making private activities yield professional dividends." Beard "arranged a publicity party for the Skotch Grill. . . . He had also recently signed on as a representative of the French cognac industry."[12] Beard had scores of such arrangements through the years—Omaha Steaks,[13] French's mustard, Green Giant Corn Niblets,[14] Old Crow bourbon, Planters Peanuts, Shasta soft drinks, DuPont chemicals, Adolph's Meat Tenderizer,[15] he knew no shame—and Craig was disgusted. Once they had met, he liked Beard even less.

Craig's opening strategy was to flatter him—for example by publicizing Beard's cooking school and quoting him lavishly: "Often in the past, [said Mr. Beard,] students enter a class with a devastating lack of belief in their ability to do more than scramble an egg. But they begin to relax after an hour or so and most of them leave the opening session feeling like junior Escoffiers."[16] The great Dean of Cookery could surely not have been more pleased.

Craig would save the private and all but invisible thrust of his stiletto for a later time. If he was going to have the extent of influence he felt himself capable of, he had more challenging obstacles than one big, fat self-promoter.

Craig Claiborne was up against an immense change in American culture. He knew that the denatured half-artificial foods that were on the rise and the way of life they were giving shape to were deadly to the soul and the body. James Beard's corruption was only a symptom of the money-first value system that was threatening more than how Americans ate. Craig had as eminent a position from which to speak as any in the nation, and he was going to use it. "The American diet is seriously in need of overhauling," he wrote in the *Times* of February 25, 1958. "Although we are the best fed and the most overfed nation on earth, our dietary lacks are appalling. There are vitamin deficiencies at every income level and 20 percent of the population is overweight."

He tried hard to make a difference, and he did influence hundreds of thousands of cooks and eaters. But while that significant minority of Americans were swept up in the love of food and cooking, and came to care very much about the quality of what they put in their bodies, there were many millions more whom Craig could never reach but the agri-corporate complex could. By the year 2000, when Craig Claiborne died, industrial food pervaded the American diet, and 69 percent of American adults were overweight, obese, or extremely obese.[17]

In 1958 Craig didn't yet know who his audience was going to be. How wide a spectrum should he try to reach? Should he be writing for those already committed, or ought he to be an apostle? How much could he assume his readers already knew, and could he teach without offending them? Sometimes, as in his jeremiad on the American diet, he seemed to be addressing himself to the nation at large. But the nation at large surely hadn't much interest in fantastically difficult apple fantasies in the shape of Venetian glass. For that matter, how many *Times* readers did?

What began to make the difference was that something in his voice apparently invited conversation. His readers started writing in, and they never stopped. He didn't always answer them, but often he did, and what counted was that often enough these people, real people, ordinary people, found their way into his columns. And where else did this happen in the *New York Times*? The paper did print letters to the editors, all so grave and weighty, as befitted the somber editorial and reportorial voices to which they were responses. But what's known now as interactivity—and taken so lightly for granted—simply didn't exist. Craig Claiborne delighted in it.

Sometimes his interlocutors came to him, virtually, in the form of their recipes, and sometimes he went to them, physically. To talk about buying fish off the dock at Sheepshead Bay, he went there, and quoted "Laddie Martin, the tanned and affable skipper of the Rocket II."[18] To describe innovative uses of the electric blender, he attended a dinner party given by "André Surmain, a local gastronome,"[19] and quoted Surmain's recipes. (Was Surmain, à la Beard, on the take from the blender maker? One has one's suspicions, and soon enough Craig would be able to sniff this sort of thing out. And then he absolutely wouldn't go.) For a disquisition on the esthetics of setting a table, he turned to a well-known fabric designer.[20] For a lesson in soufflés, he visited the Broadway actors Lynn Fontanne and Alfred Lunt at home.[21]

To the world of mute consumption of TV dinners, to the world of candy bars and snacking on the run, Craig Claiborne offered the alternative—well worn but well proved—of people sitting together at a table, sharing food that had taken some effort to put there, and talking. He considered that simple scene to be one of the bulwarks of civilization, and participation in it one of the duties, and pleasures, of belonging in civilization's long history. And so it was with a certain stiff neutrality that he wrote of such proclamations as those in a speech by the anthropologist Margaret Mead which he had been assigned to cover:

> She attacked the idea that the ritual of families dining together was a universal panacea capable of curing most dietary ills.
>
> "Too often," she noted, "such gatherings become horrors for the children involved. . . . The dining table is not the proper place for discussing manners, classroom marks and whether or not one must drink milk and eat certain foods."[22]

He would not have enjoyed dining with Margaret Mead. Column by column, Craig was discovering by elimination who his audience was: It was people whose company he would enjoy at the table. The more people he met, the wider that definition became, and the more congenial his writing.

Craig had to maintain a discreet balance between his own sophistication and his obligation to impart to his readers, without condescension, the knowledge they needed to keep up with him. How many of them were likely to know what *rillettes de Tours* were? Better to explain, plainly: "made with fresh pork, lean and fat, which is sieved and seasoned with delicate herbs which may include marjoram, sage and rosemary."[23] He did not tolerate imprecision, and wished others as well not to do so: "If there is no such word as gastro-semanticism, there should be."[24] Yet he also wanted his readers to know that they could, as he did, prepare splendid dishes with the most modest of means. Here once again he expressed the point through a meal at someone else's home: "Signora Fedora del Monaco [the wife of Mario del Monaco, a star of the Metropolitan Opera] is an imaginative cook whose New York hotel kitchen is not much bigger than a hemidemisemiquaver. Her cooking utensils consist of little more than a skillet, two kettles and a saucepan. Her source of heat is a pair of electric burners."[25]

In late 1958 Craig moved from his tiny apartment on the Upper East Side to somewhat less cramped quarters in Greenwich Village, at 133 West Thirteenth Street, but he was still in no position to entertain in the style to which he had become accustomed when dining out. It had taken him barely his first year at the *Times,* however, for a visit *from* him to be a sought-after invitation. The *toujours-au-courant* Leonard Bernsteins, for instance, turned up as his hosts in November 1958; Mrs. Bernstein, the former Felicia Montealegre, showed off her native Chilean specialties[26] (which it may be doubted she cooked unassisted very often, if ever).

It took him almost no time to develop his lifelong relish for caviar. "According to G. F. Hansen-Sturm," he wrote soon after his evening chez Bernstein, "the caloric content of caviar is negligible. 'Eating it,' he says, 'is a delightful way of getting a balanced diet.'"[27]

In the New Year Craig had a postholiday attack of gastronomic humility. He visited the sprawling Latin American outdoor market beneath the elevated New Haven Railroad tracks in East Harlem, and marveled over the "abundance of plantains, pigeon peas and chayotes" and the "culantro [cilantro] leaves, cassavas, and a pumpkin-like squash called calabaza." But he didn't find a charming Latina cook whose East Harlem apartment he wanted to visit. The recipes he printed—for roast fresh ham, *tostones de platano,* rice with pigeon peas, and a chayote-and-bean salad—came from Rigoberto Martinez, director of the Department of Agriculture and Commerce for the Commonwealth of Puerto Rico. I.e., through the mail.

§

Home cooking was fascinating, and infinitely various, but culinary art, Craig believed, was unlikely to reach greatness anywhere except in a restaurant. When he had begun to dream about the job he now held, the vision that stirred his soul was that he would be able to write about food at its greatest. Surely in New York he would find that. But his experience of the city's restaurants had been such a disappointment that in his first eighteen months that he had written very little about them. This had nothing to do with any pressure to stay away from criticism; the *Times* maintained (and still maintains) an impenetrable firewall between its advertising and editorial departments. No restaurateur, or any other advertiser, even dared asked for an article. Craig always would dine anonymously, and the *Times* would always pay for everything. He never accepted a gift, a free meal, a free glass of Champagne. The unassailable integrity of the *New York Times* was a principal reason that Craig had set his sights on working there, and didn't think about anywhere else, for the *Times's* integrity was lamentably rare. Especially in the food writing world, corruption was the norm. James Beard's antics were particularly shocking because his status was so high and his influence so strong, but in a way his commercial connections may not have been so egregious as those of many other, lesser food writers simply because his were, in many cases, impossible to conceal.

Even in major metropolitan newspapers, the opening of an important restaurant—one expected to advertise regularly—called for a "review," which was not permitted to be even slightly negative. The meals the restaurant reviewer ate were free, and lavish. The editor and publisher of the paper and their families, as well as the reviewer, would probably continue to dine gratis as long as the restaurant continued to advertise, and the arrival of a new chef, or the inauguration of an open-air terrace, would almost inevitably result in a feature article. Were the readers ever told about these deals? Absolutely not.

Home-cooking columns on the women's page were often reproduced word for word from press releases from the manufacturers of products featured in the recipes. Travel magazine writers flew first class at the airlines' expense, stayed in free suites, dined in luxurious restaurants, and contributed articles praising those airlines, those hotels, and those restaurants. All this was standard practice. And the readers were never told.

It is not so different today. Travel and food "journalism" is a much richer field, now dominated by large, highly profitable corporations. Yet the travel and food magazines they own—whose executives, publishers, and topmost editors are very highly paid and also have stratospheric expense accounts—"cannot afford" to pay the travel and dining expenses of the writers they assign to write about travel and dining. The magazines, to the extent they can, still cadge plane tickets, hotel rooms, and meals for writers on assignment. And the hoteliers and restaurateurs really have no choice but to cough up. The writer can count on the best service the house can provide, as much alcohol as the writer can absorb, and course after course of the chef's finest work. The writer and editor assure themselves and each other that their personal and institutional standards of integrity will not be swayed. But try writing what a fraud the place was, what an unfunny architectural joke those teetering constructions posing as food were—and see if your piece sees the light of day.

As for the pieces that do see print, are the readers ever told about the freebies and deals? Ha.

With a very few very slight exceptions, this system never sullied Craig Claiborne. He was clean, the *Times* was clean, and it's still clean today.

Craig wrote so few restaurant reviews simply because he detested bad restaurants, and he really didn't want to write about them. But ultimately he couldn't have a career as the food editor without reviewing any restaurants at all. He had damned a number with faint praise, but by early 1959, he was so fed up with the low standards of even the highest-priced establishments that he was ready to take the gloves off.

§

His astonishing front-page article, "Elegance of Cuisine Is on Wane in U.S.," was one long lament but for Craig's delight in Le Pavillon and his hope for the Culinary Institute of America, newly established in New Haven to train chefs in the European tradition. The piece comes to a close with one old French chef's castle-in-the-sky dream of a school for young culinary professionals in Manhattan, with three kitchens, three restaurants staffed by students, and a faculty of European chefs nearing retirement and teaching as volunteers.

"And who would finance such a project?" Craig asks, deadpan.

"Management, the unions, and the New York City Board of Education, if not Federal funds," replies the chef.

Craig leaves this preposterous fantasy floating in midair, and the piece is over.

Two big things were about to happen, both of them good.

First, the piece shook the food world to its roots. People were talking coast to coast. Restaurateurs were protesting. Diners were chiming in. And Craig Claiborne was on the map.

Henceforward, and with steadily increasing force, he would be America's leading authority on food. A good review from Craig Claiborne would have a restaurant's telephones ringing day and night; a bad one would silence them. If he had wanted the power of a *Times* theater critic, now he had it.

The second big thing was a friendship with the chef of Le Pavillon, Pierre Franey, which would change the course of his life.

§

In *A Feast Made for Laughter* Craig tells another story in which mysterious luck befalls him through no great effort or preparation on his part, rather like his hiring by the *Times*. This story is about as true as that one.

> One morning in March 1959 I wrote a memorandum to the publisher, Arthur Hays Sulzberger, with a proposal. In it I stated that I had had numerous inquiries as to the possibility of publishing a cookbook bearing the *New York Times*' logotype. I was wholly altruistic in this matter.

The reader is requested to pause a moment at this point and enjoy that last sentence.

> I told him that I felt that such a book would redound to the prestige of the paper. I added that I would be willing to produce such a book under any terms that he dictated. I said that I would edit the book for such commission as he deemed fit; for a share of the royalties; or for a flat fee.
>
> Within a day or two I received in the interoffice mail a brief note from his deputy, Ivan Veit, dated March 27, 1959. I don't think I fully comprehended the scope of that letter. It gave me the rights to the title of a book to be called *The New York Times Cook Book*.[28]

Craig said he didn't expect much to come of it.

7

Pierre

From the first moment when Craig Claiborne interviewed Pierre Franey in the kitchen at Le Pavillon, Craig was intensely attracted to Pierre, with his "fresh, innocent, boyish face."[1] But Pierre was absolutely straight, with a wife and two little kids; a Burgundian peasant, with no formal education beyond the basic, a bluff, tough, simple guy. He had come up the hard way, through old-fashioned iron-disciplined butt-kicking French restaurant kitchens, where no *pédérastes* need apply.

Pierre was also a fantastically talented cook. After Craig's formal training at Lausanne and a lot of serious practice since then, he thought pretty highly of his own skills, but when he watched Pierre in action, he realized that he still had a lot to learn.

Years later, Pierre would recall that after Craig's big front-page piece of April 1959, "Le Pavillon became Craig's postgraduate cooking school. He started coming by to visit about once a week just to watch us cook."[2]

There was an easy, comfortable feeling between them. They liked the same kinds of food. They enjoyed each other's company.

Craig remembered their first dinner together in detail: "Pierre and his wife, Betty, came in to my apartment in Manhattan, where he and I joined forces in the kitchen for the first time. The three of us dined on quail *Beauséjour* (with bay leaf and garlic cloves); a purée of celery root; watercress and endive salad; vanilla ice cream with strawberries sweetened and perfumed with kirsch. We drank toasts with a vintage Château Lascombes."[3]

Here began the most important, and most complex, friendship of

67

Craig Claiborne's life. Two forces were joined in it that would shape Craig's work through the rest of his career: Pierre Franey's culinary virtuosity and the standards of excellence that the two of them shared.

They continued cooking at each other's homes. They were having fun—and that was rather new to both of them. Craig was inveterately dissatisfied, restless, lonely. Pierre was all work, all focus, hour after hour to the point of exhaustion. Now they were laughing.

Craig and Pierre both were discovering that friendship across a divide that theretofore each of them had thought rather forbidding— the divide between their sexual identities—needn't be something to fear, and they were learning it with an ease that surprised them both. They both loved food like crazy, and that was enough.

"We spoke the same language," said Craig.[4]

"From the first," Betty Franey said, "Craig and Pierre just clicked."

(They spoke the same gastronomic language, but the issue of Pierre's native tongue was always a little difficult. In the interest of Americanization, Pierre and his family had begun to pronounce their name to rhyme with "rainy," although in good French it is more like *fra-nay*. In

In Pierre Franey's kitchen.

time Pierre would return to the correct French pronunciation, but Craig never made the switch, and to his dying day called him Frāney.)

The Franeys lived in a modest little cottage in a modest little suburb called Valley Stream, barely into Long Island from Queens, under the flight path of planes roaring in to Idlewild. It was also near Betty's parents' house. (Both her parents were French; her father, Auguste, was the room service manager of the Waldorf-Astoria.) Pierre had two hours off in the afternoons, and Betty would drive all the way in to Manhattan six days a week so that he could spend time with their little daughters, Claudia and Diane. Sometimes they would all pile into Craig's little apartment in the Village for an elaborate dinner, long and always convivial.

In 1954, Henri Soulé had opened a summertime incarnation of Le Pavillon in East Hampton, known as The Hedges, with Pierre as chef. By 1958, the Franeys had scraped enough pennies together to buy a little waterside lot in the then obscure East Hampton village of Springs, with a tranquil view of Gardiners Bay; and it was here on summer Sundays and on Pierre's brief vacations that Pierre and Betty and the two little girls would find quiet respite. Pierre would wade the mud flats for clams, trap crabs, cast for striped bass and bluefish. They ate corn and tomatoes and peppers and chickens and eggs from the local farms. They would grill the fish, picnic on the beach, sleep bundled up in the couple of drafty shingled shacks that had come with the property. The children splashed in the shallows; they all turned brown in the sun.

This was the life Pierre and Betty welcomed Craig into. When he came back home to Greenwich Village alone after a summer day at Springs with the Franeys, or no more than a quick Sunday dinner in Valley Stream—Betty would cook something from the *cuisine bourgeoise,* while the girls climbed him like a tree—sometimes Craig would weep with gratitude.

Thursday nights, Pierre and Betty would almost always drive into Manhattan to dine out with Craig. From time to time they brought Claudia and Diane, whom Craig adored. Sometimes the girls, just the two of them, would visit Uncle Craig at his apartment, which in Diane's recollection was "romantic, and exotic."[5]

These were happy times for Craig. He loved working with Pierre. He loved the Franey family and they loved him.

§

The more time Craig spent in the kitchen at Le Pavillon, fixing in his mind the finest details of Pierre's uncompromising technique, and the more dishes he tasted his way attentively through in the dining room, in gustatory bliss, the more strongly he felt a renewed commitment to the ideals of formal French cooking.

Then in the summer of 1959, Craig learned of a restaurant soon to open that would violate nearly all his hallowed precepts of classicism. The Four Seasons was going to be as restrained, as austere, and as fearlessly modernist as the stark, sleek tower in whose base it was being constructed, the Seagram Building, the masterpiece of Ludwig Mies van der Rohe. Mies's student Philip Johnson was designing the restaurant. The Four Seasons' décor and mood would change with the seasons; the Seagram family were supplying it with art by Jackson Pollock, Pablo Picasso, Mark Rothko, Richard Lippold, and Joan Miró; and the Swiss chef Albert Stockli (already among Craig's favorites for his unlikely but highly successful transformation of the Newark Airport restaurant) was planning a menu of startlingly simple dishes based on unusual ingredients and "largely unfettered by European tradition."[6]

As a rule Craig believed in waiting for a restaurant to develop and mature before he published a word about it, but he wrote about the Four Seasons even before it had opened. And then soon after its opening, he rushed to review it. The Four Seasons was, he said, "perhaps the most exciting restaurant to open in New York within the last two decades."

After Trader Vic's Queen's Park Swizzle and the poor old Continental of Paramus it was perhaps understandable that Craig should have let himself get a bit carried away. Whatever extravagance he might have wished to indulge in was doubtless abetted by the fact that he had already begun to pursue his vocation in that unique and blessed state, unknown previously to any other writer at the *New York Times*, in which his work—maybe also owing to all those dinners out with his bosses?—seemed to pass from his typewriter into newsprint free of the depredations of an editor. An editor might have noticed that apropos his most-exciting-in-two-decades remark, Craig had been dining in New York for approximately half of *one* decade; that twenty years back Craig had been nineteen years old and had never set foot on the island of

Manhattan, and had never tasted either a glass of Sauternes or a truffle. This miraculous freedom from correction would be Craig's henceforth.

His writing certainly did get over-fancy from time to time, but his air of authority was, for the most part, earned. He knew good service for sure:

> In a city where waiters are noted for an Olympic detachment [Nonexistent Editor would have changed that to *Olympian*], it is a revelation to find a corps with the pride and enthusiasm that their occupation demands. Judged on the basis of recent visits, there is probably no dining establishment in New York where training for table service is more thorough. . . .

A close reading of Craig's review[7] hints that he took particular pleasure in The Four Seasons' wine list. He named three rather grand Burgundies ("a Nuits-St-Georges, Clos des Corvées, 1953, a Fixin, Clos du Chapitre, 1955, and a Chassagne-Montrachet, les Ruchottes, 1955") "that were enjoyed recently."

> The décor is a conversation piece sufficient in itself to sustain a lively causerie through a leisurely lunch. [Would Editor have been intimidated by *causerie,* or have insisted that it was a word nobody would know and ought damn well to be changed to something in English?] . . . Typical in the cold selection is an "herbed lobster parfait." If memory serves, this contains large chunks of lobster enrobed in a devastatingly rich blend of whipped cream and hollandaise sauce. [Editor: *If memory serves?* You don't take notes already?]

He loved the food, praising the several varieties of fresh wild mushrooms available, the then-unusual use of fresh herbs from the restaurant's own herb garden, the tableside-flamed beef Stroganoff, the *quenelles de brochet* "gossamer as a cloud."

But he didn't love everything. The ghost of Conrad Tuor eyeballing student-waiter M. Claiborne's excess of mashed potatoes made a spectral visitation from Lausanne: "The service of gross portions of edibles is a barbaric custom that is all too common in American dining places," Craig wrote, and "the Four Seasons is no exception." He went on to deprecate a sauce lacking finesse, a heavy dumpling, and insufficient expertise in the sculpting of the vegetables.

At these prices, your sauce should surely be chock-full of finesse and your vegetables had better be properly sculpted. Lunch for two with wine but no cocktails averaged $25; dinner, $40. Adjusted for inflation, that would be and $184 and $295, respectively—pretty close to what The Four Seasons will set you back today.

§

In October 1959 Craig accompanied Frank Schoonmaker, "the most celebrated and by far the most knowledgeable wine expert in America,"[8] on a trip to Paris that would have burst the liver of anyone with a constitution less robust than the ones these two seemed to possess. They arrived in time for dinner at Lapérouse on October 10th and managed to fit in lunch at Le Roi Gourmet before their departure on the 21st. In between, Craig's handwritten notes[9] attest that they packed away twenty multicourse meals in ten days, some at bistros and brasseries with potent old-fashioned cooking, including Le Coq Hardi, Chez Joséphine, Chez l'Ami Louis, and Chez Allard, and others at such temples of the *haute cuisine* as Le Grand Véfour, Drouant, Taillevent, and La Tour d'Argent. The thirty-nine-year-old food editor of the *New York Times* had in fact never in his life tasted food as good as this, as beautifully served as this, in surroundings of such refinement. Even the Pavillon couldn't hold a candle to the likes of Taillevent and the Grand Véfour.

Craig did know that things were *supposed* to be this good. In his dinners out week after week in New York, although the fine-dining restaurants always fell short of his ideals, he still had learned by adumbration what was possible even if unachieved; but neither his unguided wanderings in Paris ten years before nor his resolute searching for excellence in New York had ever brought him close to this kind of thing, much less put him physically *in* it as this Schoonmaker trip was doing. Even little crowded, rustic old Allard, with its grandmotherly duck with olives, its unadorned potato omelettes, and its frankly odoriferous grilled sardines, somehow *came together* with a harmony and warmth that made Craig feel good straight through. Was it something like love? Something, perhaps, like the harmony and warmth of the boarding house kitchen in Indianola?

§

No, no, no. Hadn't that all been an illusion, perhaps necessary at some point in his history but in need of discarding now? Hadn't the boarding house kitchen been a psychological construct, part of which was the absence of his mother from it and part the presence there of the abstracted best of her—her food? Those people hadn't *loved* him. They were servants. They *had* to be nice to the little sissy boy of the house. Craig the grown-up, Craig the New Yorker, must beware that sensation of warmth: It could be false, as false as the smiles across the racial divide of the Delta, false as *all* those Southern smiles, none more false than that of his mother with her threadbare dignity stretched so thin over her desperation.

Even now, truly settled in New York, a New Yorker to his bones, Craig could not get her and her Mississippi out of his mind. He hated what his mother had been, and he remained mystified by her power. Craig's father called his wife by the sobriquet Trina; she, unvaryingly, addressed him as Mr. Claiborne.

> She would recline in the living room, unpinning her hair, throw those long, much-waved tresses over the side of the sofa, and say, "Craig," or "Mr. Claiborne," or "Finch," "Go get me a glass of ice water" . . . No *please*. No *will you*. . . . Strangely, whoever received the command got up from his book, his letter writing, his whatever, without question or hesitation, went to the kitchen, and got the ice water.[10]

He could not square Mississippi and New York. New York was home now. When his mother came to visit, her foreignness—the Mississippi inside himself—made his skin crawl. Her genuine Southernness, in New York, seemed to him an act.

She would make excuses for the Confederacy in the War of Northern Aggression. She couldn't shut up about "the magnolia-scented history of the Mississippi Delta." She couldn't hold her liquor. She droned on and on about people whom nobody else at Craig's table had ever heard of.[11]

Eventually he had had it. Characteristically, he told several versions of the story, but the gist was always the same: He renounced his mother, once and for all. Sometimes it was in the lobby of the Waldorf-Astoria, sometimes it was in her room. He couldn't even remember which year the terrible finale was—only that he was somewhere in his mid-thirties.

This was not the only critical passage of Craig's life of which his memory failed him. He remembered very little of his time at Mississippi State, just that he'd hated it and never wanted to see that campus again. He couldn't remember much about his next three years at the University of Missouri either.[12] He did not recall where or when he had left the navy either of the two times he did it, nor whether or not he had gone home to Mississippi either time.[13] He remembered his epochal piece on the decline of American cuisine as having appeared on the front page of the Sunday *Times*;[14] it had in fact been a Monday. He had forgotten much of his elementary education: "I cannot . . . add, multiply, or subtract. I count with my fingers. Until a considerably advanced age, I did not know left from right and at times would resort to feeling my heartbeat to make certain which side was left."[15]

His recollection of that "*final* and *total* estrangement from my mother"—"the most powerful and poignant moment of my adulthood"— was doubtless powerful, and meaningful, to him, but to anyone else trying to stitch together some sense of it, it has a lot more holes than cloth.

His case against her was mysterious. Her letters to him when he was at sea in the navy were "filled with gossip and remembrance, but more than that, filled with declarations of love and admiration that make the exchanges between Robert Browning and Elizabeth Barrett seem adulterated and naïve." They "served as a giant-sized umbilical cord wrapped unceremoniously and noose-like around my neck. . . . Her words leaped out tarantula-like at me and I had no defense." Hers was an "all-embracing, smothering love," which made him cry silently into his pillow "in buried fury." He had "no place to scream." He had, he wrote, ripped her letters to shreds and cast them into the Pacific.[16]

Craig's mother's immediate offenses that evening in New York had been that she had "sat too close to [me] for filial comfort," and when he had demanded of her, "Why must you be so eternally, so God-horribly a mother?" she had replied, "I can never be anything except your mother."[17]

He told her he wanted never to see her again. And he didn't. He didn't even go to her funeral.

The memories of the family confirm that Miss Kathleen was a complex concoction. During Craig's early years at the *Times*, his nephew

Claiborne Barnwell, the son of Craig's sister Augusta, was a member of the Pi Kappa Alpha fraternity at Mississippi State, and at the same time Craig's mother—Claiborne Barnwell's grandmother—had already been employed for several years as the fraternity's housemother. (Craig himself had been a member of Pi Kappa Alpha in his wretched year and a half there.) Mrs. Claiborne was greatly loved by her boys, as was the food she and her kitchen staff put on the table, which was considered by far the best on campus: fresh-baked hot rolls every night, fresh-baked biscuits for breakfast, everything homemade, no shortcuts, three meals a day—twenty meals a week, omitting only Friday dinner.

The PiKA brothers referred to her in the third person as "Mother Claiborne" and called her to her face "Claibo"[18]—hardly the term of endearment one would think of honoring a grande dame with. Claiborne Barnwell knew her within the family as "Garma," but at the fraternity house, in front of his brothers, she was always Mrs. Claiborne.

"Garma was worshiped at PiKA," he says. "The boys never crossed her. She was blind to all the drunkenness. I went to State and joined Pike because I thought I owed it to the family. It would have been a thorn in her heart if I had done otherwise. She was overbearing. A huge presence. The kitchen help were very disciplined even when her demands were exorbitant. I would sometimes be the only one to say it didn't matter if not every one of a hundred and twenty bowls of banana pudding had the same number of pieces of banana in it.

"She never raised her voice. She was a matriarch. Enforced table manners fiercely."

Another alumnus recalls[19] that Mrs. Claiborne kept the Pi Kappa Alpha house living room as her private preserve, under lock and key, with off-white carpeting and pale blue upholstery—not exactly frat-house décor—for the formal teas she would hold from time to time for the university president, distinguished faculty, and prominent members of the local community.

Pi Kappa Alpha was the dominant fraternity on the Mississippi State campus. Their hospitality was rather grand: Their dances had the best bands, and were open to anybody, but Pikes, as they called themselves, never went to any other fraternities' parties. The brothers themselves, however, were not necessarily grand: Only the very richest young men in Mississippi went away to prep school, and Mississippi State would not have been their college of choice. A few scions of Mississippi's ruling class did end up at Ole Miss—perhaps having detoured first through Princeton, Vanderbilt, or Virginia—but State, never. Kathleen Claiborne nonetheless insisted that her boys behave as gentlemen. If they didn't know how to, she made sure they learned.

"When Claibo came into the dining room," the alumnus recalls, "we all stood up, and then we'd say the blessing out loud, and we didn't sit down till she did. When you finished your dinner, you had to take your plate to the kitchen, but on the way you had to stop by and say to Mrs. Claiborne, 'I enjoyed my dinner, thank you very much,' and she'd give you a smile. By the time I was there, she was getting deaf, and some of the guys would just say, 'Well, I saw a dog get run over in the street, thank you very much,' and she'd smile just the same."

Claiborne Barnwell says: "My sister"—Kathleen Craig Barnwell Skates, known, confusingly enough, as Craig, and within the family as Sister—"was very resentful of Mrs. Claiborne. She went through a time when she was quite poor. She was living in Starkville [the seat of Mississippi State], and Garma sent her food every day—as if all she wanted was for Sister to say thank you, like 'I'm expecting you to think I'm wonderful.'"

Miss Kathleen forced Sister to sign a pledge that if she didn't practice piano every day, her dog would be taken away. Sometimes when Sister came home at night she would find a many-page letter on her pillow, filled with her grandmother's aspirations for her. One such surviving missive begins with two densely written pages of the interwoven histories of the Delta and her family, and continues:

And now as the granddaughters of these pioneer families step forward as the debutantes of 1955 with great pride they can claim a part of that glorious past although they could never visualize their grandparents living without the things they accept as ordinary necessities. In common there is much for it is their delta made possible by their families toils, a proud aristocracy sleep in many places now. . . . May you build as they built a strong Miss.

Several members of the family agree that Mrs. Claiborne was frustrated by her sense of immobility. She was capable and intelligent, but she was locked out of any possibility of worldly accomplishment—and locked out of the upper class as well—by having married at seventeen, by the hardship that ensued from her husband's business debacle, and by the social system of her time and place. Hence her letters of aspirations for her granddaughter, and surely also her clinging to her son, in whom alone her aspirations were being realized—until, somehow, what? She overdid it? Loved him too much? Clung too tightly? In any case, after that one night at the Waldorf, she was cut off from him forever.

Back in Indianola, she wrote to Craig, "I think you are ill. I want you to take this money"—a check for a hundred dollars—"and go to a psychiatrist."[20]

He did so, and continued for years, and he seemed to draw from his therapy some of the worst possible conclusions. His self-discoveries seem to have been mostly about blame. That was, unfortunately, rather the psychotherapeutic fashion of the day. The eminent and influential Swiss psychoanalyst Alice Miller, in *The Drama of the Gifted Child*, had written that "All children . . . suffer trauma and permanent psychic scarring at the hands of parents, who enforce codes of conduct through psychological pressure or corporal punishment."

All children? Even if only some were victimized in this way, much of the psychoanalytic orthodoxy of the 1950s—as set forth by Miller's predecessors for the past half-century—held that "psychically scarred" gifted children were doomed to grow up permanently depressed and insecure. Sometimes they might succeed, but inwardly their success would be no more than a pathetic and forever insufficient struggle for their parents' approval. Craig saw his life precisely depicted in that cruel theory.

And it was from his therapy that there came the most chilling, and perhaps the most telling, sentence Craig Claiborne ever wrote about himself: *"I learned to shed ties, more often than not with hideous effect but without retreat or apology."*[21]

§

His ties were already few, and not always strong. It was often up to his friends to keep a friendship going. Thank God for Henry Creel, the true gentle soul, the only one who could always soothe Craig's terrors,

Henry Creel.

calm his rages, and quiet his heart. Creel was a fellow Southerner, years older, a portly, prosperous oil executive, an expert mixer of margaritas, civilized, steady, and stable. He dressed beautifully, and lived in an elegant apartment on Sutton Place South—a tony address in what one gay wag says was known at the time as "the gentlemen bachelors' world of the East Fifties."* One of Craig's friends called Henry "the mother Craig needed." Others thought Craig wasn't sufficiently grateful to Henry, even sufficiently nice, but Henry didn't mind. Sometimes friendships don't balance out.

Sometimes things don't add up. On Craig's return from World War II, his mother had given him a book of her favorite recipes that she had written by hand. He had used it "in my bachelor days in Chicago"[22] and long after, till it was tattered and stained. Wouldn't that have been a perfect example of a tie to be shed? But he kept it all his life.

---

*An apartment house nearby with the address 405 East Fifty-fourth Street was nicknamed "Four Out of Five."

§

It was the absence of any dependency, the absence of any need, that made Craig's friendship with Pierre Franey so deeply valuable to Craig. Open-heartedness was what he found in Pierre, and it seemed as if he had not really known it before. Without the tension of a sexual relationship, without the infinitely tangled complexities of family relation, what they shared was as plain as an egg, and as rich in possibility.

Pierre seemed so—uncomplicated. Henri Soulé, Pierre's grandiose boss, was also, behind his façade of piss-elegance, a simple man. Pierre and Soulé seemed to have in common an unshakeable dedication to excellence: In their view, Le Pavillon must be the best restaurant in the United States; it must compare with the best in the world.

Pierre Franey had come to this country as a wet-eared, homespun kid of eighteen, to work in the restaurant of the French pavilion at the 1939 World's Fair in New York. He had been until then a lowly *commis* (apprentice) in the sauce department of the famous Paris restaurant Drouant, whose proprietor, Jean Drouant, had been asked by the French government to assemble a team capable of showing the world the absolute best of the world's greatest cuisine. As *chef de cuisine* Drouant had selected the well-known Marius Isnard, of the Hôtel de Paris in Monte Carlo. Isnard was supposed to be in control of the kitchen and its personnel, but in choosing Henri Soulé as general manager[23]—till then a mere assistant maître d'hôtel at one of Drouant's other restaurants—Jean Drouant had unknowingly installed a petty monarch who would soon have every last one of the ninety-eight members of the pavilion restaurant's staff reduced to absolute subjugation.

Soulé was as ferocious about excellence as about discipline. "A touch of the tyrant," Craig once wrote, "is essential in a first-class restaurateur."[24] Soulé insisted on the best ingredients—which were not easy to find in New York in 1939—and he insisted on the best possible performance by his staff no matter how hot the kitchen or how long the hours. He quickly recognized in Pierre an indefatigable worker whose focus never blurred, and he made him first *commis* at the fish station.

The Restaurant du Pavillon de France was a sensational success in the summer of 1939, with over 136,000 customers.[25] The staff went home, however, to a country gripped by terror: Germany's might was mass-ing in the east, and invasion was only a matter of time. When the crew returned to New York for the reopening of the World's Fair and the restaurant in the spring of 1940, the Nazis were already on the march across eastern France. They would roll in triumph through Paris in June. America was vacillating between isolation and intervention, riven by fear and confusion. "The Fair's billing as the World of Tomorrow," wrote Pierre, "seemed a cruel mockery in a time when tomorrow seemed so much in doubt."[26] The restaurant's second season was accordingly miserable: Lavish dining out, for Americans, had come to seem excessive in the face of global dread, and the French employees were terrified for their families, their homeland, and their own survival.

A number of the staff, including Pierre Franey and Henri Soulé, decided to stay in New York at least for the moment: The Nazi-dominated Vichy government of France was in power, the resistance against it had barely begun to take shape, and their legal status in the United States was ambiguous at best. Both the French and the American authorities had apparently lost track of Pierre.[27] Then in September 1940, President Franklin Roosevelt signed a new law that would allow visiting foreigners to acquire permanent visas—and to serve in the American armed forces.

Cooks and waiters wandered around New York, picking up work wherever they could get it. Soulé, on the other hand, knew precisely what he wanted to do. He had already run the best restaurant this benighted land had ever seen, and in his opinion American gastronomy, if it were to survive, still needed him. With financing from Jean Drouant and Drouant's investors, and credit from the French pavilion restaurant's suppliers (and also, though no one has ever been able to prove or disprove the claim, allegedly Joseph P. Kennedy), Soulé set out to create the most luxurious, and finest, restaurant in New York's history. He lost touch with his wife back in France, and hardly read the news. He was not troubled by what the war might do to the economy of New York: There would always be diplomats, generals, profiteers, refugees with suitcases full of jewelry; there would always be the rich in New York.

He hired a trio of chefs, equal in rank—in his new kingdom le Roi Soulé would brook no competition.

Throughout the year and more it took to construct the restaurant,

Soulé had nothing for Pierre to do, so Pierre had taken a job in the vast banquet kitchen of the Waldorf, his gifts wasted on excruciatingly trivial tasks (for example, "slice two thousand lemons"[28]). When Soulé called him back to serve in the new restaurant's splendid kitchen as *chef de partie* in charge of fish, Pierre readily returned. So did nineteen others from the old World's Fair staff.

On October 15, 1941, Henri Soulé opened Le Pavillon at 5 East Fifty-fifth Street, a few steps off Fifth Avenue and directly across the street from the St. Regis Hotel. There could not have been a more blue-chip address. To his opening night he invited Kennedys, Cabots, Rockefellers, Vanderbilts. For these prized customers, dinner was on the house; lesser mortals paid through the nose.

From that moment forward, Le Pavillon established, for good and ill, the pattern for expensive New York French restaurants for decades to come. Grandeur ruled, in fabrics, tableware, lighting, high polish, heavy weight. Stiff Gallic formality was the style of service. The crystal was Baccarat,[29] the silver serving wagons by Christofle.[30] Le Pavillon went through six hundred roses a week.[31] Regulars never signed a check: Soulé would calculate the tab, distribute the tips, and add the total to the customer's account.[32]

Perhaps the most snobbish gesture of all—which, alas, became the New York norm for the next forty years—was Soulé's insistence that the menus be written entirely in French. If you couldn't read French—or you happened to have forgotten for the moment that a *timbale de homard Archiduc* consisted of poached lobster with mushroom and truffles bathed in *sauce Normande,* and it may also have slipped your mind that a *sauce Normande* was a *velouté* made with fish stock, tomatoes, and shrimp butter—there would be a captain to explicate it all for you in the most mellifluously smug of accents.

And that table up front? No, it is reserved. But nobody shows. It is *réservé, madame.* Somebody whispers, *Duchess of Windsor—sometimes she comes and sometimes she doesn't.* Soulé is pouring a magnum of Dom Pérignon for Cole Porter and party, and no, they're not paying. The people who could most afford Le Pavillon were the ones Soulé charged least. Pierre Franey, in his memoir, wrote, "He would approach a customer, and say in his formal, assured way: 'Countess, I have something very special for you.'"[33]

As for Pierre: "I did not get to see a whole lot of this."[34] The kitchen was a world of *workers,* of men—all men—of a class and kind alien to the voluptuaries in the dining room, and vice versa. If you had proposed to either party the idea of an open kitchen, they wouldn't even have laughed; they'd have been baffled at the thought.

The prices were gasp-inducing. In his *Dining at the Pavillon,* Joseph Wechsberg presented a typical Pavillon bill of the early 1960s:

Cover charge for two	$ 2.00
2 caviar	16.00
1 chateaubriand for two	18.00
2 vegetables	4.00
2 salads	2.00
1 soufflé for two	5.00
1 bottle of champagne	17.00
2 cocktails	3.00
2 liqueurs	4.50
2 cafés	1.40
	$72.90
(add 15% tip)	10.95
	$83.85

By Pavillon standards [wrote Wechsler] you have not been extravagant at all. You've had the Pavillon's blue-plate de luxe special—caviar and steak. Instead of two wines, a white and a red one, you've nursed a modest bottle of Champagne throughout your meal. You've ordered no *entrée* [i.e., appetizer], no *spécialité de la maison*. By the time you've dispensed the usual gratuities and paid for your taxi, you will have spent $100 for the evening.[35]

Adjusted for inflation, that'd be $729 today.[36]

The price of caviar was not printed on the menu. Nor were the prices of Dover sole, the special cold stuffed *poularde,* the roast duck, rack of lamb, saddle of lamb. Chicken was priced by weight. The contemptuous old maxim fit Le Pavillon like a Balenciaga gown: If you have to ask, you can't afford it.

In that inveterate journal of the rich *Town & Country,* Poppy Cannon recounted a "Meal of the Month" given in honor of none other than Joseph Wechsberg and his new book celebrating Le Pavillon. The menu epitomized "all the best that Henri Soulé knows and loves—the finest of foods and the greatest of wines":

Caviar de Beluga
Wodka-Wyborowa

Mousse de Saumon Poulette
Corton-Charlemagne 1960, Louis Latour

Filet de Bœuf Financière
Pommes Macaire, Épinards en Branche
Château Cheval Blanc 1947

Poularde Froide à la Néva
Salade Gauloise
Charles Heidsieck Rosé 1955

Les Fromages de France
Dom Pérignon 1952 en Magnum

Sorbet Héricart
Friandises
Marc de Bourgogne Exceptionnel, Marquis d'Angerville
Liqueur Basque

Café

The check would have been $1,200 for the party of twenty, if it hadn't been on the house. That is a little under $500 a head in today's money. Wechsberg et al. were serious eaters, deeply appreciative that the *financière* garniture was composed "of little heaps of gastronomic jewels: quenelles of veal, mushrooms, shredded truffles, olives generally stoned and blanched, cockscombs, and kidneys. 'Also, for the most recherché,' Monsieur Soulé suggests, 'to be really fine you should have,' and he lowers his eyes and blushes boyishly, 'the—er—sex of the rooster.'" [37]

Soulé knew that only a minority of his customers at any given lunch or dinner, by contrast, were paying much attention to the food. He kept an eagle's watch, however, over those few who closed their eyes on a first taste, who ate slowly, contemplatively, who sent out the ineffable signals of a person who *understood*. One never knew—one of them might be a beatified gourmet of France, a member of the Club des Cent or the Confrérie des Chevaliers du Tastevin. One of them might be, when one least expected it, Craig Claiborne. But there was one above all who must be satisfied—his palate delighted, his esthetic sense pleased by the presentations, his standards of decorum met by the service—and that was Henri Soulé.

Soulé had known from the beginning how good Pierre was. When Pierre was drafted into the U.S. Army, and was perfectly prepared to spend the war as an ordinary G.I., Soulé, who was too old to serve in the military himself, had been scheming behind his back, and the next thing Pierre knew, he was invited to be the personal chef of General Douglas MacArthur. To the astonishment of Soulé, MacArthur, and the army, Pierre turned down that plum of a job. He wanted to go to Europe and fight for his motherland: "I had been around firearms most of my life; I was a good hunter, a good shot."

Instead they sent him to cooking school in Alabama. His instructor was a sergeant who knew nothing about food preparation. Pierre frequently corrected the sergeant's technique. When Pierre requested a three-day pass to see a girlfriend, the sergeant denied it. Pierre went anyway, AWOL. When he returned, he found that he had flunked out of cooking school.

The army made Pierre a machine gunner and sent him to France—precisely his original wish. After the Normandy invasion, he wanted to go to see his mother in Burgundy. Unfortunately, the village of Saint-Vinnemer was still behind the German lines, and his commanding officer forbade him to go. Pierre said he was going to go anyway. The officer capitulated and lent Pierre his own jeep and driver. Somehow they managed not to be killed by the Germans, and when they entered Pierre's ancestral village, the whole populace turned out, cheering, believing that their liberators had arrived. Pierre's mother had sewn an American flag, which she gave to the jeep driver in tearful gratitude. Two days later, Pierre and the driver returned safely to their unit, and soon Saint-Vinnemer was in fact freed by American forces.

The army continued north across the devastated landscape of Holland. There was little food, but Pierre and his platoon were followed by a cow and a gaggle of chickens. In an abandoned farmhouse he found a pig. A pig won't follow like a cow or chickens. Pierre found a baby carriage, and the pig cooperated. A passing general and his motorcade stopped for a look. A reporter and a photographer for the wartime paper *Stars and Stripes* found this newsworthy. It was Pierre's début as a public figure.

Thirty-five years later, the former jeep driver, having seen a cooking column by Pierre Franey in his local Michigan newspaper, sent the writer a package containing the American flag that Pierre's mother had made during the Nazi occupation.[38]

By the time he was twenty years old—after a long childhood of apprenticeship—Pierre had long since mastered every possible culinary skill: "I had labored at every station in the restaurant kitchen, taking on the tough, muscular work like butchering as well as the artistry of sauce making. I had mastered all the techniques and rules. . . . I understood, the way a painter does, what had worked for centuries and could imagine how, in a very disciplined way, to diverge from those classics."[39] When he returned from the war, he had achieved something else. "What had changed, and profoundly so, was that I felt immeasurably more certain of myself as a man."[40]

Yet this man would labor obediently under Soulé's merciless rigors for seven more years until the *maître* was confident that Pierre was ready to command the most celebrated kitchen in America. At last, in March of 1953, Soulé gave his majestic nod and there he was: *chef* of Le Pavillon. Pierre Franey had just turned thirty-three years old.[41]

The premises at 5 East Fifty-fifth Street belonged to Columbia Pictures, whose president, Harry Cohn, was a regular at Le Pavillon. Cohn was well known for his loud mouth and general vulgarity, and Soulé hated him. Cohn wanted, of course, a prominent table, and Soulé never gave him one. When the lease came up for renewal in 1957, Cohn doubled Le Pavillon's rent. He also accused Henri Soulé of anti-Semitism.[42]

The accusation rather shocked Le Pavillon's numerous Jewish habitués, among them many of Soulé's darlings. Soulé was having no more of Cohn. He found new premises in the Ritz Towers at Fifty-seventh Street and Park Avenue, and built there a new Pavillon, more spacious than the old and even grander. The next year Cohn was dead, and Soulé got 5 East Fifty-fifth back. There he established a "little sister" of Le Pavillon, the less formal but ever so chic La Côte Basque. He commissioned the Parisian painter Bernard Lamotte to cover the walls with big, bright, and lovely scenes of the harbor at St-Jean-de-Luz, in the home province of *soi-même*, Soulé. *Le restaurant, c'est moi,* he was said to have said. The executive chef of both Le Pavillon and La Côte Basque was to be Pierre Franey.

Henri Soulé was hated by some, respected by some, courted by some, envied, tolerated, venerated, and admired. But almost nobody who actually knew him *liked* him. One who did was Craig Claiborne. In a long profile[43] of Soulé that—a rare occurrence among Craig's writings—was never published, he accorded both opprobrium and praise to his subject almost entirely in the form of quotations from others. It's easy enough to sense Craig's own feelings in much of the praise, as in this from "the late raconteur and artist Ludwig Bemelmans," whose view of Soulé was obviously that of a coddled favorite:

> He is the composite of all the best proprietors and high priests of the table I have ever seen. . . . [He] seems to be stuffed with the goodies of kitchen and cellar, and on a good day when all goes well, his face, round as the sun, shines as if the pastry cook had just passed his butter brush over it. He is perpetually examining every corner of his restaurant. He . . . has a dancer's agility; even when standing still he seems to spin, aware of everything that is happening on all sides.

"The influence that he has exercised on French cuisine and French restaurants in this country," wrote Craig, "is beyond measure."

Pierre Franey was not interested in Soulé's influence. Soulé had been Pierre's boss for twenty years, and after all that time that was still all he was. As far as Pierre was concerned, there was no warmth at all between them.

Soulé, on the other hand, called Pierre Pierrot, and proclaimed that he thought of Pierrot as a son. That was not how the relationship looked to a new immigrant named Jacques Pépin. Pépin had already served as the personal chef of Charles de Gaulle, but at Le Pavillon he was only another *chef de partie,* making all of $2.60 an hour.[44] Pépin was also imbued with the fierce spirit of French labor, and in his memoir he recalled that Soulé treated Pierre Franey "with no more respect than he accorded to the most recently hired pot scrubber." Pépin was outraged to discover, only a few months after his arrival, that years had passed since anybody on the kitchen staff had been given a raise.[45]

In the winter of 1959–1960, business was sagging, and by Soulé's order, Pierre began, very reluctantly, to try to reduce costs. Pierre was humiliated, and outraged: What had become of Le Pavillon's uncompromising standards of excellence? In January 1960, Soulé demanded that the entire kitchen staff reduce their hours from forty to the union minimum of thirty-five hours per week; and there would be no overtime, ever.

Pierre knew that it would not be possible under those circumstances to produce food of the peerless quality that was his sine qua non—and had been Le Pavillon's too before this surrender to mediocrity. Pierre and his brigade unanimously refused. Soulé demanded that Pierre come to meet with him in his office. Pierre demanded that Soulé meet with him in the kitchen.

Craig was following the contretemps with high amusement, as well as complete sympathy for Pierre and his staff. "After several days," he wrote, "conversations between the two were reduced to an emissary who went back and forth between M. Soulé in the dining room and Mr. Franey in the kitchen."[46] It was a stalemate, and Craig's affection for Henri Soulé was waning fast.

On February 16, 1960, Pierre Franey walked out.

Jacques Pépin then urged his colleagues to join him in a mass resignation. "In France," he wrote, "such events were so common that there was a special term . . . *la brigade saute*—'the brigade explodes.'" But this was New York, and the kitchen workers' union was not a movement of high-minded socialists and philosophers.

That evening a pair of large Italian gentlemen who were associated in some capacity with local 89 dropped by Le Pavillon. I can assure you they were not there to sample our *poulet Pavillon*. . . . The goons cornered me in the cooks' dressing room. The snitch closed the door and stood against it as one of the union guys lifted me off the floor and slammed me against the wall, pinning me there.

The rest of the scene was straight out of a gangster movie—*You'll never work in this town again,* etc. What the tough guys hadn't counted on, however, was the non-scarability of this little guy, tough in a different way, who like Pierre had come up hardscrabble in the French restaurant system.

Once the goons were gone, Pépin calmly reminded his colleagues that if they needed to work overtime, what were those bums going to do? So work overtime if you have to, and we'll take it up with Soulé. If he won't pay you, you walk, like Chef did. Also don't forget: Anybody can get sick and have to stay home. Do you think Soulé wants a sick cook sneezing into the food? And what if an order takes a longer time than usual to prepare? The customer will be yelling bloody murder at who? Soulé, right? Then Soulé's going to yell bloody murder at you. And then what? He fires you? Fine! Because I say we quit anyway. Not all at once. One at a time. You tomorrow. After a couple days more, you. Then me. And so on, till there's nobody left.

Which is exactly what they did.[47]

Henri Soulé had no choice but to close Le Pavillon's doors. On February 23, 1960, a sign appeared in the window announcing—wishfully—that it would reopen on March 15.

There had never been such a thing as a "star chef" in America—until March 3, 1960:

LE PAVILLON SHUT IN A GALLIC PIQUE

Chef Walks Out in Feud Over
Hours and 7 Members of
Staff Follow Him

Craig wrote the whole thing up in the *Times* as comedy. "Many familiar with l'affaire Pavillon see its source in the strong emotional and Gallic temperament of the principals. . . . Both are choked with emotion at times when discussing the other. Tears well up, and the wrath begins." The piece was accompanied by two photographs. Pierre looks like a matinee idol. Soulé, shrugging, lower lip puffed out, belly bulging, looks like an *opera buffa* clown.

Craig's treatment of the antagonists is mocking, but even-handedly so. Whether he had anything to do with the decidedly uneven-handed selection of the pictures is impossible to know.

What is known is that Pierre Franey never went back to Le Pavillon, and that he and Henri Soulé never spoke again.

8

Authority

Craig always said he had no more than modest expectations for *The New York Times Cook Book*, but it was a far from modest undertaking—comprising almost fifteen hundred recipes, filling more than seven hundred pages, nearly three inches thick, and encyclopedic in scope. When it was published in 1961, the only comparable cookbook on the market was *The Joy of Cooking*, but *Joy* was much more basic, more instructive, and almost entirely American. *Joy* was essential for any cook starting out, to be sure, but it was not a work of imagination. Next to it *The New York Times Cook Book* was rather a wild ride around the world, reflecting the catholicity of Craig Claiborne's gastronomic passions.

All the recipes had appeared in the *Times* between 1950 and 1960, which meant that most of them had been published before Craig's employment there. Of those that had appeared in his columns, "many . . . were enthusiastically adapted from my textbooks at the Professional School of the Swiss Hotel Keepers Association."[1] Craig had done none of the recipe testing; the *Times* maintained a formidable test kitchen of its own. As for rigorous editing, "Oh, God, I thought, there are probably a thousand errors in each chapter. . . . Here I will make a confession of a truth known only to those who have edited and published my books. I have *never* proofread a galley before a cookbook of mine was published. I am psychotically fearful of discovering errors in recipes."[2] Luckily, Craig had a team of editors behind him, both at the paper and at his publisher, Harper & Row.

What was all his was the selection of material. The book begins, naturally enough, with appetizers, but the first five aren't even recipes. He just tells you how to serve caviar, foie gras, smoked salmon, ham, and oysters—perfect exemplars of his taste for elegant simplicity. Only then is there an actual recipe, and it is an almost absurdly difficult one: a galantine of turkey that requires skinning and de-boning the turkey; stuffing it with a forcemeat of ground veal, pork, salt pork, cream, and Cognac along with strips of tongue, strips of fatback, pistachios, and truffles; rolling the whole thing up in the turkey's skin to form a sort of giant sausage, then sewing that up with needle and thread; poaching it in stock (which, if you're good, you have made yourself) along with aromatic vegetables; glazing the cooled galantine with aspic and finally decorating it with "cutouts of truffles, black olives, hard-cooked egg whites or the green part of scallions to form any pattern desired."[3] Welcome to Craig's world.

Still within that first chapter come recipes for Schweinsulze (jellied pork loaf, requiring six pigs' feet); rullepølse (Danish spiced breast of veal); Mexican carnitas; keftedes (Greek meatballs); anguilles (eels) Quo Vadis; two versions of oysters Rockefeller; Russian pirozhki; Chilean empanadas; mushrooms stuffed with (canned) snails; quiche Lorraine ("It seems odd that this very special pie, traditional in France, was so long in gaining popularity in America"[4]), and lobster *en Bellevue parisienne* (shown in its photograph to be a work of bravura Victorian culinary architecture, "surmounted with aspic-coated medallions"[5]). There were also less flashy and less challenging dishes, for the modest or shy—marinated mushrooms, stuffed eggs, cucumber sandwiches—but Craig's hopeful premise was that "world travel on a scale unsurpassed in history is making the American palate more sophisticated."[6] That wasn't yet as true as Craig liked to believe, but *The New York Times Cook Book* was going to go far toward making it so.

That galantine—what was he thinking? Was he unconsciously, passive-aggressively trying to scare everybody off? Did he actually think anyone would take a look and go, Oh, golly, that's just the thing for next Friday when the boss is coming for dinner? Could it have been some kind of Craig-&-Pierre joke? Or was this early food porn? Cookbooks in later years, after all, would often be bought more as the stuff of fantasy than as manuals for cooking.

In fact Craig was perfectly serious. He had seen these galantines on the S.S. *France,* in the displays of hors d'oeuvre at the grand restaurants of Paris, at formal dinners for gourmet societies and royalty. And he saw just such a galantine on an elegant New Year's Eve buffet—in his imagination. There was the key to *The New York Times Cook Book*'s uniqueness and its success: What had fired Craig's imagination, he now was sharing. Hundreds of thousands of other imaginations would catch fire from his.

It is impossible to say whether the book had caught the wave of an entirely new American enthusiasm for food and cooking or had set it in motion. Craig remained resolutely modest on the question: "It was my honest belief when that book came off the press, a belief that I maintained for several years, that *The New York Times Cook Book* would not sell more than thirty thousand copies. I firmly believed that at the end of five years it would disappear from bookshelves and thus go into oblivion."[7] It has now sold some three million copies, and is still going strong.

In the book's early days it seemed to be an inescapable presence in every household of privilege in New York, and the readership of Craig's columns in the *Times* grew apace. Kids just out of college were asking their parents for *sautoirs* and chef's knives for their birthdays, and sweating for hours in their tiny kitchens to turn out three-course dinners straight out of the book, for friends who would soon be reciprocating with productions of comparable laboriousness.

You might start with billi bi: "This may well be the most elegant and delicious soup ever created," Craig wrote. "This is the recipe of Pierre Franey, one of this nation's greatest chefs."[8] In those days, you didn't get the nice clean farmed Prince Edward Island mussels of today—you had to yank and twist and scrub the scratchy beards off the little bastards one by one. And then you strain them *out?* You "reserve the mussels for another use"? *A mussel soup with no mussels in it?* Pierre's mussel-free version of billi bi is in fact insanely delicious.

Easier will be the chicken breasts with tarragon, in a somewhat sludgy flour-thickened cream sauce. Craig assures you that "White wine, heavy cream and the delicate herb known as tarragon are three of the foundations for classic French cuisine."[9] But four stores on the Upper West Side and then a trip across the park have yielded no fresh tarragon, so you settle for the rather acrid dried version; then nobody at the table knows the difference.

"One of the most delectable of desserts,"[10] *oeufs à la neige,* is also one of the most demanding of a total beginner—three recipes in one: mounds of beaten egg white poached in milk; a caramel sauce; and *crème anglaise,* which calls for the double boiler you do not own and which therefore may require two or three tries, with the sauce-making saucepan bobbing unsteadily in a larger one containing simmering water, before you get a non-curdled outcome.

Having cream in your choice of all three dishes would have made Henri Soulé shudder, but a fine white Burgundy could be had in 1961 for a song, and would absolutely sing straight through that menu. And the young, green hosts would have years—and years of Craig Claiborne's counsel—to learn the niceties of menu planning.

Luncheons, picnics, brunches, new restaurants, dinner parties. All of a sudden, it seemed, these were what people were doing for entertainment. You didn't stop going to the theater or the ball game, but now a meal with friends was a whole evening's pleasure, and you had a whole new thing to talk about—best of all, unlike family or politics, one without danger—the food.

—I must get your recipe.

—It's in the *Times* cookbook—you do have it?

—I've barely scratched the surface.

—I know what you mean.

—I was reading it the other day, and what in heaven's name is *pastel de choclo?*

—Let's look it up.

Pastel del choclo is "a hearty and unusual Chilean casserole that is somewhat tedious to prepare but well worth the effort. It contains an amplitude of chicken, beef and corn."[11]

—I don't think I'm going to try that one anytime soon.

And then six weeks later, you go to a dinner party where they're serving *pastel del choclo.*

Had Craig realized what a storm of one-upmanship he was starting? Was that what that galantine was about? No, and no. He loved the idea of inspiring a few to undertake his more daring pièces de résistance, but much of *The New York Times Cook Book* was an attempt to push the broader public well ahead of where he knew they stood. A column he published on New Year's Day of 1960 was flattering in tone—

"During the Fifties, just ended, public taste was elevated to an awesome degree"—but not very excited in its recognition that "the palate was awakened to such magnificent dishes as quiche Lorraine, beef in Burgundy sauce, coq au vin and sukiyaki." His "awesome" and "magnificent" seem a bit forced.

The wave of enthusiasm that greeted many of the more challenging dishes in the book, therefore, took him somewhat by surprise. He was delighted to find himself riding its crest, but he also didn't kid himself. This did not look to Craig Claiborne like a wholesale transformation of the American gastronomic landscape.

For every New York or college-town dinner party boasting Craig's *cannelloni alla nerone, bollito misto,* and Sicilian cream cake, there were still dozens of households barreling toward culinary perdition. "Television dinners are said to have become the principal diet of those too enamored of the medium to spare the time to scramble eggs," he had written in that same New Year's 1960 column. "Who knows? With sufficient research in the preparation of food capsules for space travel, perhaps mealtime will become a thing of the past for that segment of the public that has neither the time nor the appetite for a refined, if painstaking, cuisine."[12]

For the most part Craig was able to worry himself little about "that segment of the public," for his own following was growing so fast. To them he could patiently explain the Soulévian insistence on French-only French menus on the grounds that "In the first place, French is generally conceded to be an elegant language, [which] adds 'tone' to a menu. . . . and there is no clear, concise, unwordy translation of the dishes. The French can say in a word what would require a sentence to translate into English." Moreover, he said, "An examination of this nomenclature is a fascinating study in itself."[13]

Tyrannical as this may sound today, it must be remembered that with the investiture of John and Jacqueline Kennedy in the White House, French culture was in the ascendant, along with its formality and its sense of aristocratic hierarchy. Until Mrs. Kennedy hired the highly accomplished René Verdon, there had never been a White House chef at all: The housekeeper cooked for the First Family, and meals for state occasions came from outside caterers or the U.S. Navy. Verdon had been trained in the brutal system of old-fashioned apprenticeship in

France, and as Craig had learned from Pierre Franey, that experience had demanded "long hours, rigorous tasks, and extraordinary physical stamina,"[14] but it also meant that Verdon knew the *haute cuisine* to the last jot. The president and First Lady would dine in the White House private residence on the likes of *quenelles de brochet* and mousse of sole with lobster.[15]

The menu of the inauguration luncheon of John Fitzgerald Kennedy[16] on January 20, 1961—when, if ever, you would expect the White House kitchen to shine—is a sobering cross-section of the impacted layers of culinary cliché René Verdon was being brought aboard to displace:

Cream of Tomato Soup with Crushed Popcorn

Deviled Crabmeat Imperial

New England Boiled Lobster with Drawn Butter

Prime Texas Ribs of Beef au Jus

String Beans Amandine *Broiled Tomato*

Grapefruit and Avocado Sections with Poppyseed Dressing

Hot Garlic Bread *Butterflake Rolls*

Pattiserie Bâteau Blanche*

Mints *Coffee*

In Verdon's obituary in the *Times*,[17] William Grimes (from 1999 to 2004 the paper's restaurant critic) wrote:

He shocked Americans used to canned vegetables and iceberg lettuce by tending his own vegetables on the White House roof and arranging for the White House garden designer to plant herbs in the flowerbeds of the East Garden.

His first official meal at the White House, a lunch for Prime Minister Harold Macmillan of Britain and 16 guests on April 5, 1961, set the new tone: trout in Chablis and sauce Vincent, beef filet au jus and artichoke bottoms Beaucaire, and a dessert he dubbed *désir d'avril*, or "April Desire," a meringue shell filled with raspberries and chocolate.

*The atrocious French is *sic*, alas.

"The verdict after the [MacMillan] luncheon," wrote Craig, "was that there was nothing like French cooking to promote good Anglo-American relations."[18]

It wasn't just the food. Jackie Kennedy fairly radiated francophilia. She had spent her junior year at the University of Grenoble and the Sorbonne; she had majored in French literature, and she spoke the language fluently. Her renovation of the White House was overseen by the decorator who had restored Versailles. She dressed in Givenchy, Dior, Chanel.

Ninety-sixty-one was therefore a fine year for Craig's own francophilia. He wrote of the French ambassador's formal dinners and his wife's love of the *cuisine bourgeoise*;[19] of drinking the red wines of Bordeaux with fish;[20] of Thomas Jefferson's love of French food;[21] of a new pâtisserie in Woodside, "L.I."[22] (better known to most New Yorkers as Queens). He reviewed the newly opened French restaurant Lutèce, which he found so "impressively elegant and conspicuously expensive" that "the patron of Lutèce would do well to wear a dinner jacket. . . . A business suit seems inappropriate."[23]

He reported on the meals served to the Kennedys on their first official trip abroad by the Queen of England at Buckingham Palace and by General Charles de Gaulle at the Palais de l'Élysée ("a clear consommé, turbot in cream sauce, roast saddle of lamb Clamart . . . and a frozen coffee soufflé"), contrasting the delicacy and elegance of those menus with what the Eisenhowers had served the French president the previous year in the States: "twice a day . . . a surfeit of beef." By contrast, he wrote, "There has been admirable variety in the Kennedys' European menus, and those in charge of local state visits would do well to give them close scrutiny."[24]

Craig's first love was certainly French food of that ilk, but it by no means dominated *The New York Times Cook Book*. The range of exotic possibilities exemplified in the appetizer chapter continued throughout, and there was no lack of near-impossibilities as well, à la the galantine, but Craig had built a cookbook that could in fact be the only one you owned. It was not a manual of technique, but if you began with the easiest things and you weren't afraid of goofing, it made the perfect graduation gift for the college senior who couldn't boil an egg. Indeed, on page 302, there are directions for hard- or soft-cooked eggs, fried eggs, and, as soon as you felt up to it, *oeufs au beurre noir*. Page 307 includes "How to Scramble Eggs," and, below it, Salmon Soufflé. Amid Gevulde Kool, Ravioli alla Bardelli (with calf's brains), and Lobster Thermidor are also Minnesota Fudge Cake, Hasty Pudding, Creole jambalaya, and roast turkey with giblet gravy (accompanied by photo-illustrated instructions for carving it).

The New York Times Cook Book is a bit like one of those old general stores that display the sign "If We Ain't Got It You Don't Need It." There is a straightforward chapter on wine; there is another on other beverages, from tea to Tom Collins to glögg. There is a guide to cheeses, a guide to herbs and spices. There is a list of sources for hard-to-find ingredients ("There was only one major cheese shop in all of Manhattan," Craig wrote of 1961 in the book's thoroughly revised 1990 reincarnation). There are conversion tables of weights and measures, timetables for roasting meats. Not too modest to be left out are boiled rice, buttered cabbage, baked potatoes, roast duck, broiled lamb chops, sliced tomato salad, mashed butternut squash, and, for when Grandma was coming to see the new apartment, Ohio corn relish. The brief recipes for all of these basics are so clear and so correct that even the long-seasoned cook may sometimes find them worth checking in on: You may discover something forgotten or perhaps even never known—slipping your raw egg carefully from a saucer into the frying pan, for example, instead of the usual grease-spattering splat; or that taking the trouble to peel your tomatoes, garden-perfect as they may be, quite transforms a simple tomato salad. Pierre Franey's attentiveness to getting things precisely right, though not acknowledged in the text, makes itself felt throughout in details like those.

§

On the rebound from twenty-one years at Le Pavillon, Pierre Franey was offered a job by one of its regulars, who loved Pierre's cooking so much that he had tried to mediate the feud between Pierre and Henri Soulé and who thought that running a complex kitchen like that of Le Pavillon might not be so different from what Pierre might face in the executive position he had in mind.

The job would be nine to five, five days a week, in Midtown Manhattan, with a breathtakingly higher salary than Pierre would ever have thought of asking for; and the title of vice president. He could come home every night to his wife and family. His weekends would be his own. He could work with Craig in another state than exhaustion.

The name of Pierre's new boss was Howard Johnson. Yes, that Howard Johnson. "I know that many people now, especially at this time when the restaurant chef seems to have such a glamorous life, will see this work as, somehow, a comedown," wrote Pierre, "a mortification . . . but for me it was not; for me it was a chance to live a normal life and to take on challenges of scale that few cooks can ever imagine."[25]

Pierre hired Jacques Pépin and, from The Four Seasons, Albert Kumin. They were going to revolutionize the food at HoJo's. They intended to figure out, for example, how to turn two thousand pounds of chicken a day into real stock and honest chicken pot pie. They struggled with the challenge of creating pastry that would survive freezing. Among the givens were low-wage, poorly trained personnel who had to follow detailed and demanding instructions, and portion control and costs accounted to fractions of cents. Pierre took it all in stride. He was happy.

§

Craig was still devoted to Le Pavillon—irritating as that was to Pierre—and his undying enthusiasm encouraged a young chef there, a protégé of Henri Soulé's named Roger Fessaguet, and two of the maîtres d'hôtel, Robert Meyzen and Fred Decré, to open a restaurant of comparable ambition. Craig's review of La Caravelle was rapturous: "Rarely has a restaurant opened to such an immediately public enthusiasm," he wrote, "and rarely has it been so thoroughly deserved."[26] From that moment and for years thereafter, a reservation at La Caravelle was obtainable only by its wealthy faithful or if you were willing to wait weeks for a table.

And now they had the Kennedys.

The story[27] went that Joseph P. Kennedy—who, you will recall, may or may not have been an original investor—was dining at Le Pavillon, as he often did, when he demanded to know of its American maître d'hôtel, Fred Decré, why he kept on working for "that lousy Frenchman." Decré had soon thereafter jumped ship to establish La Caravelle in partnership with Roger Fessaguet.

Soulé had overheard Kennedy's remark, and the next time he was in the house, Soulé, always a not-so-closeted Republican anyway, made sure Kennedy overheard *him* assessing young John's presidential prospects—"Not a chance, not a chance."

Creatures of habit, and above the sniping of such small fry, the Kennedy family returned. This time Soulé—entirely contrary to his own privacy policy—somehow just happened to have admitted a photographer. Kennedy instantly envisioned the press coverage of the Democratic candidate's family gobbling foie gras at the most expensive restaurant in the country, and demanded, loudly, that the photographer be thrown out. Soulé muttered to one of his underlings—in French, but insufficiently *sotto voce* and doubtless on purpose—that even though the boy was not yet president, the old man was acting like a dictator.[28]

The Kennedys promptly transferred their loyalty to La Caravelle. It became a kind of clubhouse for the whole extended clan, and it was Roger Fessaguet who recommended René Verdon to Jacqueline Kennedy, assuring her that the First Family could then dine in their new home on a *cuisine française* of the highest order.[29]

It was of this time that Craig wrote, "The *New York Times* was the ultimate job of my life. . . . It was, to me, the grandest newspaper in the world. I am not ashamed to say that there were times when no one knew, in solitude, I was literally moved to tears when I reflected on my association with the paper. As much as I could possibly be, I was gloriously happy."[30]

As happy as I could be: That closely hedged caution was pure Craig Claiborne.

§

In midsummer of 1961, an editor at the publishing house of Alfred A. Knopf named Judith Jones was looking forward excitedly to a book scheduled for release in September that she thought was "a work of genius."[31] It was going to be the first cookbook that she, or Knopf, had ever published. After a long struggle to find the right words, Jones and the authors had come up with the title *Mastering the Art of French Cooking*.

Mr. Knopf said, "I'll eat my hat if that title sells."[32]

The job of his dreams.

But Jones was certain that she had something potentially big on her hands. She believed that Craig Claiborne's reputation had risen to the point at which a blessing from him could confer on the book the importance it deserved, and so, although she did not know him at all, she invited him out to lunch. When she urged him to review the book— even just take a look at it—Craig said he didn't do book reviews.

He was, however, quite interested in the fact that Jones and her husband, Evan, were dab hands at Manhattan rooftop grilling, and he thought that that might make for a good story.

As to that book review he didn't want to do, what he didn't say was that he had a book of his own—*The New York Times Cook Book*—due out at exactly the same time.

Finally he "offered a bargain: If the Joneses would agree to put on a cookout so he could write about it, then, in return, he promised to give his attention to *Mastering*. If he thought it worthy, he would review it."[33]

Craig did the Joneses proud, plugging Evan's upcoming book on his native Minnesota, praising their herb garden, and noting that a recent Senegalese dinner on their rooftop terrace had greatly pleased the ambassador of Senegal to the United Nations. Their sense of style met with Craig's approval, too: Their guests were "almost always seated at table. They both have a proper abhorrence for buffet suppers when plates are balanced on laps or knees." The Joneses' dinner for Craig—cockles and mussels in green mayonnaise followed by spit-roasted lamb with flageolets—showed, he wrote, that "They live by the dictum that food is fun and that cooking is a prime pleasure."[34]

Two and a half months later—spang in mid-publication of his own, career-critical *New York Times Cook Book* and perfectly timed nonetheless to do the most it could for *Mastering the Art of French Cooking*—Craig wrote that Julia Child, Louisette Bertholle, and Simone Beck had produced "what is probably the most comprehensive, laudable and monumental work" on the subject of French cuisine. "It will," he wrote, "probably remain the definitive work for nonprofessionals. . . . It is written in the simplest terms possible and without compromise or condescension.

"The recipes are glorious. . . . All are painstakingly edited and written as if each were a masterpiece, and most of them are."[35]

It can probably be safely asserted that Julia Child would have found her thousands of dévotés if Craig Claiborne had never been born, but it is equally safe to say that this review—so great had his influence grown—shone on *Mastering the Art of French Cooking* a spotlight brighter than could have come from any other source.

Craig's generosity should be noted. He could have published the review a month or two later, or praised *Mastering the Art of French Cooking* more mildly. Doing it when he did, and with such high praise, almost certainly sacrificed sales of his own *New York Times Cook Book*.

9

Attention

Henri Soulé seemed to have a real problem getting along with people. With customers he had a two-way switch: fawning or disdain. As for staff, we've seen how things went with Pierre Franey, Jacques Pépin, and Le Pavillon's whole *brigade de cuisine* in 1959. Now, in 1962, this.

La Côte Basque was supposed to be his easygoing restaurant, little sister to the big, grand Pavillon. "It was his personal charity drive, a contribution to illicit romance," wrote Gael Greene (Craig's first truly talented emulator) in the New York *Herald Tribune*. "Or as he said: 'La Côte Basque is Le Pavillon *pour les pauvres,* my Pavillon for the poor.' And, 'The Pavillon is elegant. The Côte Basque is amusing. Some people may find it quite convenient that Henri Soulé has two restaurants in Manhattan. A man may take his wife to Côte Basque and the other lady to Pavillon.'"[1]

But on Wednesday, January 24, 1962, Soulé exploded again, and his amusing little restaurant for wives imploded for good. Here is the notice he posted, as quoted in the *Times* by Craig Claiborne: "Due to insubordination by the dining crew of orders issued by me, I have no alternative except to close this restaurant as of tonight until such time that my orders will be complied with."[2] Such time was to be: never.

You might think that the Franey episode had taught him something, but evidently not. Soulé's La Côte Basque was dead. By April 1962[3] he had sold the lease, the equipment, and the Bernard Lamotte murals to the owners of another French restaurant, the once great but long-declining Café Chambord, for $260,000.[4] The sale did not rise to the level of the *Times*'s notice.

In the early 1960s the first of that decade's convention-flouting fever was already in the air. At a birthday celebration for President Kennedy on May 19, 1962, in front of fifteen thousand goggling onlookers, Marilyn Monroe took the stage at Madison Square Garden wearing a sheer, flesh-colored dress so tight she had actually had to be sewn into it, and nothing else but her shoes. Her breathily lascivious delivery of "Happy Birthday, Mr. President," could not have been an apter sign of the dawn of the Age of Diminished Impulse Control, nor her lover Jack Kennedy an apter president. (Mrs. Kennedy, by the way, was not present, and Ms. Monroe's dress would be auctioned in 1999 for $1.26 million.[5])

Craig caught the sixties fever too. His career-long assistant at the *Times,* Velma Cannon—a dignified and elegant lady of ninety-odd years now—remembers: "I always knew he was gay, but I didn't care what he was. Sometimes I did worry, though, in the early days, that he might be a little—promiscuous. I'd call him up at his apartment about a little proof correction or something, and for a while it seemed like it was always some different young man who answered the phone."

"I have always been impetuous," Craig wrote in his memoir, "and do not regret the trait."[6]

Arthur Gelb, for many years the managing editor of the *New York Times,* was, quietly, Craig's protector and defender. "He didn't realize how homophobic the place was," says Gelb. "The publisher and many of the top editors just didn't like him. Was that because they were homophobes? Probably. And Craig was obsessed with sex. I had to tell him, Please, tone it down. He talked too much. Fast, with a little stutter.

"To look at, he really didn't come off that way, though. He was always very well dressed, very conservatively dressed. And there was nothing pompous about him.

"And I'm convinced he never planned his great role. It all came organically. Other people made plans for him. It was like that all his life. He thought like an artist. His ideas came instinctively. He was not well organized. He was impulsive. A genius. Had ideas in his dreams.

"My wife and I used to dine with him quite a bit. He loved a good dinner, obviously. He never devoured his food—only tasted. He would chew it, roll it around in his mouth, savor it. Never finished his plate, never. And yes, he did drink too much, and it got worse as time went on."[7]

Alcohol usually seemed to attend on Craig's experimental whims.

Nearly always the disinhibiting consumption was his own, but one of the nuttiest adventures of his life was due to someone else's drinking. In 1962, on one of his sudden and inexplicable inspirations—harking back, perhaps, to his fizzled romance twenty years before with the mysterious Mrs. Wood—he decided to get married. His fiancée was a woman who "moved effortlessly" among people of "'mixed' psyches and sexual inclinations."[8] She had given up drink, which worried Craig, especially because the reason she gave him was that "when she drank she tended to 'blow up.'" What allowed him to set his uneasy apprehension aside was how compatible—to his astonishment—they were in bed. She "was aware of my sexual tendencies." She accepted Craig's proposal "with what I considered alacrity. I promised to be as faithful as I could but added that my vows were chancy."

His bride-to-be (he never revealed her name) didn't seem to have much desire to see her old friends, until one time when she did invite one woman to dinner. "The conversation at that meal," Craig recalled in mock delicacy, "was to be quite intimate."

Sensing major frivolities in store, he prepared an elaborately festive dinner—a multi-dish Swedish smörgåsbord to start, to be followed by roast leg of lamb with tomatoes and mushrooms, salad, cheese, and "an opera torte with a cream filling and almond paste topping."

The supposedly teetotal fiancée's preparations consisted of belting down three shots of bourbon in rapid succession. There would have been cocktails when their guest arrived, and then with the smörgåsbord came the traditional shots of ice-cold aquavit, each tossed back, as is traditional, in a single gulp.

Craig's lady love, with each new surge of alcohol through her system, pointed out to him various errors and character faults of his which she had previously neglected to mention. Craig sat reddening in silence as the insults intensified. His failure to respond—his inveterate defense against attack ever since learning it from his childhood friend David Sanders in Indianola—made her angrier. He tried to calm her. The guest, sensing the low likelihood of a good outcome, gathered her things and departed. Craig withdrew to the kitchen to do the dishes, in particular to look after one of his few truly valuable possessions, a set of six Baccarat crystal goblets from which they had drunk the Burgundy and the Bordeaux that he had so carefully selected.

The scene unfolds as follows.

Fiancée flees to bedroom.

Craig puts record on phonograph, Bernstein's *Candide*. Song is parody of opera but does *sound* like opera. Fiancée hates opera. Song title—wicked Craig!—"Glitter and Be Gay."

Fiancée exits to kitchen. Screams. Sound of shattering Baccarat crystal.

Re-enter fiancée. Punches Craig hard in chest. Craig falls backward onto sofa, breath knocked out. Does not rise.

Exit fiancée. For good.

§

Nineteen-sixty-two was the first year Craig began reviewing restaurants regularly, and on May 18 the paper published his first Directory to Dining, with brief capsule reviews of five restaurants. The evaluations were limited, none longer than a hundred words. The bistro Gaston had "one of the most inspired French kitchens in town." Marchi's was "one of New York's most unusual" Italian restaurants because it didn't have a printed menu. Tien Tsin had probably the finest Chinese kitchen in the city. Sayat Nova had good "American cuisine," but that was a typo—it should have said Armenian. King of the Sea had to settle for being "perhaps Manhattan's best known seafood house."

"Such a listing," the column noted, "will be published every Friday in the *New York Times*." There was no byline, but Craig Claiborne was the only food writer the paper had, and the style was unmistakably his. Therefore, given that he continued to decline to write about places he really didn't like and there were always bound to be more than a few of those, from this point forward Craig was going to have a hell of a lot of dining out to do.

Pierre and Betty Franey were among his most frequent dining companions. Although Pierre and Betty knew about his secret life, Craig made sure it was invisible to the family as a whole—for so it had to be, not only for him but for nearly every other gay person in the country. His life with the Franeys was pure Americana, just with better (and French) food—birthdays, holidays, little trips here and there, always with the kids. The third, Jacques, was born June 30, 1962.

On Christmas Eve of 1962, the Franeys' doorbell in Valley Stream rang, and Diane, then eight years old, opened the door. "It was a dark night, and snowing," she recalls, "and there was Craig with a cocker spaniel puppy in a Champagne basket, with a bow around her neck. Her name was Baba au Rhum. I was overwhelmed, I was so happy. Baba was our dog for the next fifteen years. Whenever my father went to Craig's to work, he always brought Baba with him."

Craig seemed to be becoming a model of good citizenship. He quit smoking.[9] He took driving lessons.[10] He started French lessons.[11] He began to keep meticulous records of the dinners he served, with each course described and each guest named. On the advice of his accountant, he began to keep an appointment calendar, which tells us, for example, that on January 2, 1964, he bought a "radio for Betty & Pierre"[12] and that lunch with the *Times* photographer Bill Aller on February 11, 1964, at Chez Napoléon, was "6.80 + tip."

The Franeys had had their little cottage in Springs for five years, and for Pierre, driving all the way in to Manhattan so often to work with Craig at his apartment in the summertime had been getting old. When Craig got his first $10,000 in royalties from *The New York Times Cook Book,* Pierre, having seen how much Craig loved the tranquility and sea air of the South Fork, urged Craig to think about finding a place of his own. In early 1963 Craig was spending a weekend on the East End of Long Island, and, even though he'd seen it all before, this time he was so taken with the dunes, the calm waters, the sailboats in the distance, that when he heard there was a lot for sale a mile and a quarter down King's Point Road from the Franeys' house, with a wide view across Gardiners Bay, he rushed to see it—at midnight. He made an offer in the morning, and signed up a contractor the same day.[13] He wanted a house fast, and so decided on a Techbuilt—a prefabricated construction kit pioneered by the architect Carl Koch. The result was a stark modernist wedge with a tall wall of glass to bring inside the ever-shifting silvers, grays, blues, and thousand greens of the water and the restless sky.

There was something indescribable in the light of the East End that had drawn great artists to it: The nineteenth-century landscape masters William Merritt Chase and Jasper Cropsey and the wild mid-twentieth geniuses of the New York School—Jackson Pollock and Lee Krasner, Mark Rothko, Willem de Kooning, Robert Motherwell, Larry Rivers, Franz Kline—had all pursued their vision in the town of East Hampton. Now Craig Claiborne and Pierre Franey would make the East End's

Baba au Rhum, Diane and Claudia Franey, Craig,
and the King's Point Road house under construction.

farms and fisheries famous for a particular beauty of their own. And the house, as offhand and careless as Craig's creation of it may have seemed, would be the scene of some of the most delicious meals ever cooked in America.

There would be a firehouse-style steel spiral staircase down to small bedrooms beneath, and a long counter dividing the big open living space from a long open kitchen; the kitchen would be the heart of the house. After a first approving glance at the plans, Craig never even asked the contractor a question till the project was finished ten months later. He bought a houseful of furniture in a manic spree through Bloomingdale's.[14] Soon he also had a lovely swimming pool, in which he never swam. The best he could do was hold forth in his floating armchair, margarita in hand, watching in delight as the Franey children and others splashed all around him. He himself could not swim.[15]

Craig with Jacques Franey, King's Point Road, East Hampton.

"He'd stand at the edge of the lawn and look at the beach," recalls Claudia Franey, "with his trunks pulled up over that pale, pale little belly. But he never went in. Every hair in place, always."[16]

"He couldn't do anything physical," Diane laughs. "Couldn't hang a picture. Couldn't use a screwdriver. Either my father would do it or he'd have to call somebody.

"He couldn't handle money, either. When he'd find something he liked, say an antique, he'd have to call his accountant and ask, 'Do I have enough money to buy this?' And if he did, he'd write a check.

"He would take us on trips, because our father wouldn't let him pay him, or maybe it was the *Times*. That's how Craig would try to repay Papa for all the work he did. He took us on a skiing trip, and we said, 'Aren't you going to ski?' And he said, 'It's too cold.'"

Craig kept his apartment in Greenwich Village, but once he had King's Point Road set up to his satisfaction, in December of 1963, it was home. He had had a complete array of restaurant kitchen equipment installed, with a spectacular collection of heavy, tin-lined French cop-

Pierre loved gardening. Craig did not.

per pots and pans. The idea of a professional kitchen in a private home was then unheard of. As he wrote about it and pictures of it appeared with his articles in the *Times,* yet another idea of Craig's began to catch on that would later grow to immense proportions.

"The *New York Times* paid for every last penny's worth of that kitchen," Arthur Gelb recalls, in a rueful tone suggesting that there were a great many pennies involved.

Pierre dug and planted a kitchen garden, which Craig loved having but never touched. Diane Franey: "He couldn't stand to get his hands dirty."

§

It was the nature of his job that Craig was meeting more and more people. Some of them were bound to be personally interesting to him, and some of those were potentially friends. Three sorts of friendships began to emerge.

One was with other gay men, both sexual relationships and simple friendships, about which he neither wrote in the paper nor spoke outside the insular world in which those friends and Craig found their ease together. That isolation would change as the times changed, but in the early 1960s the gay world even in New York—except in certain fields, such as dance, fashion, and the stage—remained a world apart. "One reason I found it easy to accept Craig," says Arthur Gelb, "was that my wife, Barbara, was the daughter of S. N. Behrman, the playwright, and so in the early years of our marriage, I'd been plunged into the life of the theater, where homosexuality was no big deal. But at the *Times* it was still a big deal."

Indeed, when (at Gelb's behest) the *Times* ran its first-ever feature story on what it called "the presence of what is probably the greatest homosexual population in the world"—that of New York City—the piece had necessarily been written by a heterosexual reporter, Robert Doty, because, as Gelb wrote in his memoir *City Room,* "If there were then any gay reporters on the *Times,* they had not as yet declared themselves."[17] The headline was not exactly gay-friendly: "Growth of Overt Homosexuality in City Provokes Wide Concern." But they ran it on Page One, and the lid was off the secret code: "There is a homosexual jargon, once intelligible only to the initiate, but now part of New York slang. The word 'gay' has been appropriated as the adjective for homosexual."[18]

Craig found friends among another group as well: professional chefs. He liked to write about chefs as people. In an article for the Sunday magazine headed "Chez Three Chefs," he asked, "What pleases the palate of a first-class chef when, on his *jour de repos,* he dines in the quiet and peace of his own home?"[19] Craig certainly knew the answer from his many Sunday dinners chez Franey, but for this piece he visited three other French chefs, Léon Chauveau of the Drake Hotel, Roger Fessaguet of La Caravelle, and Jean Vergnes of the Colony, to sample the "plain but excellent cuisine" of their wives. The honesty and simplicity of the three chefs' appreciation of such unfussy food, an appreciation that saw no conflict with the refinement that was their professional pride, appealed deeply to Craig. Fessaguet and Vergnes would become lifelong friends of his.

Craig's writing about chefs was among the early stirrings of the new American idea of the chef as a personality. He had planted the seed when he first wrote about Pierre's heroic stand against Henri Soulé in 1959, little knowing that the chef-as-star would grow over time into a virtual cult. One wonders what René Verdon or Pierre would make of an ambitious young chef today fresh out of the Culinary Institute of America and desperate to make it big in New York or L.A.—and already seeing himself on the Food Network, too—who considers it job one to find the right publicist. One recent contestant on the television program *Chopped*—a competition of professional chefs—thought himself to have an advantage because "The lighting is perfect for my skin tones."[20]

The third and widest field in which Craig made friends was artists—one good reason up front, no doubt, being their acceptance, taken for granted, of people's idiosyncrasies. As the young Franeys had found, Craig was cultivating quite a crop of those.

In Edward Giobbi Craig found a distinguished artist, a sensational cook, and a friend for life—although their friendship would prove a complex one. No other of Craig's friends put up with as much guff, sometimes tantamount to abuse, as Giobbi did; and Craig loved no one else so like a brother.

Naturally it started with food, and a piece in the *Times*. They met serendipitously. Giobbi and his wife Elinor lived in exurban Katonah, New York. They invited a neighbor to dinner who wrote about food. She knew Craig, and asked if she could bring him along. Giobbi recalls: "I just threw together a big plate of antipasti. We had—we have—a garden. It's a farm. Chickens, rabbits. I made chicken two ways. I do that a lot. You start with a sauté, which is most of the work, then I finished half of it with chestnuts, Marsala, and onions, the other with shellfish, tomatoes, and peppers. I cut the chicken in small pieces—it looks more impressive."

Craig was knocked out, and asked if he could come back to do a piece for the paper. Giobbi—whose paintings hung in such museums as the Whitney, the National Portrait Gallery, and the Museum of Fine Arts in Boston—had no ambition to be known for his cooking. "But I said sure. He wanted me to make the same things. This time he brought Pierre. He wrote up the antipasti."

And he wrote up the Giobbis—"the young artist, who works in colors as vivid as his conversation . . . his wife, Elinor, a pretty, soft-spoken woman from Memphis, Tenn. . . . [their] three young children, all of whom have inherited his warm smile and engaging manner. . . .

"Like most good cooks, and Mr. Giobbi is an outstanding amateur," Craig wrote, "he came from a home in which good food was part and parcel of family life." Giobbi had grown up in Connecticut, but his ancestral home was in the Marche region of Italy, where his parents had been born and to which they had now returned. Ed and family spent much time there, and his father had sent the homemade wine that Craig and Pierre drank with the antipasti he served them: roasted peppers, chilled eggplant caponata (though Craig did not use that still unfamiliar term), stuffed mussels, and pasta with a quite nontraditional, richly buttered marinara sauce.[21] Craig's piece rather oddly included canned tuna as part of the antipasto platter.

He might better have considered leaving it out, for it was impossible for a reader to serve the tuna that Giobbi served. "Every summer we'd go to Provincetown and I'd buy about a two-hundred-pound fish—it was only five or six cents a pound—and take it home and can it myself, in good olive oil. It was unbelievably good. No resemblance to commercial tuna."

Craig had found another family to idealize. In Elinor he found a deep cultural kinship—for Memphis is historically much more closely related to the Mississippi Delta than to any part of Tennessee. She was also a member of the old-line upper class to which Craig's mother had so frustratedly aspired. Best of all, Elinor was a partisan of Freudian psychoanalysis, and through the years the two of them would share the secrets they otherwise divulged only in their therapists' sancta sanctorum.

In Ed Giobbi Craig had found not only an easygoing, eccentricity-tolerant companion but also a cook who without the least formal training could work elbow to elbow with Craig and Pierre at counter or stove and it was—easy. "It didn't take long till we really were like family," Giobbi recalls. "Before he'd go on a trip, he'd always call us, and he'd call us when he got back. He was so sentimental, and so generous. If I looked at a book in his house, the next week I'd get a copy in the mail. One time we were all in Italy, and I was admiring these plates in a shop window. Some famous designer—they were expensive. And in a toy store there were some trucks that my son liked. Christmas Eve, twelve plates for me, and one of those toy trucks.

"At Christmastime every year we'd play an LP of Dylan Thomas's 'A

Child's Christmas in Wales,' and Craig would just sit there with tears pouring down his face. But then for Christmas Day proper he would always go away somewhere—St. Barts most often—alone, most often. I think it was his heartbreaking memories of his childhood.

"But then he could be so terrible, too. One time Pierre and I went with him on this trip, a professional trip, reporting, and he was having an affair with a married guy from upstate New York. Pierre and I complained to him about what an idiot the guy was, and what an idiot *he* was to have anything to do with the guy. Well, late that night, drunk, he busted into my room, screaming. I mean he totally lost it. Screaming. I couldn't take it. Five o'clock in the morning, I packed up and left. I quit the trip. He didn't speak to me for three months. Three months of silence.

"Finally, he wrote me a letter. Didn't apologize. Oh, no. Just a letter inviting the family and me for the weekend. To the kids he was Uncle Craig, and they had no idea what was going on. So we went, and everything was fine. He wasn't going to apologize, though. You had to take that with Craig."[22]

§

In his work Craig's temper was always even, his tone mild, his judgment lofty but never unkind. On May 24, 1963, he introduced a rating system to his weekly column of restaurant reviews: Like the *Guide Michelin* of France, he would award one, two, or three stars, or none. He described his ratings thus: "One star denotes restaurants of more than routine interest; two stars denote those of superior quality, and three stars pertain to restaurants regarded as among the finest in the city." (The use of the first-person singular remained rare in the *New York Times,* and it rubbed Craig the wrong way anyhow. Hence the awkwardness and vagueness of that passive "is regarded," implying, as it does, that a lot of people think so. The opinion, of course, was Craig's alone. Much better would have been *The New Yorker*'s wryly unroyal "we" and the active verb "regard." But that was then.)

In this first employment of stars Craig accorded one to Del Pezzo, "a most agreeable and unpretentious Italian restaurant," and two to Jimmy's Greek American Restaurant, a little lunch-only spot in the Financial District, "far and away the best Greek restaurant in the city," where "guests serve themselves from a small and very neat kitchen." He did not say anything at all about the food at the Black Angus. That of La Petite Maison he called "competent." He gave neither of them a star.

For all his friendship with their chefs, Craig remained disappointed in the quality of New York's supposedly best restaurants. His great screed of April 1959 apparently hadn't made much difference. Four and a half years later, he published a long piece in the Sunday magazine[23] at least as censorious: "The food of the city's most celebrated dining salons, with one or perhaps two exceptions," he wrote (the one of course being Le Pavillon, the "perhaps" other probably The Four Seasons), "is neither predictably elegant nor superb. More often than not it is predictably commonplace." He assailed "some of the proprietors of the city's best-known restaurants [who] are businessmen attracted to the industry because of its 'glamour' . . . and are not trained, in any sense, in what might be called the grand tradition." (The new owners of La Côte Basque, for example—whom Craig did not deign to mention in this piece—were a theater producer and a former nightclub owner, who seemed more interested in entertaining their celebrity friends than in the quality of the food or the service.)

Craig went on to decry the sameness of the menus, the hors d'oeuvre "of the open-and-serve or slice-and-serve school," the "nondescript breads, overcooked string beans and soggy carrots," the pâtisserie not made in house but *bought* "from a pastry shop in Queens, or wherever."

New York restaurants' knowledge of cheese was deplorable, their wine prices obscene, and the service, *ach!* That was always a painful subject for Craig, who could still envision himself at Lausanne poised with the starched napkin just so over his arm. He could barely imagine how Conrad Tuor would shudder at the sight of these bumbling, arrogant— Craig could find them worthy of no better term than *plate carriers*. "In New York the average waiter would make a very good bus boy, the average captain a very good waiter, and the average maître d'hôtel an acceptable captain." He *never* used the unspellable nonsense word *mater-dee*.

In the autumn of 1964, without saying why, he changed the three-star system of his weekly Directory to Dining to a four-star one.[24] "Four stars," he wrote, "pertain to restaurants regarded as among the finest in the area." He didn't revise what one, two, or three stars meant. The attentive reader was therefore left with only the existing definitions, which included "Three stars pertain to restaurants regarded as among the finest in the city."[25] So if you were a stickler, three and four stars now denoted exactly the same thing—the only hair of difference being "city" versus "area." The confusion would not be made taxonomically clear until Craig redefined his star ratings in the privately published *Craig Claiborne Journal* eight years later. But if you were a regular enough reader of Craig's reviews—and most of his readers were—you could more or less iron out wrinkles like this for yourself.

§

The *New York Times* was not in those days the national newspaper it has become. Even in the semirural hamlets where New Yorkers spent their weekends, getting the Sunday *Times* was always something of a scramble, with advance reservations necessary for the few copies that made it to the general store on the green. In Chicago or Los Angeles you had to wait for the paper to arrive at particular downtown newsstands late on Sunday afternoon—the *New York Times* was printed in *New York*, there was no electronic transmission of its image to remote printing sites—and in many a city the only place it could be had at all was the airport. If you were more than a few minutes late, it was almost certainly sold out.

Despite the difficulty of getting hold of a copy, and perhaps to some extent because of it, there was no other newspaper with anywhere near its charisma. The *Times*'s integrity, its intelligence, the depth of its staff, the breadth of its coverage, the quality of its reporting and its writing, and its editors' access to the most powerful people in every field set it apart; its influence was unparalleled. Certain of its writers—James Reston, David Halberstam, Anthony Lewis, Hanson Baldwin, Arthur Krock—were major forces in the life of the nation.

But the job of the food editor was as local as the crime beat. People coming to New York certainly did want to know where to eat, as attested by the popularity of Craig's *Guide to Dining Out in New York* (first published in 1964 and often updated); and the *Times*'s imprimatur on Craig's encyclopedic cookbook of 1961 surely helped in its impressive sales. The absence of the words *New York Times* on his *Cooking with Herbs and Spices* of 1963 showed quite effectively how important that imprimatur was: Even given that book's admittedly much smaller scope (in the foreword he writes, "Let it be said that this is a modest volume"), its sales were a disappointment.

What to do? Travel. Go anywhere, write about food everywhere. Okay, how about Alaska? From his notes:

> No farms. No cattle. Milk is brought. . . . Cribbage board of walrus tusks. . . . Very few servants . . . dirt roads. . . . Grilled, rather tough steak served by waitress with names like Marge Millie and Helen and a jukebox. There are classic salad accompaniments like shredded carrots with raisins or tossed iceberg with a mixture of thin mayonnaise with tomato catsup.[26]

You gotta love "very few servants." Yet on this one trip Craig managed to post no fewer than six Alaska stories to the *Times*. He reported on the town of Ketchikan, where "restaurant-going for pleasure is not a thoroughgoing enterprise" but which "boasts the largest single collection of totem poles in the world."[27] He dined on and described leg of venison served with thirty cloves of raw garlic.[28] In Juneau he ate at Mike's, one of the total of two restaurants in town, where the service was "classic bad,"[29] and also sampled a highly regarded home cook's moose liver with kelp chutney.[30] Little of this was likely to be of utility to his readers in New York, but it would be equally amusing to a reader anywhere in the country (with the possible exception of Alaska), and Craig, in his comical misery, was clearly having a fine old time.

The Alaska escapade had been largely serendipity. Craig's next project was a painstakingly staged production that required long planning, complex arrangements, and precise execution. It would also show Craig Claiborne in a new light—no longer only as a mere reporter but as a personage.

Across Gardiners Bay from Craig's and the Franey family's houses on the shore loomed one of the strangest anomalies of the American landscape, the 3,300-acre, entirely private Gardiners Island, which had been bought from the Montaukett Indians in 1639 by an English settler named Lion Gardiner. It was granted to him in perpetuity by King Charles I, and it had been owned and occupied by his descendants in an unbroken line ever since. The king named Lion Gardiner Lord of the Manor, a title which, despite their having been American citizens for the last ten generations or so, had been claimed by each succeeding male heir. It was Robert David Lion Gardiner, Sixteenth Lord of the Manor—who absolutely forbade any trespassing on his private domain—to whom Craig Claiborne appealed in 1965 for permission for a picnic on the beach.

"Craig who?" replied the Lord.

Craig explained who he was, and Pierre, and told Gardiner that they wanted to gather together some of New York's finest chefs and create a picnic of extraordinary refinement, for a piece in the *New York Times,* and wouldn't the Lord of the Manor and his wife like to come?

Turned out the Lion was a true *fin bec,* a member of food and wine societies, and thought it was a grand idea.

Craig didn't tell him he was going to call *Life* magazine and see if they would also like to cover the picnic.

On the strength of the prospective publicity in *Life,* Craig persuaded Abercrombie & Fitch* to lend him a huge barbecue grill. In similar fashion he cadged from Baccarat a loan of two dozen very expensive crystal wineglasses.

Craig and Pierre enlisted White House chef René Verdon, Roger Fessaguet of La Caravelle, Jean Vergnes (no longer at the Colony, now cheffing for the Irving Trust bank), a guy named Armand Innocenti to play the accordion, and Jacques Pépin (whom Craig identified to Gardiner as the former chef to Charles de Gaulle, of course, but also, rather amazingly but quite truthfully, as "a sky diver who jumps from airplanes on weekends and a student of philosophy at Columbia University"). All were encouraged to bring wives, kids, grandparents, friends.

Two days of shopping, late nights of prep. They had command of a five-hundred-horsepower monster boat lent by the Lord of the Manor as well as a putt-putt rented at Montauk, and it still took three trips to get all the goodies assembled at Bostwick Point. "Just ahead of you," Mr. Gardiner explained [as quoted by Craig], "is the largest virgin oak forest in America. It was there before Columbus discovered America."

Driftwood and flotsam were gathered, tables improvised, white cloths

---

* At that time, not a mass merchant of cheap teenwear but more or less the opposite: the nation's finest purveyor of fishing tackle, shotguns and other hunting equipment, and outdoor gear of all kinds.

spread, fires lit, Dom Pérignon opened—compliments of the Gardiners (Mrs. a lissome beauty some years younger than the Lion). "Isn't it delicious in this crystal?" Gardiner said. "You can feel the bubbles through the glass." Craig had brought Beaujolais and—picture those French chefs' *moues* and rolled eyes—Almadén Mountain White Chablis. Was that really the best the vaunted oenophile could do?

Jean Vergnes grilled fifteen mustard-coated *pigeonneaux à la crapaudine*—squabs ingeniously flattened and folded so as to resemble *crapauds,* or toads. Pierre poached a striped bass—freshly caught from Gardiners Bay—in court-bouillon, and for it made a *sauce rouille*. He also made a Mexican ceviche and served it in a giant clamshell that Craig had brought for the purpose. That morning at Craig's house, Verdon had refused to make his *pâté de campagne* without pork liver—it would not be authentic—but after a heroic search Mme Fessaguet had found some, run out of gas, and made it back, on foot, just in time. Fessaguet boiled lobsters in seawater and stuffed them with sieved hard-boiled eggs, shallots, chives, parsley, and their own livers, coral, and roe.

Jacques Pépin and Mrs. Robert Lion Gardiner
at the Gardiners Island pique-nique.

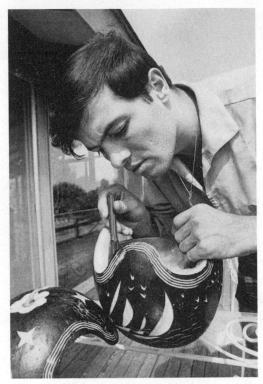

Pépin carving watermelon.

Pépin carved two watermelons into baskets and filled them with mixed fruits macerated in apricot jam and kirschwasser. There were also mussels in *sauce ravigote,* a boiled-beef salad, marinated weakfish, potato salad, green bean and tomato salad, Brie, goat cheese, and Camembert. Children swept a net through the surf for whitebait, which were quickly dipped in batter and then fried in hot oil.

Meanwhile the *Life* photographer and the anonymous writer—there were no bylines in *Life* in those days—swooped and circled and tried, insofar as possible, not to get in the way. Craig was everywhere at once, wielding bottle after bottle of Champagne.

With these words of the Lord of the Manor Craig ended his piece in the *Times*: "Gardiners Island hasn't seen a feast like this since Captain Kidd ate suckling pig with my forebears nearly 300 years ago."[31]

Back home in Springs, Craig washed and polished the borrowed Bac-

Captain of the pique-nique.

carat glasses with particular care, grateful that not one was so much as chipped. Above them on the wall he rehung a Provençal pottery platter that had also done duty at the picnic. At three o'clock in the morning, the nail on which the platter was hung somehow worked its way loose, and Craig woke for the second time in recent times to the distinctive sound of Baccarat crystal shattering.[32]

The story in *Life*, "A Most Magnifique Pique-Nique"—much more important to Craig than his own, smaller piece in the *Times*—appeared in the issue of August 25, 1965. The photo spread was lavish, but Craig's picture did not appear in it. No matter. His mission had been accomplished. He had shown that his doings could now command national attention.

10

Olympus

In October 1965, Henri Soulé had his revenge, and Craig was on the spot to write it up.

SATURDAY NIGHT AT LE PAVILLON,
IT'S CHAMPAGNE AND KENNEDYS
by Craig Claiborne[1]

Not only Saturday, either: "Twice over the weekend," he wrote, "the family chose his elegant and august restaurant as a point of farewell feasting for the departing French ambassador, Hervé Alphand, and his wife." On Friday night the hostess was the late president's sister, Eunice Shriver. On Saturday—never mind that Jacqueline was no longer First Lady, the LBJs could do as they officially wished—Mrs. Kennedy would see her favorite diplomat off in her own fashion at "a place where the Kennedys can go with guests and remain relatively unstared at."

The Kennedy family had, as we know, abandoned Le Pavillon and its arrogant monarch back in 1960, in favor of the new La Caravelle, the chic and decorous new creation of Soulé's upstart protégé Roger Fessaguet. Now Soulé had them back, and to Craig Claiborne—for whom Henri Soulé was almost an obsession—this was news worthy of the *New York Times*.

Craig's piece was reminiscent of one of his first for the paper, his breathless-boy coverage of the dinner for Queen Elizabeth in 1957. He reveled in the details of patrician swank—Mrs. Kennedy's "simply

123

designed jonquil-colored matelassé dress," their dinner of Dom Pérignon, caviar, *navarin d'agneau,* and Château Pétrus 1953. Robert F. Kennedy "arrived too late for caviar," and "W. Averell Harriman and two other couples" dropped in later. "After café filtre and more Champagne, someone proposed a discothèque.

"'Arthur,' someone volunteered.

"'Le Club,' someone else said.

"'Arthur.'

"'Le Club.'

"It was 11 o'clock, Le Pavillon was almost empty, and the party rose to go. They walked through the restaurant's revolving doors and into a crowd of more than a hundred bystanders, some of whom had waited an hour for a glimpse of the Kennedys."

Pierre could go on not speaking to Soulé and vice versa, but as far as Craig was concerned, Henri Soulé was still "France's foremost gift to American gastronomy."[2] For Craig, his fan-clubbish gush about the Kennedys—so he would tell you—was just for fun. But prestige such as the presence of the Kennedys conferred on Soulé—and such as coverage of their presence in his restaurant by the *New York Times* amplified— sustained Soulé, and that was important to Craig. Soulé, in Craig's view, was a great artist, a figure of historical significance. Even his absences and failures were significant, because they would affect the course of fine dining in America as surely as his successes did. Soulé's disasters also made good stories.

The story of La Côte Basque was emblematic. After Soulé's staff-shattering tantrum in 1962, he had sold La Côte Basque to the owners of the once great and now less than mediocre Le Chambord, who had given their new acquisition the hopelessly unwieldy title of "Le Café Chambord at La Côte Basque." Within a little over two years they had run it into the ground, and when the restaurant closed in August 1964, the *Times*'s unsigned but unmistakably Claiborne-voiced coverage described it as having "fallen upon evil days." The writer had rather wickedly sought out Roger Chauveron, the highly respected founder of Le Chambord itself, who considered that it too had been run into the ground by the same two owners; Chauveron averred that "the lack of personal direction was the main problem of his former restaurant." In case you didn't get the point, the piece added that "The Chambord, whose association with La Côte Basque came about recently, had not in recent years known the glory that it had enjoyed for two decades after it opened during the Christmas season in 1936. Under the aegis of Mr. Chauveron, it attained worldwide renown."

On September 1964, Le Café Chambord at La Côte Basque declared bankruptcy, with liabilities of $322,467.00—most of that being debt to Henri Soulé—and assets of $0.00. The significance of this whole scenario for Craig was that it was setting the stage for the great man's return.

For the better part of a year, Craig had been working on his long manuscript about Henri Soulé.[3] It resembled more than anything else a *New Yorker* profile—too long for the *Times* or any other magazine, too short to be a book. He couldn't have sold it to *The New Yorker,* however, since that magazine had already published a biographical profile of Soulé, by Joseph Wechsberg, in 1953. Wechsberg's profile also formed a substantial portion of his 1962 book *Dining at the Pavillon,* so it's hard to imagine that there would be a prospective publication anywhere for another piece covering much of the same ground. It is the only significant work that Craig Claiborne never finished, and never published. Nor did he ever explain why he gave it up.

He never explained why he took it up in the first place either. It may have been purely emotional. The tone of many of the quotations Craig chose was frankly adulatory: Soulé was "the greatest in the world. . . . His heart is as soft as chocolate mousse . . . an enormously sentimental man . . . absolutely single-minded." Craig's own words were equally laudatory: "He is a towering figure . . . [with] a singular distaste for the moneyed-without-manners. . . . Le Pavillon has the grace, grandeur, elegance and style that is essential to a restaurant of its genre . . . [It] is the finest French restaurant not only in America but in the world."

But no one's opinion of Soulé was higher than his own, and Craig's veneration was so blind that in quoting him he allowed Soulé to be once again hoist on his own petard: "I have only one boss, and my boss is God."

In December 1964, Craig's review in the *Times* of the new restaurant Le Mistral was overshadowed by a much longer piece[4] that ran alongside it describing "what might be called [Le Mistral's] professional bloodlines. Like several others of recent vintage and comparable elegance, its lineage can be traced to one man—Henri Soulé, owner of Le Pavillon and the man who has without question been the most towering figure in America where French restaurants are concerned."

What followed consisted largely of highlights from Craig's manuscript, which was still in progress at the time. There was a brief biography and curriculum vitae. There was the characteristic anecdote, "told of Robert Meyzen, one of Mr. Soulé's protégés and an owner of the fashionable La Caravelle Restaurant. It is said that when Mr. Meyzen once seemed more aggressive than usual, one of his staff remarked, 'Who does he think he is, Henri Soulé?' to which a colleague answered, 'Eh bien, and why not? Soulé thinks he's Charles de Gaulle.'" And there was the inevitable summary encomium: "The influence of Soulé on the American restaurant world will never be measured, but if one travels in restaurant circles there is a phrase that recurs like a timeless refrain: 'You remember him; he worked under Soulé.'"

Beneath the article proper was displayed the family tree of Soulé's many successful ex-employees, some of whom had left to find their glory with his blessing and many without it. No question, a lot of them had done very well, in principal positions at many of the best restaurants in New York: La Caravelle of course (owner), as well as The Four Seasons (chef), La Grenouille (owner), Lutèce (maître d'hôtel), Le Veau d'Or (owner), La Potinière and La Potinière du Soir (owner), El Morocco (captain), Le Manoir (owner), and the St. Regis Hotel (chef). Others had established luxurious restaurants in Miami. There was excellent French food to be had in the Catskills of upstate New York for years because so many of the French chefs of Manhattan went skiing or played *boules* there on vacation or in the brief pauses that passed for their weekends, and a few—some of them also Pavillon alumni—had stayed to start their own country restaurants. Also among the Pavillon's descendants were the escapees to corporate America—Pierre Franey, Jacques Pépin, and a good half-dozen of their old Pavillon colleagues all now at Howard Johnson's; others had found positions at Campbell Soup, Nestlé, and Air France, where they may have made some brief difference before those companies plunged back into their great native ocean of mediocrity.

William Grimes, a successor to Craig at the *Times* in an altogether different era (1999 to 2004), had quite a different take on Soulé. "The influence of Le Pavillon was not all for the good," he wrote. "Sternly traditional, it inscribed, as though in stone, a style of service and an approach to cuisine that . . . was French cooking and French service by the rule book, immune to change. In time, it would come to seem fussy, antiquated, and, as the forces of globalism revolutionized French cuisine, almost a parody."[5]

Soulé reopened La Côte Basque—the real thing once again—on May 18, 1965. In the New York *Herald Tribune*'s Sunday magazine *New York* (the predecessor of today's freestanding magazine of the same name), Gael Greene covered the countdown of the days leading up to the opening in the anxious-ecstatic style for which she was becoming famous and which positively fed on Soulé's chilling insolence. "It was like the return to the concert stage of Vladimir Horowitz. . . . [Soulé on the phone to a supplicant:] 'Oh you would? And where have you been for the past three years? We haven't seen you at Pavillon.' . . . '*Laissez tomber le cheesecake!*' . . . The room is criss-crossed by waves of hysteria. It is the hour of the *quenelles*. . . . Soulé draws himself up to a full and overwhelming five-feet-five. [Soulé to an innocent customer who has dared to do something that would be perfectly ordinary anywhere else:] 'Ladies do not drink at Henri Soulé's bar.' She leaves, broken, humbled, demoralized."[6]

This was a time when being an asshole was considered in certain New York circles to be a mark of social superiority. Craig Claiborne never deigned even to recognize such a repugnant value system, yet he forgave it entirely in Henri Soulé. Perhaps he was allowing himself to enjoy it vicariously, as Gael Greene did, but in Craig's case without writing about it.

The ways of snobbery are infinitely many. As egalitarianism tightened its hold on the cultural élite of the 1960s—the sort of people who wrote editorials for the *New York Times,* for example—New Yorkers whose claims to importance were merely social or monetary were in something of a panic. Soulé could never have survived on the custom of Kennedys and Vanderbilts, but he was astute enough to know that as long as he had them, and as long as the press made that fact well known, then the socially insecure but financially capable—of whom New York had so many—would keep Soulé securely on his throne. An amazing thing to think about is that he accomplished all this in what was inherently the role of a servant.

The Kennedys, Harrimans, Marlene Dietrichs, Cole Porters, et al. were delighted to play their part in Soulé's game—there was a lot of free Champagne and caviar disbursed, and it was nice to see oneself looking so grand in the rotogravure—and it sold newspapers too. Craig's own place in the scheme was curious: He may have enjoyed the social-envy aspect of the game to some extent, but to him at bottom it was still about the *food*. He wanted Henri Soulé to succeed because nobody, in Craig's experience, had ever had a restaurant in America to compare with Soulé's.

He knew that the revival of La Côte Basque was a critical moment in the sixty-two-year-old maestro's career, and therefore, perhaps, in the future of food at its best in New York. He gave Soulé two months to get the kinks worked out. After that generous interval, Craig's review[7] opened with a curious feint: "A towering superlative, like a little knowledge, is a dangerous thing. But the present temptation is to state without equivocation that Henri Soulé's recently reopened La Côte Basque . . . is the handsomest restaurant in Manhattan." Handsomest? Could a compliment from the great *restaurant critic* have been any more left-handed? What was more: The reopened restaurant looked exactly like the original. It took Craig fully half his column inches to get to any mention of the food. That, he said, "lacks the fire that transforms mere excellence into exquisiteness, the noble to the exalted." Summing up, he seemed to have trouble with his English: "The kitchen soars neatly"—soars neatly?—"but it should be celestial." Rotten writing, but clear enough. The great Soulé had disappointed his most passionate, and most prominent, advocate. It must have been hard for both of them.

Craig was a critic pure and simple—he cared only for the performance, didn't want to see behind the curtain. Gael Greene wanted to know everything, and what she knew about the rebirth of La Côte Basque would have shocked the purist Craig to his toes. In her account of the last-minute flurry she reported: "The potato chips have arrived, as have currant jelly by the gallon and enough Accent to flavor all the watery vegetables in all the roadside beaneries of America for a year."[8] Accent—*monosodium glutamate?* No wonder, indeed, that Craig had tasted mediocrity.

It was not a good time to incur Craig Claiborne's displeasure. He had wanted the status and power of the *Times*'s critics of books, music, and the theater, and now he had it. *Time* magazine accorded him commensurate recognition:

The slight man with the crinkled, smiling eyes is not the sort of celebrity for whom headwaiters snap to attention. When he walks into a Manhattan restaurant, hardly anyone notices. But he notices everything. Is the decor adequate? Does the headwaiter seem anxious to get on to someone else? Is there any single offering out of the ordinary on the menu? Is the wine overpriced? Is the busboy attentive to such details as discarded swizzle sticks and filled ashtrays? Are the service plates set just right?[9]

Time made it clear that there was no one more important on the American food scene than Craig Claiborne, and it portrayed him as something of a bloodless hanging judge—a role he hated. "When he says good, it is very, very good for the restaurant's business. When he says bad, it can be horrid." Craig may not have liked it, but that was true.

The magazine did at least note that he loved a good bowl of chili as much as a perfect *oeuf en gelée*. It noted, too, his undying affection for Le Pavillon. But the article's emphasis was on the destructive power of Craig's disapproval.

§

Neither *Time* magazine's high opinion of Craig nor his own disappointment in the cuisine of La Côte Basque meant more than zero to the pets and petted of Henri Soulé. *Hoi polloi* clamored for tables and were duly rebuffed. The social-clambering set forked over whatever they had to to pass in review past the chosen few at the choicest spots in front. Those chosen few, at lunch nearly all ladies, also sat in front at the fashion shows and wore those same clothes in the pages of *Women's Wear Daily* and appeared without fail in what were still called the society columns. Soulé's *brigade de cuisine,* under pressure from the boss after Craig's review, labored to produce dishes of exquisite delicacy, but his favored ladies picked at their *omelette aux truffes* and mousse of sole with two sauces without tasting any of it. They were too busy gossiping about one another bare-fanged with Truman Capote—little suspecting that dear Truman would chop them into socialite *tartare* in his now-legendary story "La Côte Basque 1965."[10]

It was none other than René Verdon who, having just resigned as

White House chef, delivered the Kennedys' last poke to the Lyndon Baines Johnsons' presidential eye, shiv courtesy of the food editor of the *New York Times*:

> Although the chef, an amiable, portly man in his early forties, would make no comment about the dining habits of the Johnsons, it is certainly true that their taste in food is considerably less sophisticated than that of the Kennedys.
>
> The Kennedys were partial to such dishes as quenelles de brochet, or delicate poached forcemeat balls made with pike, mousse of sole with lobster, and braised chicken with Champagne sauce. . . .
>
> Although Mr. Verdon was reluctant to discuss details . . . he would admit that some of the dishes he had been asked by memorandum to prepare had seemed unaccustomed to his Gallic palate.
>
> This would include a cold purée of garbanzos or chick peas, which he described for his taste as "already bad hot."[11]

§

On January 27, 1966, Henri Soulé died, apparently in an instant, of a heart attack. Pierre Franey said that it happened in the men's room at La Côte Basque.[12] Others—gleeful, it would seem, with the poetic justice of a scene that *might* be apocryphal—contended that he had been on the phone yelling at a union official.[13] Craig's admiration, in his tribute in the *Times,* overflowed—an admiration that, far from deprecating Soulé's irrepressible impudence, exalted it:

> Henri Soulé was the Michelangelo, the Mozart and the Leonardo of the French restaurant in America. He was a man of towering standards with cool disdain for the commonplace and the sham. . . . He was scorned for the vagaries of his temperament, his touch of the tyrant in search of perfection and his characteristic disdain for those who would climb social ladders via his red carpet.
>
> Once a dominating grande dame for whom he took an immediate dislike arrived and, after being seated, demanded that she be moved elsewhere. Mr. Soulé refused with the explanation that all the other tables were reserved.

"That's your table," Mr. Soulé said, indicating where she sat.

"But I don't like this table," she insisted.

Pursing his lips and staring her straight in the eye he asked, "Tell me, good woman, did you come to eat at Le Pavillon or did you come to argue with Soulé?"

Soulé frequently spoke as though Soulé were a third person, someone outside himself. . . .

His like may never be known in this country again.[14]

A person of our time may find it hard to know what's so great about this kind of behavior on the part of a restaurateur talking to a paying customer. If it had been comical, delivered with a self-mocking wink, that would have been one thing, but Soulé's arrogance was deadly sincere. That Craig saw no reason to excuse it, that in fact he found it entertaining, tells us something important about Craig Claiborne, something that takes us back to his mother: As democratic as he wished to show himself to be, and as he believed himself to be, here we see him identifying with a social type that takes pleasure in humiliating those whom it can get away with nailing into place.

What makes this case peculiarly difficult to make sense of is that Soulé's background was so humble and his actual position—however you measured it, in social, financial, or intellectual terms—was below that of any customer or even would-be customer whom he might choose to demean. If there had been a little more make-believe and humor involved, we could peg him as a modern jester, but there wasn't the slightest bit of either. What can be seen fairly clearly is that there is a satisfying inversion at work—the first shall be last—particularly satisfying to the seeker of status who himself is deeply uncertain of where he or she stands. Thus might it be to a projected Miss Kathleen inside Craig: She cannot admit the uncertainty of her status, but she can unconsciously enjoy the comedy of the cruel upstart hammering down a less worthy upstart. All we have to do is identify with Soulé and we win, too.

Satisfaction is to be had, however, only if the game takes place entirely below the level of consciousness. To persons of self-conscious refinement there was always the self-excusing distinction drawn that you didn't humiliate those *far* below you. You didn't humiliate waiters, or the poor. Craig liked to believe that he himself would never knowingly humiliate anybody at all. You had to get your kicks—that is, give them—by smiling on the antics of Henri Soulé. This worked only as long as you weren't on the receiving end, in which case they wouldn't be amusing at all. But that was the fine point: You could smile, even laugh, because *you* had *not* been his victim.

§

Craig's inner mother may never have relaxed enough to recognize it, but his status was rising higher. It wasn't only that he was rising in his field. What the *Time* magazine article hadn't said, and what almost nobody recognized, because the change had come so subtly, was that he had virtually *created* his field. Not so many years before, not so many people had cared very much about food. Now a lot of people did. Behind that phenomenon will forever lie the irresoluble chicken-and-egg question, and there are plenty of intervening variables as well, from the G.I. Bill and the Boeing 707 to Julia Child and the Zeitgeist, but one fact remains immovable, *viz.*, that in the second half of the 1960s there was one reigning authority of the food world (new idea, itself) and Craig Claiborne was it.

In September 1966 the *Times*'s weekly Directory to Dining finally added Craig's byline. His personal approval had become a seal of legitimacy.

Time magazine's issue of November 25, 1966, put Julia Child on the cover—she was on television now, and probably at least as well known as Craig, if not more so, but he never showed a hint of jealousy. In 1964 he had devoted a long piece in the *Times* to a visit to her in her Boston kitchen, and in it, going even further than in his initial review, had written that *Mastering the Art of French Cooking* "may be the finest volume on French cooking ever printed in English."[15] Julia Child was beloved, but Craig Claiborne was the authority.

The extraordinarily long piece in *Time*—five thousand words—was all about her, and not about him at all, but it drove home the point of how big the phenomenon they had set in motion had gotten:

The concern with good eating, which first became evident after World War II, has now swept across the nation. Cooking schools everywhere report themselves oversubscribed. Supermarkets have found that their gourmet counters are their handsomest profit earners, and are rapidly expanding them. "Sixty percent of the items in this store weren't here ten years ago," says the manager of Chicago's Stop 'n' Shop. . . .

A decade ago, the typical market offered half a dozen cheeses. "Today," says Ed Kiatta, manager of Larimer's in Washington, D.C., "if you don't have at least 50 assorted, high-powered imported cheeses, you're not in business." The same is true of herbs and spices. Once a store could make do with a dozen old dependables; today, supermarkets carry more than 100 items, with such old standbys as sage being displaced, as "too strong," by such postwar newcomers as fresh tarragon, fennel, thyme, dill and coriander.

Craig was famous enough that he could even kvetch in the public print about his position. Interviewed by *Editor & Publisher* magazine, he had the nerve to complain, "I eat in ten restaurants a week and feel like the Peruvians. They say they are excavating their graves with their teeth."[16]

And he didn't mind throwing a punch now and then, especially when the legacy of his sainted Henri Soulé was at stake. Craig's story about the new management of Le Pavillon—overtly a news article, not an opinion piece—seems to open quite neutrally: The head of the investment group that had bought the restaurant, Claude C. Philippe, "says he intends to preserve the traditions and style established by Mr. Soulé." But that carefully chosen *says* prefigures a paragraph farther on, in which, while vaguely attributing the words to others, Craig describes Philippe as "dominating, agile, arrogant, and intense. . . . with volatile charm [and] ruthlessness. . . ."

Characteristically, Craig keeps his dagger behind his back till late in the piece. He tells us that Mr. Philippe "became assistant to [maître d'hôtel] Oscar Tschirky, better known as Oscar of the Waldorf," and when Tschirky died,

> He in turn became Philippe of the Waldorf. In October 1958 the colorful figure was indicted by a federal grand jury on four counts of income tax evasion. He subsequently became known as Philippe of the Astor, Philippe of the Commodore, Philippe of the Summit, and Philippe of the Americana. In September 1960. . . . he was fined $10,000, the maximum that could be imposed, for evading $25,472 in income taxes.[17]

The story also notes that La Côte Basque was not part of the Pavillon deal, and was going to continue with its present staff under the management of "Mrs. Henriette Spalter, a longtime associate of the late master restaurateur." Now there's gentle euphemism. Madame Henriette, as she was known to all, had been the hat-check girl at Le Pavillon and also, for years, Henri Soulé's mistress. In his will Soulé had left to Spalter half of his now quite valuable house in Montauk, Long Island—the other half going to his sister in France—while leaving to his wife, Olga, also in France, whom he hadn't laid eyes on for years, $2,500 in cash "plus half of his residuary estate in trust."

In his will Soulé had also bequeathed a gold watch to his "dear friend J. Edgar Hoover," for whom, at Le Pavillon, he had seen to it that "there was always a bottle of vintage Romanée-Conti at the table."[18]

There was another gold watch in Soulé's estate—a magnificent one, from Cartier. He had actually given it to Craig a little over a year before, when Craig had reviewed Le Mistral and published the family tree of Soulé's legacy in the restaurant world. "I knew that I couldn't keep this watch," Craig wrote in his memoir, "even though I was fully aware it was given to me not as a gesture of being 'bought' but of genuine gratitude and affection."[19] Craig had promptly phoned Clifton Daniel, the *Times*'s managing editor, who said he wanted to take it up with the publisher. Both Craig and his boss had no doubt of the outcome—their consultation with the publisher was purely *pro forma*: Craig had to give it back. Daniel wrote a letter to Soulé explaining the paper's policy. So did Craig, his letter accompanying the watch in its red leather Cartier box. For months, terrified of what wrath he would meet with, Craig didn't show his face to Soulé. When at last he did, Soulé gave him a hug and said, "If you ever leave the *Times*, or when I die, that watch is waiting for you." Which it was, in the safe at Le Pavillon.

The legacy of Henri Soulé had become an integral part of Craig Claiborne. When it was defiled, Craig felt it inside himself. You could feel his dolor when for the first time in his career he published a review of Le Pavillon, now "taken over"—note the choice of term—"by another management"—ditto—"under the direction of Claude C. Philippe and a group of investors." He bemoaned "a shrimp cocktail with an uninspired cocktail sauce and a presentation that resembled what one might expect at a hotel banquet." You could almost see Soulé's ghost smirking over Craig's shoulder as he wrote, "With a restaurant of Le Pavillon's reputation and cost, even the minutest details loom large, and thus one is aware of the seeds in the lemon quarters served with the salmon. . . . [In the days of Henri Soulé] red roses, white carnations, and the like were arranged in impeccable patterns. Last week there were carelessly thrown-together carnations and asters in dreary-looking dime store cups with handles."[20]

Some months later, on August 20, 1967, on Barry Gray's radio program, Craig continued extempore in the same vein, and this was more than Claude C. Philippe could bear. He fired off a letter on August 28—a long one—that began "My dear Craig," wandered through a number of vague and disconnected complaints, and then settled to its point: "I quite understand that you, as some others, cannot bring yourself to think of Le Pavillon except in terms of the late Henri Soulé. . . . [Y]ou seem to have decided it was not worth mentioning that for over a year after the death of Henri Soulé no other restaurateur in New York or Paris saw fit to accept the challenge of taking over the restaurant and following his great traditions, and that possibly I am deserving of some small praise for having had that courage. . . ."

Philippe closed in futility incarnate. Did he think Craig Claiborne was going to apologize, retract his review, and write a new one, or what? "I am not at all concerned with the fact that you seem to have picked a feud with Le Pavillon as you have with other restaurants in town," he wrote, "but as a reporter you bear the obligation of giving your readers accurate reportage of any situation. . . . [T]he consensus of opinion is that the Pavillon's cuisine has never been better."[21]

Craig may have surprised Claude C. Philippe by actually writing a letter in reply, under his *New York Times* letterhead. Its text, dated August 31, 1967, in full:

Dear Philippe:*

In the first place I don't know where your notion came from that I "seem to have picked a feud with Le Pavillon," which to my knowledge is untrue. A feud to my mind would involve a certain amount

---

* Craig seems to have forgotten that this is the man's surname, or is pretending to. Or maybe he is thinking of him as "Philippe of the Pavillon."

*of passion, and I feel quite dispassionate about the matter. I have
always felt that a restaurant will flourish or perish in New York in
direct proportion to what it offers the public.*

Sincerely,
Craig Claiborne
Food News Editor[22]

Things were different where Soulé's inheritors were upholding their
heritage. Fred Decré and Roger Fessaguet were well established on their
own in 1967 as owners of La Caravelle, "perhaps the city's most distinguished French restaurant," but they were also both Pavillon alumni,
and when they opened Le Poulailler near Lincoln Center—a neighborhood in desperate need of fine dining—it was to accordingly high standards that Craig's review held them. After some weak praise of a few
good things, Craig found disillusionment in "dried, thin, tawdry slices
of ham . . . miserably overcooked vegetables . . . too much garlic . . .
lemon halves served with seeds unremoved"—he really *hated* those—
"and cold, stale French buns." He seemed to be speaking directly to
Decré and Fessaguet when he wrote, "These are tedious, niggling small
points that one might tolerate in a lesser establishment with lesser management." But he wanted them to know that his sympathy would not be
stretched as far as the "maître d'hôtel, formerly of Le Pavillon, who on
last view in that salle à manger [that is, under the aegis of the contempt-
ible Claude C. Philippe] was sporting a red pencil in his vest pocket.
At Le Poulailler he displays a larger collection of yellow pencils and
looks even less dignified and more like a well-dressed minor clerk in an
undertaker's office."[23]

Which was to say: Soulé would never have tolerated such vulgarity—
gentlemen, *try* to remember.

And when the master's memory was honored, as Madame Henriette
was doing with such propriety and finesse at La Côte Basque, Craig's
heart swelled. The best thing she had done was to bring in Martin Decré,
brother of Fred Decré[24] of Le Poulailler but also, and much more important, formerly Soulé's maître d'hôtel and right-hand man at Le Pavillon.
It was only a short review in his Friday Directory to Dining, but Craig
said that "La Côte Basque is flourishing happily now . . . and the food is
excellent," and he gave the restaurant his rare maximum four stars.[25]

Le Pavillon continued its decline. On the first day of March of 1968, the *Times* reported, "Less than a dozen people were having the $8 prix fixe luncheon. Only five tables in the two front rooms were occupied. The main dining room was closed."[26] The writer of the story was Marylin Bender, not Craig Claiborne. Claude C. Philippe—for some reason Bender called him Claudius—was, permanently, out. Stuart Levin, formerly of The Four Seasons, was, unenviably, in. The restaurant had lost $50,000 in the last year.

Craig reviewed Le Pavillon two and a half months later. "If anyone is tired of reading about the life, times, vanities and vicissitudes of Le Pavillon Restaurant," he wrote by way of opening, "now may be the time to turn the page." One pictures Stuart Levin's eyes closing in pain. When he read on, however, he found that "While his advent will never be heralded as the Second Coming, there does seem to be a discernible improvement since [Levin's] arrival. . . . In one respect Le Pavillon remains on a par with the best in New York, and that is the kitchen. The chef, Roland Chénus, is capable of dishes of great glory." Craig proceeded to praise a number of them, "beautiful" sole, "near-celestial" striped bass, "fantastic" veal chops, "auspicious . . . délice of veal Francomptois. . . . succulent, white, nonpareil." But "it is my earthbound duty (read punishment) to be captious and carping about some small detail, and it can be noted that kidneys, recently prepared at table by the maître d'hôtel, were cut into too large cubes, although the mustard sauce was good." Small detail indeed—and at least the guy was apparently no longer sporting a pocketful of yellow pencils.

"The last time this department reported on the status of Le Pavillon"—in the reign of Claude C. Philippe—"note was made that the splendor of flowers in profusion was not what it was in Soulé's time and they were arranged in what looked like 10-cent store mugs. They are now arranged in what look like oversize old-fashioned glasses." The service was "impeccable," the wines "overpriced." Stuart Levin's manner of dress was described, albeit indirectly, as looking "tacked on." Nevertheless, all things considered, especially the food, he must have been relieved.

Le Pavillon would survive for another four years.

§

In 1968 Craig's fame was at its zenith—his celebrity still new enough that he made good copy, his position now secure enough that writers could make the sort of absolute pronouncements that editors and their headline writers earned their paychecks for.

For *Time* magazine's choppy, knowing style, critic Claiborne was perfectly suited:

[At the Republican National Convention] Craig Claiborne, New York Times food critic, made the rounds of Miami's restaurants and found their cuisine good for laughs but not for digestion. Affronting his gourmet tastes at one restaurant was a mousse au chocolat crowned with whipped cream and as a final insult, perhaps, a maraschino cherry. At another establishment, Claiborne complained that a wedge of Camembert cheese had been served cold. The waiter offered to "run it under the broiler." "Now I ask you," wrote the exasperated critic, "isn't that worth the price of the meal?"[27]

For Gael Greene, New York's restaurants were high drama, and on her stage Craig was a diva. Craig in life wasn't a diva, but that's how Greene scripted him.

Chefs love him, owners hate him, diners obey him. . . . Craig Claiborne is, at 47, New York's most powerful food critic, and probably the nation's testiest food taster. A pan from Claiborne really smarts. Let him expose frozen Alaskan crab masquerading as fresh lump crabmeat, and the howls reverberate. . . . Craig hates piped-in music and piped-in décor, too small wine glasses, too large portions ("gross . . . excessive . . . quite vulgar").[28]

Let us not forget: 1968 was the year of the whole world going kerblooey. Vietnam in tragic straits: Khe Sanh, the Tet offensive, the My Lai massacre. Martin Luther King Jr. shot in April, Bobby Kennedy in June. Black Panthers, black pride, the once proudly arm-linked hope-dreaming civil rights movement broken into factions of blame and resentment. Prague Spring. Spring in Paris: *Sous les pavés, la plage*—under the paving stones, the beach—*soi-disant* revolutionaries ripping up cobblestones, chucking them at their baffled class-brothers the cops. Lyndon Johnson lost the presidency without running for it; Nixon won it: two men whose very physiognomies—so ugly, so patently mendacious—told evil fortunes. Percipient Americans groaned. Truly a world was upside down in which Jacqueline Bouvier Kennedy married Aristotle Onassis.

It was a good time to stay home, smoke pot, and cook dinner for your friends. It was a good time to go out for dinner and drink a lot of wine. It was a good time to care about the nuances of good food and wine. It was precisely the right time for Nora Ephron to write "Critics in the World of the Rising Soufflé" for *New York* magazine.[29] In Ephron's story, mere writers—she dubbed them, semi-neologistically, the Food Establishment—were portrayed as battling knights on the bloody plain of sheer imagination.

The scene was a party at The Four Seasons, for the début of the "massive, high-budget venture" of the Time-Life series of cookbooks under the superintendence of Michael Field, who

> was a wreck. A wreck, a wreck, a wreck, as he himself might have put it. Just that morning, the very morning of the party, Craig Claiborne of the *New York Times,* who had told the Time-Life people he would not be a consultant for their cookbooks even if they paid him $100,000, had ripped the first Time-Life cookbook to shreds and tatters. . . . He said that everyone connected with the venture ought to be ashamed of himself. He was rumored to be going about town spreading the news that the picture of the soufflé on the cover was not even a soufflé—it was a *meringue!* . . . He referred to Field, who runs a cooking school and is the author of two cookbooks, merely as "a former piano player."

This was a whole new take on Craig's world. In his own experience it had been a fairly nice place. When there were disagreements, or even resentments, they were, as in most people's lives, private matters. Ephron had conveniently misquoted Craig. His actual description of Michael Field had been "former concert pianist."[30] Sort of a different tone. But it was too late for subtle corrections. Craig and Julia and James Beard, and Paula Peck and Nika Hazelton and a bunch of other people whose bylines some people might have read but whom most people really hadn't heard of were public figures all of a sudden, or were being treated as such by Nora Ephron and *New York* magazine.

Ephron's was a long, long piece, and its grains were sifted with talmudic fineness. "Things in the Food Establishment are rarely explained . . . simply," she wrote. "They are never what they seem. People who seem to be friends are not. People who admire each other call each other Old Lemonface and Cranky Craig behind backs."

After a very long history of the food world and a very great deal of "Bitchy? Gossipy? Devious" innuendo, Ephron finally settled down to a sober look at the actual person who "speaks softly, wears half-glasses, and has a cherubic reddish face that resembles a Georgia peach . . . [and who] is probably the most powerful man in the Food Establishment."

> He has been able to bring down at least one restaurant, crowd customers into others, and play a critical part in developing new food tastes. . . . Six years ago, Claiborne began visiting New York restaurants incognito and reviewing them on a star system in the Friday *Times*; since then he has become the most envied, admired, and cursed man in the food world. . . .
>
> The fact of the matter is that Craig Claiborne does what he does better than anyone else. He is a delight to read. And the very things that make him superb as a food critic—his integrity and his utter incorruptibility—are what make his colleagues envious of him.

What happens in journalism is that when one magazine runs a story that's fun and interesting and a lot of people talk about it, other magazines follow, wanting—not the same story, just sort of. Editor to writer: Could you do something with our twist on it? This is more of a family magazine, so could we have something, oh, more homey, and personal? Hence, the *Saturday Evening Post*:

> On nights when he does not go out, even if he is alone, he cooks a full-course dinner, shaves, showers, changes into a suit and tie, puts wine and linen napkins and candles on the table, and music on the hi-fi, and dines in solitary splendor. . . .
>
> "I can't imagine anything I don't have," he went on. "I'm like Alice in Wonderland. I'm not interested in travel or money. East Hampton is the dream house of my life. My job at the *Times* was the impossible goal I set myself, and here I am, I have it for life. Pierre Franey and his family

are my family—I'm godfather to their children. Pierre and I meet every Thursday and we cook together, though I really act as his assistant. My house in East Hampton is very close to theirs, and we see each other all the time. All my life I'd been miserable and anxious and frightened. Now I have everything. All I want is for it to continue."[31]

Monkey see, monkey do—*Newsweek,* four weeks later:

Gourmet dining—at home or on the town—has become a new status symbol for the successful citizen, and a growing source of anxiety. . . . Authentic restaurant critics are flourishing. . . . The most influential of them all is Claiborne—and he can be acidly dyspeptic. . . .[32]

§

Craig Claiborne could look back on the 1960s with immense personal gratification. When he did so in the *Times,* however, there was as much pique as pride. He took delight in Julia Child, the proliferation of Japanese and Chinese food (especially sushi and Szechuan), La Caravelle, La Grenouille, Lutèce, and the Kennedy White House. But his list of laments and damnations was long: inflation (illustrated by the catastrophic increase in the price of caviar, from $36 to $50 to $60 for 14 ounces*), cyclamate, monosodium glutamate,† President Nixon's "predilection of some sort for cottage cheese garnished with catchup," "something masquerading as cream called Coffee Rich," chocolate fondue, "which must be the all-time nadir among things to cook," and, to be sure, the death of Henri Soulé.[33]

Craig's fiftieth birthday was coming up in September of 1970. Everything he had dreamed of for himself had come to pass. He had created a world, and now he ruled over it. He could do what he wanted. Oh, and that Time-Life cookbook series that he supposedly disdained? He and Pierre were doing the *Classic French Cooking* volume. Let the Food Establishment, or whatever you wanted to call them, make of it what they would.

---

* Adjusted by the actual rate of inflation, however, $50 was barely an increase at all.
† It is devoutly to be wished, and probably the case, that he never read Gael Greene's account of the massive amount of MSG stocked for Soulé's reopening of La Côte Basque in 1965.

Pierre Franey, with a little wicked sense of humor about Craig's imperial position in what both of them were damned well not going to call the Food Establishment, got in touch with Jacques Pépin and few other of their chef buddies and hatched a plan for Craig's birthday. The S.S. *France* was going to be in port in New York, and Pierre persuaded Craig that a piece about the kitchens would be a good idea. Pierre knew the chef, he told Craig, so he'd set up a tour.

The prior January Craig had discovered "the finest French restaurant in the world . . . not, as one might suppose, in Paris or the provinces of France"[34] but in the first-class dining room of the S.S. *France*. You could have as much caviar as you wanted, anytime you wanted it, for no extra charge. He thrilled to the menu's *foie gras en croûte*, langouste with freshly made mayonnaise, *ballotine de canard*, its "fancifully marbled terrine of chicken," medallion of brill with *sauce Périnette*, roast saddle of lamb, stuffed squab with truffle sauce. He was simply over the moon. "The incredible thing, too," he continued, "is that if there is nothing on any given menu to tempt the palate . . . almost any dish of classic or regional cooking can be commanded a few hours in advance, and it will be made with brilliance and no particular ceremony." He mentioned "an unlisted rack of hare" and "an intricately put together chartreuse of pheasant."

Ever since Lausanne, Craig had loved great service almost as much as great food. The problem was that he hardly ever got to see any. On the *France*, however, he did: "The service staff . . . from the principal maître d'hôtel, Louis Pellegrin, to the least ranking busboy (neatly turned out in starched linen uniforms) is awesome. . . . The impression is that they are the elite of France. . . . They go about their work with a willingness and desire to please that is rare, matched with an uncommon precision in style."

Salvador Dalí was aboard, along with his pet ocelot Babou, for whom a special meal was prepared thrice daily, each preceded by an elegantly printed menu. A photograph of the surrealist and his pet engaged in a tug-o'-war over a silk scarf at the dinner table accompanied Craig's piece, as did a reproduction of one of Babou's menus, of which one of the six possible courses was "La Gâterie 'FRANCE' (Haricots Verts—Poulet Haché—Riz Nature Arrosé de Jus de Viande et de Biscottes en Poudre)."*

* Translated: The Little Treat à la "FRANCE" (Green Beans—Chopped Chicken—Steamed Rice Sprinkled with Beef Broth and Powdered Biscuits).

There's also a photograph of the chief bartender wearing some sort of Napoleon hat apparently made out of a napkin and tucking his hand into his jacket Napoleon-style. Despite all the elegance, the *France* seems to have been a pretty fun-loving sort of ship.

For his birthday bash, Pierre and Jacques led the entirely clueless Craig into the cavernous kitchens of the liner, which were beastly hot from the pilot lights of all those stoves. Then they steered him into the first-class dining room.

The room erupted in a roar. There was Julia Child. The mountain of James Beard. Everybody from the *Times*. There was Henry Creel, dear Henry with that Cheshire grin, who'd told him they were just going to have a quiet little birthday dinner à deux, the liar. And there was—God, look at that cake—four tiers of spun sugar and ribbons and rosettes and candles and an airmail letter addressed to him all in marzipan. And the whole long row of the *brigade* in their whites and tall toques at attention behind a buffet of indescribable splendor, the kind of baroque extravaganza of *galantines* and *ballotines* and *pâtés en croûte, chartreuses, bavarois,* and *pièces montées* that had all but disappeared from this dreary sublunar world.

He was here. He had done it. All that he had dreamed of having, he had. These people loved him, most of them, not for who he was—they didn't really know who he was—but for what he had done. That was fine, that was splendid. For this moment he could allow himself to be proud, to be happy, as proud as he could be, as happy, until a qualifying clause should arise, as it surely would. Craig Claiborne had invented a new Olympus, and today he was at the top of it.

In their dark dress uniforms with gold buttons and gold epaulets, the officers, the captain of the *France*—shades of happy navy days. All his friends, his fellow writers (what feud?), the chefs, the waiters, Ed and Ellie Giobbi, Jacques Pépin, the Franeys, there must have been a hundred and fifty, all of them laughing, now singing, all of them there *for him*. Of course he wept.

11

Quits

Midmorning after his birthday fête on the *France,* Craig awoke with a terrible hangover. He woke most mornings these days with a hangover. Henry Creel said, Dobey, you're drinking too much. Craig called Henry names—with the right intonation, "master of the margarita" could be said quite nastily—implying that he was just as bad. But Henry knew when to stop, and they both knew that.

Craig had always had drinks before dinner, usually more than one and often more than two. Three wasn't uncommon, four not unheard of. Five was getting pretty festive. Six was getting drunk. Seven would have poleaxed almost anyone else alive, but Craig had been known to handle that number and still be able to walk.

Henry's margaritas were a favorite, Scotch was a reliable friend, and Craig loved an expertly made dry martini. He took pleasure in instructing bartenders in the subtleties of cocktail perfection. With dinner he drank wine no more than steadily, and did not draw attention. For after, he had always loved his Port, Cognac, *eau de vie,* liqueur; rarely only one.

His prodigious consumption of alcohol had hardly ever showed. Recently, however, Craig had taken a liking to stingers after dinner: "a copious amount of Cognac blended with white crème de menthe and shaken vigorously in a cocktail shaker with an abundant amount of ice,"[1] then strained into a cocktail glass. They went down quite easily, and quite often he had several. Now people were noticing. His face would flush, his eyes turn aqueous, his speech go torpid, trailing off sometimes midsentence. Sometimes he would be suddenly angry and his manners would fail him—he would say terrible things about people, say terrible things *to* them.

When Henry or his friends upbraided him, he said, Look, I'm doing my job, aren't I? I enjoy myself. I love my life.

He liked to recite a quotation from *Old Men Forget,* the autobiography of Alfred Duff Cooper, the British poet and politician who had been notorious for his eloquence, sexual adventures, gambling, and drinking.[2] Craig had the passage memorized word for word:

> I can truthfully say that since I reached the age of discretion I have consistently drunk more than most people would say is good for me. Nor do I regret it. Wine has been to me a firm friend and a wise counselor. Often wine has shown me matters in their true perspective and has, as though by the touch of a magic wand, reduced great disasters to small inconveniences.
>
> Wine has lit up for me the pages of literature, and revealed in life romance lurking in the commonplace.
>
> Wine has made me bold but not foolish; has induced me to say silly things but not to do them.
>
> Under its influence words have often come too easily which had better not have been spoken, and letters have been written which had better not have been sent.
>
> But if such small indiscretions standing in the debit column of wine's account were added up, they would amount to nothing in comparison with the vast accumulation on the credit side.[3]

Craig was even more forthright when he spoke to himself. "I sometimes turn to my reading lamp," he wrote, "and say a few well-chosen words (to my later embarrassment, but I have never yet had to apologize to a table lamp for how much wine I've drunk)."[4] He typed this on a sheet of thin brown paper, and stuck it in an unmarked manila folder and forgot about it. He hit the keys so hard that the comma and the period punched holes in the paper.

On another sheet of the same cheap paper at another time he typed, "I have many times over the years drunken [*sic*] myself on a morbid evening into a blind oblivion. I know that I have courted danger in times of intoxication on countless evenings, most of them best and blessedly for my own sanity perhaps, not remembered." This too ended up in an unlabeled folder.

The Boston University archivist Howard Gotlieb collected the papers and other artifacts of hundreds of public figures—ultimately more than two thousand—from Martin Luther King Jr. to Bette Davis, from Groucho Marx to George Bernard Shaw. On June 15, 1970, Gotlieb wrote the first of several letters to Craig Claiborne appealing to him to add his papers to what was to become the Howard Gotlieb Archival Research Center within the B.U. library.[5]

Papers? Craig replied. I don't have *papers*.

Gotlieb patiently persisted, as he had done with so many of the refractory subjects of his interest. Look, just anything you have. Empty your cabinets. Any old things. Things you might consider junk.

Okay, okay. Craig filled he didn't know how many boxes with things he considered junk. Old letters, blurry snapshots, pocket calendars, travel itineraries, bar bills, menus, clippings, credit card receipts, rough drafts—he really didn't look.

And that is how those musings on brown paper came to be quoted here, and how more than a few other pieces of the story of Craig Claiborne's life were fitted together.

§

For all his public success, Craig's private life in the late 1960s was something of a mess in more ways than his drinking. Although in later years he became rather prosperous, he never learned to handle money. His salary at the *Times* even as he rose to celebrity and influence remained relatively modest—$20,500 gross in 1967[6]—but his book-publishing output was substantial, and that would always be where the bulk of his income came from. He published *The New York Times Menu Cook Book* in June 1966, a major undertaking, 727 pages long, with 1,200-some new recipes and 400-plus menus. It was meant as a full-fledged companion to *The New York Times Cook Book* of 1961, which itself was still selling very nicely. In 1969 came *Craig Claiborne's Kitchen Primer*—a rather lightweight hodgepodge of recipes plus instructions in technique but a surprisingly strong success. In 1970 the Time-Life *Classic French Cooking,* cowritten with Pierre Franey, was distributed to a gigantic ready-made subscription readership. *Cooking with Herbs and Spices,* a revised and expanded and still dull version of Craig's 1963 non-seller, was also published in 1970, and could not but exceed its predecessor's performance.

The thing about book royalties is that they come only twice a year (accompanied by statements of impenetrable obscurity purporting to explain why the check isn't nearly as big as you expected). So every six months Craig would have more money than he knew what to do with, and then he would more or less blow it.

In April 1967, for example, in another mad sweep through Bloomingdale's, he replaced pretty much everything in the King's Point Road house, charging it all to his store account, to be repaid in monthly installments of $134. The harvest, featured later that year in a photo spread in *Long Island Home* magazine, was ghastly: a ship's-wheel barometer on the wall, a wastebasket with a brass eagle plaque, a cheesy model of a clipper ship, a scattering of wall-mounted starfish and seashells, and, oh, Lord, the bedroom—a virtually fluorescent orange bedspread, a white shag rug. All this is hard to reconcile with his taste in clothes, which was impeccable. Craig also decided he needed a wildly expensive Tandberg tape deck—an additional $104.83 per month.[7]

Four months later, in August 1967, Bloomingdale's put Craig on notice that he was in arrears on his payments. His accountants, David Joseph & Co., stalling for him, replied that there would be no further payments until the store supplied properly itemized receipts with each bill. Unfazed, on October 10, 1967, Bloomingdale's sent Craig a formal letter informing him that his unpaid debt now amounted to $1,426.79.

He had a very good deal on his New York apartment rent at $194 a month. On the Long Island house he had two mortgage loans, with payments of $193 and $172 a month respectively. On the Island you had to have a car, of course; that payment—he'd bought a Land Rover—was $166. The accountants got Bloomingdale's to simmer down and continue taking $134, and there was still the Tandberg, call it $105. That made $964 a month. Craig was probably taking home about $1150. If there hadn't been another royalty blast around the corner, he would have had a major problem.

If for a moment he didn't have a money problem, he would create one. One in particular was a doozy. On June 15, 1968, he wrote a check to the United States Internal Revenue Service for unpaid taxes in the amount of $4,250—and it bounced.[8]

As limitless as his foolishness with money, however, was his native generosity. For Christmas in 1966 he had bought a watch—at Bloomingdale's—for every member of the Franey family (save Jacques, who was four years old). He would pile the Franey kids and as many other kids as they wanted to invite into the Land Rover and drive them all to Montauk for pizza with the top down, opera blaring from the big new speakers he'd had put in, all of them laughing and screaming, jouncing over the back roads, no adults allowed.

When Craig's mother retired from her job as Pi Kappa Alpha's house mother at Mississippi State, she was still as hard up as she had ever been; his sister must have told him, for on August 18, 1966, Craig directed his bank to deposit to the account of Mrs. Kathleen Craig Claiborne at the Bank of Indianola the sum of $150 on the fifteenth of every month. That arrangement did not last long, however. Among the little nothings that Craig tossed in a box and sent to Howard Gotlieb at B.U. there is a handwritten note on Bank of Indianola notepaper that reads

JE [initials]
Claiborne 10/3/66
mother died
no more remittances

Many years later, Jim Abbott, the former editor of the Indianola *Enterprise-Tocsin* and an insightful observer of the culture of the Delta, would say, "Being gay was not Craig's great offense to Mississippians. It was not coming to his mama's funeral."[9]

In July 1967 Craig's brother Luke died, and he didn't go to that funeral either. In January 1968, in a letter to an old friend of the family who had written inquiring about Luke, he wrote,

I am sad to say that Luke had a pretty rough go of it during the last years of his life. He really seemed to be hounded by fates and furies and, truth to tell, self-defeating. He was a colonel during the war and married a young Hawaiian girl named Virginia Owen. They had three children, two boys both of whom are now in the army and a very young daughter whom I have never seen. . . . They lived first in Indianola then in Hawaii and finally in Pago Pago, American Samoa. I think that Luke had a problem with alcohol. He had high blood pressure and died quite suddenly. . . . I do not have Virginia's address. To be wholly candid about the matter, I was never very fond of her. . . .[10]

In August 1968, with royalties again burning a hole in his pocket, Craig decided on a change of address that on Manhattan Island carried metaphysical weight. Back when he lived on West Thirteenth Street, in his first New York apartment, that had been the *echt* Greenwich Village, of poets, trust-funded wannabes, dopers, topers, old Italian ladies in black, bright little eighteenth-century houses. In his next and more hygienic abode at 20 East Ninth Street, east of Fifth Avenue, in what was still technically the Village, he had been in bourgeois habitat, in the ambit of New York University, where apartment houses were dark and respectable and the men with goatees and berets also wore neckties.

But now he was moving *uptown*. To a true Greenwich Villager this was apostasy. To many other, more northerly Manhattanites the shadowy zone between Fourteenth Street and Trinity Church was where People *Not* Like Us, Dear, lived, presumably in squalor. For the good citizens uptown to see, now, that that wonderful Craig Claiborne of the *New York Times* was buying a proper co-op apartment in a proper building like the Hampshire House, well, that was something that ought to have happened a long time ago.

Central Park South! Thirty thousand dollars, cash. Six hundred forty-six a month maintenance* was steep, but *look* at that view, not to mention the twenty-four-hour doormen's Ruritanian-palace-guard uniforms. This was tone. The only problem was: He hated the apartment.

The closing on the Hampshire House apartment took place on August 29, 1968. Two days later he celebrated the new home he despised with a rather boisterous dinner in East Hampton, an occasion duly commemorated: For some time now Craig had been documenting his din-

---

* "Maintenance" is what people in a New York City cooperative apartment pay for their building's staff, upkeep, insurance, and taxes, and against the underlying mortgage of the building.

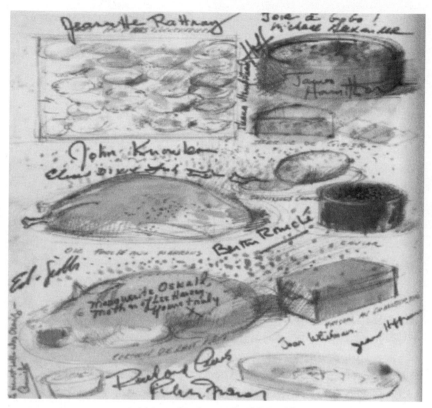

A watercolor menu by Ed Giobbi.

ner parties in big blank-paged leather-bound books from Mark Cross. There was nearly always an artist present: Ed Giobbi was the most frequent contributor, and Jacques Pépin, among his many talents, was also a quite good watercolorist. The menu was always chronicled, often in both words and pictures, and so were the names of those present. In thirty years of festivity, Craig accumulated a large stack of these volumes, each bound in a different color of soft leather.

The Howard Johnsons were there this night in August 1968, for the invention of a new species of stinger and an unfortunate consequence thereof. "I discovered that my cupboard contained no white crème de menthe," Craig recalled, "but an ample supply of the green variety. I made [stingers] with the green liqueur and poured out glasses for my guests. Howard drank his and a moment later said, 'Son, that was good.

Let me have another one of those green things.' After that, stingers were generally made with green rather than white crème de menthe."[11]

Gael Greene was also at the party, on assignment for *Look,* and she painted a vivid picture of the scene:

> The weekend is a fete of wine, champagne, stingers, and feasting. . . . Craig is alternately manic—acting out *West Side Story*—and pensive: "If I should die today, I am happy. I have everything I want." The funeral is planned: "I'm to be cremated. Listen! Here's the part in the Verdi *Requiem* where Pierre throws my ashes over the cliff into the bay."[12]

Greene left before Craig got really crazy—tossing back more of the new concoction known from that evening forward "by several names in my menu books. It is referred to as green things, green stuff, and, in French, *les choses vertes*."[13]

Diane Franey hadn't yet turned fourteen, and her parents had sent her and Claudia home, but she had seen an earlier version of the scene. "Craig had this routine," she remembers, "where he would dance to 'The Jet Song' from *West Side Story*. He had the whole thing down. He'd light a cigarette—he didn't smoke, he'd have to bum one—and you know how it starts, with just the finger-snapping? He'd lean against the wall, smoking that cigarette and snapping his fingers, tapping one foot, becoming a Jet. And then as the song went on, he'd sing along with it and dance, wilder and wilder, and then for his finale he would go *headfirst* down the steel spiral staircase to the basement. The big thing for us kids would be to run out the side door and down the hill to the downstairs door and see who got there in time to catch him."[14]

But what happened this time, after all those stingers, and in the absence of the young Franeys, was that he crashed headfirst into the concrete floor. As the crowd rushed to Craig's aid, his head was bleeding copiously, and everyone—including the prostrate performer—was convinced that he had broken his skull. In fact he had only split his scalp open.

Closing the wound "demanded 27 stitches at 2 a.m.," Craig recalled, attributing the accident to "ample imbibing."[15]

On October 14, 1968, Craig wrote to his accountant, David Joseph, the unsurprising news that "I do not know my present financial status," but he did want to know if he might borrow $4,000 to renovate the new apartment that he hated so much. Also, "I will have to have a dinner jacket for that return trip on the *France*"—the trip that would become his story of "the finest French restaurant in the world,"[16] which in turn would spawn his glittering fiftieth-birthday party.

He got his four thousand and did the fix-up at Hampshire House, but he still detested the place, and was soon looking for something else. Eventually he found the apartment of his dreams in a famous building called the Osborne, at Fifty-seventh Street and Seventh Avenue, cater-corner from Carnegie Hall. It was only a studio—one bed-sitting room with a little front hall, a tiny kitchen, and a bathroom, and that was it—but his fellow tenants would include Leonard Bernstein, the theater director and critic Harold Clurman, the pianist Gary Graffman, the art dealer Sidney Janis, the *Vogue* editor Leo Lerman, the cabaret star Bobby Short, the opera singer Cornell MacNeil, and the epitome-of-

The Osborne today.

suave actor (and alcoholic wife-murderer) Gig Young.[17] And it couldn't have hurt that some number of the residents, whether celebrated or not, were gay.

To buy the Osborne apartment he needed another $30,000. Did he have it? He did not. But Chemical Bank was presumably confident that the Hampshire House apartment would eventually realize that much. The bank was also aware—as David Joseph was, but none of Craig's friends seemed to be—that despite his semiannual splurges Craig had been quietly socking away some of that book money. The bank's confidence was evidently not absolute, however, since the thirty thousand came in the form of a demand loan—that is, they could ask for it back whenever they wanted. The reason Craig didn't have the cash was that he had been quietly investing his sock money (in the New York Times Company and, who knows why, Simplicity Pattern), but he was good for it if he had to be. He wasn't as dumb as his friends thought.

The Osborne loan closed on November 29, 1968, and Craig was on a plane to Paris that night. On December 1, having dined well, with equally agreeable liquid refreshment, he was ensconced in a suite at the Ritz—all this on the *Times*, of course—and was writing a letter to Jeannette Rattray, the publisher of the East Hampton *Star,* who had become a dear friend and confidante of the particular sort that only a sympathetic older lady can be. He had advanced from addressing her as Mrs. Rattray to this less formal

My Dear Mrs. R.,

Can you imagine what it is like if you were born in Sunflower, Mississippi, to walk along the Quai d'Orsay and realize that tomorrow morning you must telephone an old friend, the American ambassador to France; to know that you recently talked to Charles Ritz, son of César Ritz, who has postponed his departure to the airport so that he might have a small talk; to return to a magnificent suite and find a bottle of Champagne on ice; to fight back tears—

Paris is, of course, my spiritual home. There is the most extraordinary comfort, a mystic relationship that I can't understand nor explain. The view of the garden from my window as I write is somehow all related to a very real past of which I have no temporal recollection. But the emotional identity is far too profound for fantasy. Not only the garden, of course, but the Seine, the quais, the Opéra, Place Concorde, Place Madeleine—

Alone, I walked back via the Louvre and the small boat basins, stumbling over my joy . . . watching a small child launch a tiny sailing vessel with red sails, marveling at the strict alignment of the arches from the Arc of the Carrousel to the Arc de Triomphe, and having a tremor or two just seeing that Paris sky, unlike any other— anywhere. A man saw me pause to make a note or two and he came over to ask if I were taking down the number of his license plate. How could I say in French or in English what I was really doing? I wanted to put my arm around him but I only laughed and said I was an American and this was my first day in Paris.

And to top it all, Pierre arrives in the morning.

Fondly,
Craig

Sounds like a man who loves his job, right? Well, yes. But no. That is, he did love his job, but he was starting to not love his life. He often said he did, but when he did he was lying. He also was starting not to like himself. Snob, he called himself if he was drunk enough—although that wasn't true either. Incapable of real warmth except with kids—an oversimplification with a few grains of truth. Incapable of trust, afraid of the emotional risk—sort of true. Overcomplicating everything—what does that mean? Changing shrinks as if that would change his life—yes. Drinking to drown the shame of being a drunk? Absolutely.

Craig did not know why he was starting also to dislike his beloved New York, but he was. He sought a hidden motive inside himself, but there were good reasons in the city itself, and they showed themselves in its restaurants. There was a meanness creeping in. There was envy, an ever-harsher one-upmanship. Craig had always bristled when ignorant people from elsewhere talked about New Yorkers being rude—he said you just had to know how to hear them, they were brusque and funny and sweet; but now it was too often true.

He refused to blame Henri Soulé, but the restaurants of Le Pavillon's alumni were among the worst offenders. Lutèce—its democratic and always polite André Soltner the definitive anti-Soulé—proved the case by its contrast.

On Christmas Eve of 1968, Craig's colleague Marylin Bender opened a piece in the *Times* with this: "Anyone willing to pay $60 to $100 for dinner for four, or say $50 for lunch, in one of the dozen or so New York restaurants that are renowned for haute cuisine and clientele to match can reasonably expect to receive more than he bargained for these days. A gratuitous insult is likely to be served with the meal."

Bender took special aim at one of Craig's particular favorites, La Caravelle. People would show up with reservations and then not be seated, she said. They'd call for a table and be denied. People were threatening to report La Caravelle to the Better Business Bureau. Robert Meyzen—former maître d'hôtel at Le Pavillon and now partner, in La Caravelle, of Craig's pal Roger Fessaguet—proudly allowed himself to be quoted saying, "When I have Mrs. Lytle Hull and Mrs. Burden, why should I take Mrs. Somebody from Kalamazoo? If I don't feel like taking someone, that's my privilege."

Bender also noted that women "are treated as a sub-species of inferiors by restaurateurs."[18]

By 1970, in the now two-year-old *New York* magazine, Gael Greene was offering a flamboyant alternative to Craig's dignified and scholarly style of restaurant criticism. She was also, passionately, a consumer advocate. The snobbery that he disliked but was still loath to condemn in print made her blood boil:

> It hurts so nice! The card-carrying Manhattan masochist thrives on a diet of flageolets and flagellation, so often the *spécialité du jour* in the posh Pleiades of restaurants where the snub is often more creative than the cuisine. . . . You bring money, lots of money, in your Hermès *sac* or your Vuitton duffel. But mere money will not spring you from the bitter frostbite of Siberia, from neglect, glazed ennui, under-age wines, snarled lectures on gastronomic propriety, and other lessons in humility. . . . Money will not melt Robert Meyzen of La Caravelle: "You cannot buy a table—not for $200," Meyzen has said. "If you belong here, you get a table." . . . Overtipping the waiter is wanton. It is impossible to overtip the maître d'. . . . Perhaps you can get his son into St. Bernard's. . . .[19]

The villain, again, was Meyzen. And Greene was publishing this only three months and change after Craig had published his imperial look back at the 1960s, the piece in which he had declared one of the decade's finest contributions to have been the opening by Henri Soulé's inheritors of such grand new French restaurants in New York as La Caravelle.

§

Craig was itchy, restless, irritable. He went to his bosses and said, Look, Pierre contributes more and more, I couldn't possibly do this job without him, I know I've said this before, but really we've got to do something for him. We've got to give him a co-byline. And a salary.

—But yours is the name that sells newspapers, Mr. Claiborne.

—It's a matter of fairness. Soon enough he'll be just as well known. We could put it in smaller type if you insist.

—We'll get back to you.

They didn't. Craig had to call.

—Mr. Claiborne, we can't do it. I'm sorry.

§

In 1968 Craig had found his captain from Korea, the skipper of the USS *Naifeh,* John Smits, whom he really had adored. Smits was married, still in the navy but living in New Mexico. Craig had gone out to visit John and Ann Smits and their boys. He expected to hate the desert, but he was exhilarated by the clarity, the dry, clear air. One night Craig and the Smitses stayed up late and Craig said he thought he might buy land there, build a house. Then he forgot about it.

In January 1970 he went out to see John and Ann Smits again, and this time he looked at a house. He didn't know. He did know he wanted to get away. From New York. From the bullshit, the metastasizing incivility. Maybe from the paper. On January 28, 1970, he wrote to his accountant—and by now also all-round advisor—David Joseph:

Dear David:

Within the next several weeks I will receive in the vicinity of $20,000 royalties from Alfred Knopf, Inc., for the Kitchen Primer. And at the same time approximately $23,000 from Harper & Row for the Times Cookbook, Menu Cookbook, etc. . . .

This is by way of preface to an idea I can't get out of my head. For several years now I have had a strong desire to buy property in New Mexico, and in the specific town of Lincoln which is like a museum. It has historic value, Billy the Kid was killed there and the town has many artists, writers and so on, some of whom are friends of mine. . . .

It is an adobe style house with three bedrooms, a large living-dining room, with a caretaker house nearby. This is on 11.5 acres, enclosed with a stone fence. Half the property is in orchard, the remainder in alfalfa. There are water rights, whatever that means, and the cost is $42,500.

I have explained my royalty situation to [the broker]—at least the fact that I have no money for such an investment and she has proposed that I send a $500 option.

I sincerely believe that real estate out there will zoom within a few years. . . .

One final thing. I want to go to the Caribbean for a week. I have had a lousy chest cold and I feel grey and sallow. . . .

Water rights, whatever that means? What that means, Craig, old buddy, is you ain't ready for prime time in the West, where whiskey's for drinkin' and water's for fightin'. The house, the real estate broker says, is at 6,500 feet elevation and is therefore "always cool in summer." That "stone fence" you mention? Concrete block. "New Mexico territorial architecture," broker says? Photograph says, Sure, if your "territory" is a desert subdivision. And *only* fifteen miles to Ruidoso and ten to Hondo or Capitan! If you can't get your foie gras in Capitan, surely they'll have it in Ruidoso. (Try it.)

Oh, and that $500 deposit? Five *thousand*, please. (But the tractor is included.)

David Joseph suggested that the Caribbean might be a good idea.

It was rare for Craig to slam his fist down and make a firm and final decision against one of his terrible inspirations. More frequently he just let them wither away. That seems to be what happened to his plan to move to the New Mexico desert.

§

Here was a bracing taste of New York. No other place on earth could have produced a Fred Bridge, or even tolerated him. Craig did a piece about this lunatic and his cookware store on East Fifty-second Street,[20] which had catered pretty much only to professionals till Craig started recommending the huge, unwieldy, tin-lined fish poachers, heavy mandolines, hammered-copper stock pots, and such that Bridge specialized in. He carried only the best, and charged unconscionable prices to the nonprofessionals, but because Craig Claiborne had said they needed those fish poachers, or those French-made pea scoops or balloon whips or *bain-maries,* Craig's followers came crowding in, and Fred Bridge repaid their enthusiasm with abuse. "I'm not interested in people who come in here to break my chops," he said. In fact he was unspeakable to nearly everyone who entered his shop. In a time when gut-chilling rudeness was rife in New York, Fred Bridge may have been the rudest person in town. Craig didn't care—Bridge was nice to him. The Robert Meyzen syndrome.

Craig didn't feel guilty about that. What he did feel guilty about was having so much power—the fact that one piece of his could change the course of a restaurant, a vegetable, a person's life.

> Many's the sleepless night I've lain in bed worrying about the stellar worth of one restaurant or another, about whether I was justified in referring to a chef's mornay sauce as pure mucilage, or whether that unaccustomed flavor in the hollandaise was actually basil or rosemary as I had judged it to be. [21]

Craig asked David Joseph for an assessment of his financial condition. From the accountant's cautiously worded reply Craig persuaded himself that he could live on his book income for a while, and he had a great idea for a money-making venture. The *Craig Claiborne Journal.* Just him and Pierre. They could do it out of his house in Springs.

It was Pierre, in fact, who had first planted the idea, back in October 1968, with a note attached to an anonymous newspaper clipping. Pierre's note read, "Looks like a good way to make money quickly." The clipping was headlined "And In Frisco New 'Claiborne' Guides Gourmets." It was about a newsletter in San Francisco called *Jack Shelton's Private Guide to Restaurants* that had started in 1967 with five hundred subscribers paying ten dollars a head per year and was now up to five thousand subscribers. Fifty thousand bucks a year in a city a tenth the size of New York.

All through 1970, Craig couldn't stop thinking about the idea of doing his own private newsletter.

It wasn't as if that's all he thought about, however. Every so often, his job was great. In the fall, he found a superb home cook named Marcella Hazan, with degrees in natural science and biology; he loved writing about her, her husband Victor, and their twelve-year-old son Giuliano. Mrs. Hazan was about to begin giving lessons in Italian cooking in their apartment on West Fifty-seventh Street.[22] There was also a trip to Paris, where he met Richard Olney, "a man possessed of an uncommon palate for food and wine," who was, "by his own definition, a hermit," living in Solliès-Toucas in Provence, alone, with no heat but his fireplace and wood-burning stove, and without a telephone. Craig loved Olney's new *French Menu Cookbook*, and lavishly praised it in the *Times*.[23]

But still he itched.

> I was bored with restaurant criticism. At times I didn't give a damn if all the restaurants in Manhattan were shoved into the East River and perished. Had they all served nightingale tongues on toast and heavenly manna and mead, there is just so much that the tongue can savor, so much that the human body (and spirit) can accept, and then it resists. . . . I found myself increasingly indulging in drink, the better to endure another evening of dining out. . . .

He had never been to Africa. In December, off he went. Far out in the bush, albeit in relative luxury, at the Mount Kenya Safari Club, the best he could say of the food was that it wasn't bad, though the bloody marys were "sensational."[24]

On the beautiful and at that time still remote Swahili island of Lamu he sought out a family well known for its luxurious $200-per-head-per-day safaris. The paterfamilias was drop-dead pretentious. "We always take a staff of 20 people for four people on a safari," he said, including "a pair of skinners" and "four gun bearers." They always served a four-, five-, or six-course meal in the bush: "When we come back to camp at sunset, there are 'toasties' around a campfire—things like chopped game liver on toast or something nonsensical made of fish or cheese. . . ." Craig's piece sagged with his boredom.[25]

At the famous game-viewing lodge The Ark, Craig ignored the food and concentrated on the sights—and the sounds, in which, despite himself, he heard his own ennui creeping in: "You can hear the buffaloes grunting and chewing the grass and the crickets doing their thing, whatever that is." He found some tart amusement in viewing the upright-walking primates indoors, in particular one Nairobi resident with firm views on elephants: They "have such piggy little eyes and scruffy old tails," she told him. "And I hate that scruffy old skin that hangs around their bottoms." As an old Africa hand, she was of course an expert in pachyderm biology: "Elephants have a huge mass of bone in their heads," she said, "and no brain."[26]

Things got marginally better in Ethiopia. In Asmara he found, to his astonishment, good Italian food—handmade pasta, local prosciutto, fresh fish from local waters, and antipasto "much more interesting than one is apt to find in most Italian restaurants in Manhattan."[27] The traditional Ethiopian food in Addis Ababa, he wrote, "is, to my mind and taste, among the world's most interesting, and it is taken in the most convivial manner."[28] In the Addis Ababa Hilton, where you might not think of seeking out the native heritage, he discovered indigenous wonders, unlike anything he had ever tasted:

> There's incense in the air, and we were feasting on things called yebeg alicha, a tender lamb dish flavored with Bishop's weed and saffron; doro watt, the Ethiopian chicken and hard-cooked egg dish with a light pepper sauce; and menchet abish, a ground beef dish that tasted lightly of cinnamon and pepper. The gomen watt, made with spinach and shallots, was delectable, and the native drink, tej, made with gesho hops and honey, was fascinating.[29]

And so did he return home refreshed by all this novelty and fascination? The furthest thing from it.

It had been a particularly frustrating trip, perhaps the most frustrating of my years with the newspaper. With the exception of Ethiopia, the food had been dreadful and the writing of copy had been particularly hard going. . . .

When I came back, I felt depleted, if not to say dejected and slightly morose. . . . On the second day, the phone rang. It was a copy reader from the news desk telling me that I had to rewrite the game farm article to make it "more food-y." It gave me a nasty jolt. For better or for worse, over the years my copy had always been edited with a very light hand. I felt as if I were being punished. But I wrote two more paragraphs, both manufactured to fit the demands, and telephoned them in.[30]

§

Christmas approached, and New Year's. New Year's was always a time of joy for Craig. Most people hated New Year's, he knew. He always made a lavish dinner for friends, as many as he could manage, and he saw in their desperate and brittle gaiety that the holiday was hard for many of them, and he understood. He always got plastered himself. But it was complicated. For Craig New Year's was always both a happy time and a serious time, a time to look back and a time to look forward. New Year's Day, with its hammering hangover, was a day for sober assessment.

Here he was, fifty years old, at the top of a profession that he had created, the king of a kingdom he had created, and bored stiff. Maybe the idea of the journal wouldn't pan out, but he had to do something different. Pierre came over. They talked. They decided: Yes. They opened a bottle of Champagne, and it subsumed the hangover.

The *Times* was not pleased. They offered him a raise. They needed him.

—What about Pierre? Last chance.

—No, look, Craig, really.

He said he would stay until spring, and then—out the door.

12

Prodigal

Craig's last piece in the *New York Times* before his departure consisted of a single bland paragraph in the Sunday magazine. There was something almost contemptuous about it, it was so trivial—it seemed like something he might have found when he was cleaning out his desk. The dateline was May 16, 1971, but the subject was a visit he had made "several years ago" to "the ranch of the Dudley Doughertys in Beeville, Texas." There were two recipes, the first for roasting half a baby goat with dried oregano, the second for an ordinary salsa, and that was it.

After resigning that January, Craig had given not the slightest hint in the paper that he was soon to leave it. There was no piece about the next great phase of his life, the *Craig Claiborne Journal*. There was no note of farewell to his readers. He just stopped, and walked away.

He was tired. Besides the dozen or so restaurants a week he now had to sample, besides the relentless production of columns he held himself to, besides the calling and waiting and calling again and backing-and-forthing and all the dead ends that all those so often entailed, Craig had also been working for the last three years on *The New York Times International Cook Book*, another project of a scope unprecedented in its genre. It represented thousands of miles of travel, countless hours of labor, and the worldwide variety of Craig's sphere of culinary acquaintance, many of whom had figured in his columns. In the preface he thanks 182 people in addition to Pierre—among them Elizabeth David, Mr. and Mrs. Shelby Foote, Victor (though not Marcella) Hazan, Nika Hazelton, Maida Heatter, Madhur Jaffrey, Diana Kennedy, Mrs. Jacques

Lipchitz, Dione Lucas, Richard Olney, and, tied for best name, Pablo Zappi-Manzoni and the Marquesa Mercedes Ocio de Merry del Val. All the great cuisines are represented, as are those of Barbados, Fiji, Norway, Poland, Israel, Armenia, and Dahomey. The French section, at 213 pages, is a cookbook in itself; the Italian and Chinese chapters are extensive as well. Craig found the work so exhausting that he vowed never to do another cookbook.

Once the *International* was out of the way and he was winding down at the *Times,* he should have been devoting his every waking moment to the *Craig Claiborne Journal.* There was money to be raised, planning to be done, writing to be done. But an unexpected romance intervened.

Craig had always loved Chinese food, especially that at the formal and sophisticated end of its spectrum, which was almost unknown in New York. When someone had suggested to him that a woman named Virginia Lee was a master of the art and he then visited her for an interview, dish after dish of supreme elegance was put before him. He could not believe that this "strikingly handsome, smiling, and dignified Chinese lady who looked much too grand and refined ever to have handled a cleaver"[1] had done all the cooking herself, but she had. He was entranced.

That very morning, strongly encouraged by Craig, Lee decided to start taking in students. Craig said he would publish her phone number in his piece, and he would like to be the first to sign up, right now. Every week, for many weeks, he took the subway downtown to Lee's daughter's apartment in Chinatown. It was like when he had first seen Pierre Franey at work in the kitchen at Le Pavillon—he couldn't get enough of Virginia Lee.

"Having heard so much over the years of the many 'schools' of Chinese cooking," he would come to write, "and the seemingly endless nature of each, I was blindly in awe of Chinese cookery and therefore—with rare exceptions—avoided trying my hand at it. It seemed to me simply too vast to undertake." But Lee was such a good teacher, she broke the processes into such discrete and straightforward steps, that Craig found the work no longer in the least mysterious, and a new, very old world was opening to him.

Lee was "one of the great natural cooking experts of this age."[2] Never mind his vow never to do another cookbook. The journal could wait. This was "a book that had to be written."

The Chinese Cookbook, published in 1972 with the coequal byline of Craig Claiborne and Virginia Lee, was by far the clearest, widest-ranging, and most authentic exposition of Chinese food ever published for Americans. There was much more to explain than had been the case with anything Craig had written before—the Chinese way of planning a meal, the use of Chinese tools and equipment, the various Chinese ways of thinking about food. Nor was the philosophy easy for a Western mind. The book admittedly could do no more than touch on the major cultural and linguistic groups of China, but in 1972—the year of Richard Nixon's famous trip to China, the totalitarian Mao Zedong regime's first real opening to the West—the fact that there was such diversity in China would be news to most of the readers of *The Chinese Cookbook,* and what it did convey of the systems of thought underlying Chinese food was also little understood in America.

There still is no better Chinese cookbook in English. It is uncompromising in the boldness of its choice of dishes—cold kidney and celery, chicken skin salad, chicken with fish flavor, pigs' feet casserole, sea slugs with pork sauce, in addition to all the now-familiar classics—and at the same time the book is patiently basic in its instructions. Although there are of course hundreds, indeed thousands of Chinese dishes necessarily not included, once you have learned the techniques the book teaches, you can make virtually anything in the Chinese repertoire.

The sustained effort and concentration *The Chinese Cookbook* required also showed Craig that as tired as he might have been feeling, he had by no means exhausted his possibilities. The book was exactly what he needed to energize him for the risk of going solo with the *Craig Claiborne Journal.* He raised the money—actually, much of what was at risk, in the event, was his own. He found a designer he liked. He settled on a simple, modest format, confident that his reputation would be sufficient to get the journal off the ground, and that the excellence it would embody—what came down to the hard work he would put into it—would sustain it.

Warner LeRoy, the gold-sequined, gossip-column-courting impresario of the East Side kitsch palace Maxwell's Plum—picture a three-hundred-pound Elton John—threw a cocktail party for the launch of the *Craig Claiborne Journal,* having it be known that the Plum's kitchen staff of forty-six had worked for ten days (on and off, anyway) to produce the thirty-four-foot-long buffet and five-foot-high ice sculpture of an eagle. Four hundred of his and Craig's closest friends ate, drank, and posed for the cameras.[3]

It seemed a somewhat off-key début for *la* quite conservative *vraie chose,* with its few quiet black-and-white drawings and its coolly arch-Claibornean voice. Volume One, Number One, of the *Craig Claiborne Journal* was dated March 15, 1972, and was spiced with the proprietor's characteristic *bons mots:*

- "It would be interesting to know which did the most for the other's image, chickens or Henri IV."
- "This journal is dedicated to the proposition that there's only one voyage for each of us on this planet. And we might as well enjoy it."
- "Disraeli once wrote a line spoken by his Mr. Mountchesney in *Sybil.* 'I rather like bad wine. One gets so bored with good wine.'"

The journal was printed on heavy beige paper, a standard sheet folded vertically so that it presented itself 11 inches high and 4¼ wide, corresponding to two newspaperlike columns. It cost $36 for twenty-four eight-page issues a year, which was decidedly expensive—about a dollar a page, that would be today—but Craig obviously presumed you would wish to hang on to every one, for it came pre-punched for a three-ring notebook.

One signal characteristic distinguished the *Craig Claiborne Journal* from anything we might recognize as a "food magazine" today—its utter lack of vulgarity. The principal reason for the journal's high price was the absence of advertising. That absence obviated all the corruptions that are the bread and butter of food magazines today—their pandering to advertisers in their choice of subject matter; their behind-the-scenes deals in the form of advertiser-paid junkets, cruises, clothes, cars, hotel suites, massages, facials, rare wines, meals beyond the reach of anyone else but the very rich; the invisibly advertiser-funded "product placements" in their photographs; the chaotic style-and-design jumble that makes their editorial matter and their advertising ever more difficult to distinguish; the "all-star weekends," "celebrations," "seminars," "best-ofs," "festivals," and "lifestyle events" all starring their editors and the star chefs they and their star-making machinery have made stars, all

sponsored by their advertisers. That stained time had not yet come, and the *Craig Claiborne Journal* would bear no shame for its coming when it did.

Craig's journal was a simple, plain thing. The first number offered several recipes, a number of wry observations, a lesson in French gastronomic nomenclature, a tip on a great mail-order rye bread, and—most surprisingly, since he said he was so sick of doing them—four restaurant reviews. He gave three stars to an opulent new Indian restaurant named Ramayana; one to the "excellent" but "so déjà vu" Les Pléiades; two to a "Chinese fish and sea food house" ("an interesting idea") called Hong Kong Aberdeen; and two to the venerable but newly revived Saito, where the food was "good" but the décor looked as if it had been "put together with Band-Aids and Scotch tape." All were in Manhattan.

Finally, without awarding stars, Craig reported on two restaurants he had enjoyed on a recent visit to Corsica. He was amused by La Grange, where "on our first visit we were the only guest in the house . . . a small radio plays throughout the day and the chef at times comes into the dining room to read his newspaper." He was pleased as well as amused, for the same take-it-easy chef "will prepare on request the best bouillabaisse to be found south of Marseille." And he had a gustatory lifetime-first at the Auberge Pisciatelli, where "we"* dined on spit-roasted, un-gutted blackbirds.

The restaurant critic who had so deprecated the job of restaurant critic was, in short, back at the old stand.

§

And where was Pierre? In the background of the recipes, surely, but nowhere to be seen. Each issue began with a column headed "One Man's Taste." The journal was Craig Claiborne's, not Craig and Pierre's.

Over the next few issues it became more personal still. In the edition of June 1, 1972, Craig felt compelled to express his displeasure over some truly idiotic ads recently run by the American Medical Association headlined "How to Kill Yourself"—"adding that you can achieve

---

* After all those years of tortured third-person passive at the *Times*, he had at last adopted *The New Yorker*'s less awkward singular-plural first person.

this end by eating, drinking and being merry. I have news for the American Medical Association. I am a staunch defender of moderation in all things. Including eating and drinking. But I fully intend to continue to eat. And drink. And be as blissfully merry as my old bones will allow. I count eating and drinking among the chief pleasures of life and without pleasure who wants to live to 102. Dear AMA: Just don't ask me to dine. Not with you."

If he was whistling past the graveyard, he would damn well do it with gusto. By the next issue—June 15, 1972—he had been to Paris, dining with the Count Philippe de Lafayette. The city never failed to work its charms on Craig: "Old-fashioned and corny as we are, we always find Paris itself a bit intoxicating. . . . Having decided that Champagne or beer [was] the ideal beverage for *andouillettes,* [we] settled for Champagne throughout the meal. All of which led to a rather pleasant state of euphoria, and after coffee and Cognac we waltzed or pirouetted to Maxim's for a nightcap. . . .

"If what we dined on represents the demise of the French table, we are delighted to bask in its crepuscule."

Two weeks later: "We have what might be called an almost incontinent lust for the life we lead."

In the issue of July 15 he was again reporting on his trip to Europe, this time on some sybaritic dining in Milan—at Giannino's, "expertly made martinis," *gamberetti* that put him (again, as in Paris) in "a state of euphoria," "splendid meat-filled ravioli with prosciutto and cream," "excellent *animella con piselli,*" "small, elegantly conceived veal rolls," and "a wildly good *gâteau St-Honoré*"; at the Gran San Bernardo, "the perfect risotto," "simple and fantastic" *spaghettini con vongole,* "quite special" *persico alla Murat,* "beautiful" *zabaglione,* and "a splendid vanilla soufflé with chocolate sauce"; and disappointment across the board at Milan's most celebrated restaurant, Savini.

The *Craig Claiborne Journal's* rules on freebies and favors were as rigid as those of the *New York Times.* All this expenditure was coming straight out of the journal's pocket, and Craig Claiborne did not scrimp. In Paris he had been unable to avoid being given a discount on his suite at the Bristol, but it still set him back 778 francs for his three nights there, and he had entertained three guests for dinner one evening—a dinner he did not write up—for an additional 327. His Paris

hotel bill alone, then, at current U.S. rates, would have come to $1,134. He ordered the best wines, and drank a lot of the best Champagne and Cognac as well. He also flew first class.[4]

A fine indicator of Craig's approach to money management comes from the summer before. On August 1, 1971, his personal checking account balance was $11.98. He had written only one check during the preceding month—for $150.00, to Cartier.

The journal was an unlimited first-class ticket. Craig could go where he wanted, eat what he wanted, drink what he wanted, write what he wanted to write, put in the journal whatever he felt like putting. He rather liked an interview he had given to *On the Sound* magazine, and so in his issue of October 1, 1972, he ran a transcript of it. Asked about his gardening, he had replied, "My plot is not well tended. People come and throw things in the ground, but I don't do a damn thing. Pierre grows a lot of stuff, so I steal from him. I'd much rather go shopping."

On October 15, 1972, having given long and deep thought to the matter, he favored his public with a full disquisition on the practice and esthetics of the eating of oysters:

When you are ready to dine, and not a moment earlier, open your favorite oysters—only the fattest and fleshiest ones to be sure—and make sure that each is still alive by exploring its reflexes. This is quite simple—simply touch the edge of the lamella;* if it does not retract, the oyster has expired. Remove the living creature from its shell—in the most delicate manner possible—and bring it immediately into your mouth with no extraneous trimmings whatsoever and in a trice, with your teeth, perforate its liver.† If it is an oyster of proper freshness and quality, the whole of your gums will soak in it, your mouth will be filled with its juices, the true criterion of an oyster than has reached its peak.

You should rest for a moment in that state, then slowly swallow the juices and finish off the mastication and deglutition‡ of the mollusk. After that, invigorate yourself with a mouthful of good, dry white wine,

* You will have studied up on your oyster anatomy so that you know what and where the lamella is.
† See preceding note: ditto the liver.
‡In addition to your book on oyster anatomy, you will need an unabridged English dictionary.

munch a piece of black or white bread, buttered or not, this solely to neutralize the tongue in order to savor to the fullest the oyster to follow. . . .

§

These, among the privileged of America, were days of private pleasure. Cocaine, the definitive private high, was on the rise as the drug of choice. Marijuana had been a drug of laughter, sharing, sex, and eating. Coke was paranoia, too expensive to share, more often a deterrent to sexual performance than an aid, and the ultimate appetite suppressant: You didn't want to eat, you might want to make love but usually couldn't, what you really really *really* wanted was to talk—about yourself.

Authority could not hold. LBJ gave up. The Beatles broke up. Nixon fucked up. Claiborne quit, and seemed to have disappeared. Le Pavillon closed, its passing weightily chronicled by the *New York Times*[5] but unmentioned in the *Craig Claiborne Journal*. The food world was no longer Craig Claiborne's kingdom. It was a dozen, a hundred principalities, like Europe after the fall of Rome—centerless, fluid, impossible to see much of from any single vantage point, and ungovernable. Studio 54 supplanted Le Pavillon; beat supplanted melody.

People continued to cook well and eat well and drink well, of course. Great wines were being made, fine restaurants born, and *something* was happening, more people *were* interested, in a way, in some way, but they didn't quite seem to be paying attention. And not so many seemed eager, exactly, to fork over $36 a year for this modest, rather fussy little journal.

At the end of twelve months Craig had about a thousand subscribers,[6] then the number went up, then it went down. The journal announced its editor's discovery of the salad spinner[7]—one of those wonders of which you wonder, as of suitcases with wheels, How come these haven't always existed? He discovered a wondrous French machine called the Magimix,[8] soon rechristened, for the American market, the Cuisinart. He identified "foods that are purely and simply reprehensible," including, in his opinion, grape jelly, pretzels, maraschino cherries, marshmallows, marzipan, and oatmeal. The last reminded him of a story of an American and a Frenchman, strangers, seated together on an ocean liner. When the American is served oatmeal at breakfast, the Frenchman inquires, "Excuse me, sir, is that something you've eaten or some-thing you're about to eat?"[9] A buck and a half an issue for this?

Craig installed a proper test kitchen, at immense expense. He had never been satisfied with the installation on King's Point Road any-way. "This is all very simple, really," he said to the reporter assigned to cover his 1973 Bastille Day celebration of the new setup. The usual suspects—Jacques Pépin, Jean Vergnes, Pierre Franey—had gathered to create another classic Claiborne feast, and evidently the occasion and the equipment had been considered *Times*worthy: "a grill, rotisserie, two ranges, two ovens, a large wok for Chinese cooking, three sinks, a six-door refrigerator-freezer, a central counter area with pots and pans overhead, a walk-in closet for utensils, and two walls of cabinets."[10]

Craig was zooming back and forth across the globe, always in the front of the plane. He was most certainly obligated to sample, on his readers' behalf, the *Guide Michelin*'s newly crowned three-stars in France: Taillevent and Le Vivarois in Paris, Jacques Pic in Valence, and Chez La Mère Charles at Mionnay, the venue of the masterful young chef Alain Chapel. The food at Taillevent, no surprise, was "splendid, peerless . . . superb . . . of devastating goodness . . . ecstasy." Vivarois, on the other hand, reminded him of "a very modern dentist's office"; the *coq au vin* there was "respectable but nothing to do a pirouette about," and the kidneys were "cut into too-gross pieces, undercooked and served in a too-thin sauce"; the vegetables, at least, were "good." At Pic, "throw-ing caution and money to the wind," Craig dined on a mousse of *foie gras* and woodcock, "a whole truffle marinated in Cognac and baked in a puff pastry turnover," a baby rooster in a sauce of saffron and cream, "many fine cheeses," and "uninspired" desserts. In the hands of Alain Chapel he "exulted in most of the fare"—including a "sublime" *pâté* of eel and a "remarkable *gâteau de foies blonds*" [*de volaille*] that "all but defied the laws of gravity"—but he was "painfully disappointed" by the famous house specialty of a truffle-studded Bresse chicken steamed in a pig's bladder. Moreover "the maître d'hôtel . . . was disturbingly aloof and the service over-all left a good deal to be desired."[11]

"Throwing caution and money to the wind" was the basic research policy of the *Craig Claiborne Journal*. How else could you get the true Craig Claiborne, and your own money's worth? Did you really want him just grubbing around for the best dim sum below Canal, prowling Ninth Avenue again for Greek olives, or reporting on "the marvels of Fort Wayne"? He *did* go to Fort Wayne, by the way, where "a lot of the citizens idle their time away on the town's wooden benches," and he found "the best pizza we've ever eaten and an extraordinarily good dinner in the French style."[12] What the hell he was really doing in Fort Wayne, Indiana, and why, he never disclosed.

The financial records of the *Craig Claiborne Journal* are not among the papers Craig donated or bequeathed to Boston University or the Culinary Institute of America, or anywhere else in known creation, but it is safe to assume that it was not a profitable venture. In the year 1973 alone the journal was buying thousands of names to whom appeals for subscriptions were to be sent—these, for example, from Prescott Lists, Inc., of 17 East Twenty-sixth Street, New York:

5,000	Henri Fayette Greeting Card buyers	$125.00
31,711	Sherry-Lehmann 1971–1972 customers	$1109.89
5,000	*On the Sound* subscribers	$175.00
12,000	*New York* magazine subscribers	$420.00
3,000	*Washingtonian* magazine subscribers	$105.00
12,000	Epicures' Club 1972–1973 buyers	$360.00
3,000	*Philadelphia* magazine subscribers	$90.00
5,000	Hammacher Schlemmer mail order buyers	$175.00
10,000	Manhattan Wealthiest Names	$250.00[13]

The occasional odd job began to look pretty good—especially one like twelve days away from Long Island's dank November cruising the Caribbean on the good old S.S. *France,* giving cooking lessons with Pierre. Craig's pals Sam Aaron, head of Sherry-Lehmann Wines & Spirits, and Burgess Meredith, the actor—also an East Hampton neighbor and a serious oenophile—were going to come along to do wine tastings. Pierre Androuet and André Pajolec, two of the world's leading cheese experts, would be leading cheese tastings. The ship's master chef, Henri le Huédé—one of Craig's idols—and his brigade of 180 would sustain them all on cuisine more exquisite than anything Craig and Pierre would be demonstrating.[14]

Spouses and companions were invited as well—Betty Franey, Florence Aaron, Kaja Meredith, even Henry Creel. It went without saying that there would be all the caviar, foie gras, truffles, martinis, margaritas, Champagne, Burgundy, Bordeaux, and stingers the *professeur* could fancy. Also they paid good money.

§

Craig's excellent Caribbean adventure was nonetheless no more than a short-acting analgesic. The *Craig Claiborne Journal* was dying.

Craig, however, as ever, was a survivor. He had been busily negotiating with the *Times* all fall. They did want him back. They had always wanted him back. Raymond Sokolov, a scholarly and knowledgeable critic, had been Craig's successor as food editor and had done an excellent job, his research and his voice very much in Craig's own style. Sokolov had been followed, however, beginning in May of 1973, by the disastrous John L. Hess, whose attitude toward restaurants was that of a pit bull to poodles with bows in their hair.

At "the very first New York meal [he had] eaten in the line of [his] new duty as a food critic . . . a dinner held the other night by a society of food and wine lovers at a leading hotel," Hess ripped his way through "undrinkable" café brulot, "a showy stunt" of a fish mousse, a "quarrelsome salad," "insipid" cheeses, an "inferior" soufflé, and "lifted-pinky cuisine" in general.[15] Over the next few weeks he attacked "lobster rubbery and tasteless . . . French fries thick, soggy and tepid . . . a paper cup of what looked like toothpaste . . . little paper kerchiefs soaked in deodorant";[16] "filet mignon bland, apparently tenderized, and quite cold . . . Swiss steak on noodles reminiscent of a hundred airline meals . . . electronic mass-feeding stations that do practically no cooking at all";[17] "damp, puffy bread . . . tasteless pickled mushrooms, a 'gazpacho' of canned vegetable juice . . . strawberry shortcake with synthetic whip, a canned fruit tart and weak, poor coffee" . . . "a dreary, dirty and noisy shop" . . . "gray, inedible eggplant." "We cannot report on the main course," he wrote, "for we left as soon as we could pry an exorbitant bill from a surly waiter."[18]

Why did he choose places like this to write about? What was the point? Of course there was terrible food in the world, plenty of it, but if you half paid attention you could avoid it. As Craig had said in the *On the Sound* interview that he'd published in the *Journal*: "You walk in there, you look at the menu, you know the food's not going to be any good, so you walk out."[19] Hess, on the other hand, either lacked that faculty altogether, or, as seems more likely, knew exactly what he was in for and actually *liked* to go in, eat the bad food, and then raise hell.

No wonder the *Times* wanted Craig back; no wonder he wanted to come. The editors and he agreed that he would not be required to write restaurant reviews. But he would be the food editor and responsible for setting the tone of everything the *New York Times* had to say about food. John L. Hess, already smelling like fish left out too long, would not be around much longer. John Canaday, the paper's art critic would be the new restaurant reviewer.[20]

The *Craig Claiborne Journal* was deep in the hole, and the *Times* agreed to dig it out; Craig was going to repay them over the next four years with royalties from books to be published by Times Books. Although they would maintain an office for him at headquarters on West Forty-third Street and he would hang on to his apartment in the Osborne, the *Times* was fine with Craig's mainly working from home in East Hampton.

And at long last Pierre would get credit. The byline on the pieces they did together would read "by Craig Claiborne with Pierre Franey."

Making light of the whole thing, Craig and the paper mutually agreed on an ad that would run to announce his return. In his half-glasses, white-collared blue shirt, and French cuffs—and what is surely the Cartier watch left him by Henri Soulé—Craig is dressed like an investment banker, but the look on his face is purely that of the cat who has swallowed a spit-roasted canary. The headline, which can be taken at least a couple of ways, reads, "He sometimes bites the hand that feeds him."[21]

§

Craig's employment would officially resume on January 13, 1974.[22] He and Pierre gave themselves a celebratory lunch on December 30, 1973—striped bass with *sauce gribiche* and Champagne, preceded by "a few pre-prandial bloody marys." "The more bloody marys we drank," he recalled, "the more painful and consequential the demise of that newsletter seemed to be. I think there were a few tears. . . . I stood on my feet somewhat unsteadily and raised a toast to the passing.

"What I wanted most but needed least in life at that point was one more drink." But what he did was drive to a bar in Bridgehampton, where he found his fellow Mississippian and fellow hard drinker Willie Morris. They passed the afternoon in Scotch and talk of the Delta. About seven they switched to "extra-dry martinis, straight up with a twist."

> At nine that evening I drove back to East Hampton and at the stop light in the center of town I was stopped by the police for drunken driving. I was handcuffed, fingerprinted, and tossed into a cell. . . .
>
> I called the news desk and got Arthur Gelb, an old friend and an assistant managing editor, at home.
>
> "Arthur," I said, "I'm in jail."[23]

13

La Nouvelle Cuisine

Craig Claiborne's first piece after his return to the *New York Times* was called "A Last Meal."[1] And that is what it really was about, though he didn't seem to be contemplating dying. Craig was still on his ultra-luxe kick, and especially so now that the *Times* was paying again. If he *were* about to die, his last meal "would not be a solitary one. I would wish to share it with my closest friends—seven of them. The cost? Well, the price of caviar being what it is (about $90 a pound at this writing) and the price of Romanée-Conti being what *it* is ($200 a bottle), this coveted menu of mine—unstinting in any area—would hover around $900."*

Fresh caviar
Vodka, Stolichnaya

Striped bass with Champagne sauce
Montrachet, Marquis de Laguiche, 1970

Stuffed squabs Derby
Château Ausone, 1947

Braised endive

Watercress and Boston lettuce salad

* Adjusted for inflation, $3,944 in 2012.

Brie cheese
Romanée-Conti, 1959

Grapefruit sherbet
Champagne, Dom Pérignon, 1966

Derby, for the squabs, meant stuffed with foie gras, truffles, rice, and their own livers, with a brown sauce based on a stock made from their necks, feet, and gizzards. *Roux*-thickened and in no other wise fancied up (no mushrooms, no Port, no Madeira, no orange peel), it sounds rather plain for such a grand meal, but in the hands of Pierre Franey it would doubtless be unctuous, concentrated, and balanced.

Pierre, as agreed, was now officially visible. Craig's last paragraph read: "Readers will note a duality of names above, a duality that gives me great satisfaction. Pierre Franey, one of the world's master chefs, who has contributed to these pages in the past, is now my esteemed collaborator." There was a full-page photograph of the two of them in front of the new kitchen's sleek black ranges, Ausone on the counter, Pierre bast-

"A duality that gives me great satisfaction."

ing squabs, Craig clutching carving fork and knife in his fists, both of them grinning.

The byline read "By Craig Claiborne with"—not *and*—"Pierre Franey." Gradations of hierarchy were matter of close calculation at the *New York Times*. New York City was like that in general in those days, but especially so in the theater district—the *Times* offices' neighborhood—where marquee billings mercilessly ranked the stars and their lessers. A second full-page picture showed Craig in his wine cellar. There was exquisite calibration in the pairing of those photographs, the one of the partners, the other of the maestro alone.

Before Craig's food editor's chair was quite warm, he had ousted John L. Hess from the De Gustibus column and taken it over himself. It was never clear whether that title was meant to mean only "about taste," the literal translation of the two words, or whether it was intended as shorthand for "De gustibus non disputandum [est]," the likelier interpretation, owing to that saying's longstanding common usage, meaning "There is no arguing about taste."

Hess had started the De Gustibus column with what may have been a sort of backhand shot at his predecessor, Raymond Sokolov. Hess's first De Gustibus had run on June 18, 1973, just a few weeks into his tenure as restaurant critic and three months after one of Sokolov's Sunday columns, published February 4 of the same year. Sokolov had opened thus: "*De gustibus non disputandum*. What a ridiculous idea. If we don't argue about taste, what is there left to dispute?" There's a nice irony in the fact that if Hess chose the title as denoting something he actually *meant*—that is, if he really intended to say that there *was* no arguing about taste—what Hess had immediately started doing, and kept doing till Craig booted him in January 1974, was argue about taste, mainly by finding bad taste wherever he could and then sneering at it.

Whatever convoluted use John L. Hess made of the column's name, we can be pretty certain that Craig didn't give it much thought. He was not a Latin scholar. Don't forget, he still couldn't do arithmetic. He had to check his heart to see which way was left.

John Hess, as might well be imagined, would have his revenge. He and his wife, Karen, had a great deal to say about Craig in their cowritten book *The Taste of America*. Of Craig and Pierre's "last meal" of January 1974, they wrote that "the wines had been chosen as pretty much the highest priced in each class, and there was no suggestion that a reader might drink a very enjoyable wine at much lower cost."

They pounced on Pierre's recipes and ripped them to shreds. "The fish was pasted with . . . floury *velouté*; the *foie gras* and the truffles in the squabs were canned and hence a pointless extravagance; instead of the classic *demi-glace,* the sauce for the squab included tomato paste and flour, and there was sugar in the braised endives."[2]

This is worth taking on point by point.

- No suggestion of a cheaper wine. This was a *last meal,* and those about to die don't usually think of saving money.
- The fish wasn't *pasted*. It was *napped* with an old-fashioned *sauce velouté* (the word means "velvety" in French), which is always thickened with flour—one of the classic sauces that Craig had learned at Lausanne and one that Pierre had used for years at Le Pavillon.
- Yeah, the *foie gras—pure,* the recipe specified—came from a can. At that time that was just about the only way you could get foie gras in New York, and it really wasn't bad.
- The recipe calls for chopped truffles. It doesn't say canned or not. In any case canned truffles can be lousy or they can be pretty good. Pierre undoubtedly knew which were the good ones. Craig might have been more specific, but brand names were generally a no-no in the *Times*.
- Re the sauce: The pigeon stock was much more appropriate than a veal *demi-glace* would have been; and yes, it was thickened with flour and butter, again simply an old-fashioned technique from the *haute cuisine,* no longer fashionable but perfectly delicious. Both the *roux* and the tomato paste or purée are always part of the classical *sauce espagnole,* of which Pierre's squab sauce is a variant.
- Sugar in the endive? Endive is bitter. So what?

There will be more to come from these Hesses, and more in response to them.

§

In June of 1974, in Paris, Craig fell under the spell of a madly colorful Frenchwoman named Yanou Collart. She had large, liquid eyes with long, long lashes and a lingering gaze of focused charm. She knew—everyone. When she walked into a dining room, heads turned, murmurs followed. Friend of Jacques Brel's, Craig jotted in his notebook. Former fashion model. Had fainted while driving her Mercedes in Liguria and wrecked it. Had introduced Bal à Versailles, at ninety dollars an ounce the world's most expensive perfume—Joy was only eighty-five. Represented thirteen of the seventeen Michelin three-star restaurants in France, not for the money, *non non, mon cher* Craig, for the love only. Had recently taken John Lennon to the Moulin de Mougins; he gave her a waterbed.[3]

Craig's head spun. He adored her. Yanou told him, Craig, we have in France a *nouvelle cuisine*. A revolution, nothing less. You must meet the chefs, they are geniuses, they are all my friends. But now, first, do you know Taillevent? Of course you do. But perhaps you have not had the best of Taillevent. I will arrange.

> Rarely in a lifetime—including a quarter century of serious dining— have we found a restaurant with such a distinguished sum of virtues. . . . It can seriously be questioned if better cooking existed before, during or after the age of Escoffier.

> If ever the word "impeccable" could be applied to the table service of a restaurant, the word is deserved at Taillevent. . . .[4]

After the excesses requisite to reporting from Paris on cuisines both *ancienne* and *nouvelle,* Craig's constitution was in such a state that even he of the iron-clad liver was feeling a need for purification. In the time-honored European manner, he elected to seek it at a luxurious hot-springs spa, the famous old Grand Hotel e la Pace at Montecatini Terme in Tuscany: "Although we had been assured that our livers were models of resilience, we thought this visit might provide them a respite of seven days without alcohol. After all, we reflected, not a day had passed in 20 years that it had not been dosed with a goodly supply."[5]

With his imminent deprivation painfully in mind, Craig made the most of the trip to Tuscany. He began the day in Paris with a bloody mary and a split of Champagne, followed by a quick Scotch at Orly.

Between planes in Milan he had another Scotch, a beer, and then another Scotch. At the little airport of Pisa, he tossed down a double Scotch. "We arrived at the hotel an hour before dinner so we changed clothes and went downstairs to discuss our plight with our universal friend, the bartender. Tomorrow, we told him, we're quartering the calories and giving up both wine and booze for seven days running. He was marvelously sympathetic. 'Have a drink,' he said."[6]

His private notes continue the story: "It's eleven p.m. After a few sips from a white & red Chianti [whatever that may have been] there is ahead a glorious heavy. . . ." The next several words are illegible, but then, as the hour grows later, his handwriting somehow becomes clearer: "A bottle of President Gran Spumante Crystal Sec RICCADONNA . . . a superior Italian sparkling wine . . . Bartender is no help. We had celebrated in some depth. A Scotch & soda here. A martini there & sandwiched somewhere unfathomably a Manhattan . . . Slept like a baby."[7]

§

Craig and Pierre's cowritten columns continued the rhythm and pattern of Craig's longtime practice in East Hampton. There would be special guests at Craig's house for the weekend, usually talented home cooks or professional chefs. Craig and Pierre and the guest chefs would shop the farm stands or small grocers, the butchers, and the fish markets of the Hamptons for the provender with which that little world is so richly blessed. Often they would shop with no particular aim but finding what was freshest and most interesting, and let a menu form itself in their imaginations as they went along. Pierre and the guests would spend Saturday prepping and cooking, while Craig sat behind his big IBM Selectric hollering at Pierre. Not a handful, dammit! A cup? A cup and a half? *What?* Don't tell me, "Roast in a hot oven till done"—How long did you cook it? What temperature? What are you doing with that cheesecloth? You didn't even mention that! (The other chef jabbers for three minutes in French, and Pierre shouts a ten-second translation in Craig's direction, meanwhile tending four pots and two ovens and rolling out puff pastry.) What did he *say,* Pierre?

—Until finally he could hammer out a recipe comprehensible to their readers.

Then that night, there would be a party. Henry Creel would be there, mixing his famous margaritas; Henry was also the chief dishwasher. Betty, Claudia, and Diane Franey would usually come early to help set up, sometimes with little Jacques in tow. A stylist and a photographer from the *Times* would be arranging the food and rearranging the people and getting in everybody's way. Music—Broadway cast albums, Verdi, Rossini—was always playing. Almost always, Ed and Ellie Giobbi or Jacques and Gloria Pépin, or all of them, would be there, and Ed or Jacques would have watercolors at the ready to record the menu and usually also to paint some impression of the meal in one of Craig's big leather-bound books. (Jacques and Gloria had been married at the house on King's Point Road, in 1966.[8]) There were other more or less regular dinner guests, many of them residents of the East End—writers, artists, show folk, just-folks—and nearly always there were New York chefs, nearly always French of origin and training, who would roll up their sleeves and pitch in. There were usually newcomers as well, sometimes well-known ones, for these were coveted invitations, feathers in one's social cap. Equally often the newcomers would be known only to Craig—his feelings about his invitations' prestige value were mixed.

Seldom, except for Henry, were his guests gay; almost never were there gay couples—the *Times,* in those days, would have frowned on that. But in the old-fashioned sense of the word, the doings were certainly gay.

The revels in that kitchen often began as early as five in the afternoon with a Scotch and soda or another not-so-innocent potable. Our young bodies seemed immune to the perils of alcohol and we imbibed to the fullest. A typical menu during those fun-filled years would be an hors d'oeuvre followed by a soup followed by a fish course followed by a main course followed by salad with cheeses followed by dessert followed by coffee and Cognac or a stinger.

With the fish course there would generally be bottles of chilled white Burgundies; with the main course, a few great Bordeaux; and with the cheese course, a bottle or two of great red Burgundies. With the desserts, the finest Champagnes.[9]

Our young *bodies*. When he wrote this, Craig was clearly thinking back to his earliest Saturday night revels in East Hampton; but the format had been set then, and continued well into the 1970s without the slightest diminution in imbibing-to-the-fullest. Florence Aaron was a regular all through the years with her husband Sam, the wine merchant and maven—they had a house in Montauk—and she recalls: "We drank ourselves almost unconscious, even before dinner sometimes. Then wine. Sam of course would bring superb wines. Then the stingers. We were all so loaded I don't know how we got home."[10]

Near the back of the next Sunday's *New York Times* magazine would come the evening's synthesis: a few words from Craig on a theme, perhaps a suite of dishes, a word-portrait of the guest chef; a drawing or a photograph or two; and a handful of recipes, perfected by Pierre for home cooking and double-checked in the *Times*'s test kitchens.

And most of the time, after all that preparation, production, and party, that was it. Rarely, Craig might briefly recount the prep, the dishes, and the dinner itself. If one or another of the guests contributed significantly to the food—Ed Giobbi, say, or Roger Fessaguet—mention of that would be made. But for the most part, these elaborate and expensive feasts, though financed by the *New York Times,* were not intended to find their way into print.

In the King's Point Road kitchen.

184

Other regular elements of Craig's grand Long Island evenings were not recorded in either his leather-bound books or the nation's newspaper of record: the third, fourth, fifth, who knows which round of stingers; the late, loud, blotto voices lifted in song; Craig grabbing the genitals of flabbergasted male first-time guests just to see what would happen. Florence Aaron: "I remember Don Hewitt came to the party one time, for the first time—you know, the producer of *60 Minutes*—and sure enough, Craig grabbed him by the balls. He was *outraged*. Everybody else just laughed, and said, 'Join the club.'"[11]

§

"I have always been impetuous," you may recall Craig's having said. As he approached his middle fifties, he was getting more so. It probably would not have occurred to another writer to stroll through Saigon sampling street food in the midst of the Vietnam War, but in the late fall of 1974, having assigned himself a five-week gustatory tour of Asia, Craig did precisely that.

"Up and down the street," he wrote, "are soldiers with their guns and walkie-talkies and jeeps and many of the cross sections have rolls of barbed wire on the side and at the ready, but after a day or so both the soldiers and the barbed wire become another random part of the landscape."[12]

Another random part of the landscape. Once again, as under bombardment in the Mediterranean, as in the midst of floating mines and North Korean shelling, an utterly real and immediate war became some sort of—scenery. What captured Craig's attention were the chopped shrimp on sugarcane skewers, the curried eel soup, the deep-fried crab, the snails stuffed in fresh ginger leaves—"due a relatively high rank in the hierarchy of the world's most sophisticated foods"—and the ubiquitous, complex soup known as *phở*. "There remains in Saigon today," he wrote, "a deep-rooted respect for food conscientiously prepared on almost every level."

He was pleased also to see the persistence of French influence. "French bread baked in Vietnam is some of the best in the world, and local bakers can turn out croissants on a par with some of the best to be found on the Champs-Élysées." The restaurant Chez Henri delighted him. Henri was "a short, puffy-faced, portly man . . . Gallic to the core" who turned out a *civet de lapin,* a mutton stew with white beans, and *andouillettes* "of a commendably high order." But Craig drew the line at one of Vietnamese cuisine's basic seasonings, fermented shrimp paste, "perhaps the most malodorous of all things allegedly edible. It is something to be shunned or better yet, interred."

Until near the end of his stay, the war continued to seem "as remote as another continent." Then he dined at the restaurant Binh-Trieu Quan, which was situated in a lotus pond on the outskirts of Saigon. The restaurant prided itself on its *cuisine vietnamienne la plus raffinée* and its "atmosphere rustic and restful." As he was paying his check, "which amounted to just under $5 for two," Craig heard, "somewhere north of the place," a sound so urgently real that he could not fail to recognize it—artillery fire.

As unflagging as Craig's impetuosity was his diligence. Week in and week out, he was researching, writing, cooking, dining, opining—in a single short month plunging into history (Charles Monselet, Paris, 1858, "the first newspaper food columnist"[13]); working up recipes with Pierre (stuffed vegetables "Not Just for Leftovers,"[14] chicken in tarragon and champagne sauce,[15] the Swiss chef Albert Kumin's Black Forest cake[16]); praising new books (*The Nitty-Gritty of Smoke Cooking*[17]) and new cooks (David Liederman, "A Young American's Palate Gets an Education at Troisgros"[18]); discovering a young woman's new venture in Connecticut ("Lots of Books, Lots of Pots—and Some Cooking Classes, Too"[19]); and as ever, engaged in dialogue with his readers ("The Great Indian Pudding Controversy Continues,"[20] a cocktail called The Bee's Knees,[21] a Southern émigré psychiatrist's homemade herb vinegar[22]). He was ceaselessly *working.*

And it paid off. His columns were syndicated in more than four hundred newspapers besides the *Times,* some of them beyond America's borders.[23]

No job gave him greater pleasure than blazoning the excellence of an individual whom he could introduce to his readers. This, he knew, was how he could continue to fulfill his original mission of advancing the nation's gastronomic culture.

To the country that knew of Mexican food only its almost parodic image in tamales and gloppy enchiladas, he had introduced Diana

Kennedy, and written the foreword to her cornucopian *The Cuisines of Mexico,* with its all-important plural. He really wanted squeamish Americans to try her tostadas of jellied pig's feet, and he printed the recipe. Her resourcefulness enchanted him: He loved that after failing to find in any market in New York the herb *epazote*—which was essential, in her view, to proper Mexican cooking—she discovered it growing wild in Riverside Park.[24]

The most important introduction Craig would make in his mature career—most important to him personally and most important to the direction of serious American food—came to him in stages in the middle 1970s. In some ways neither Craig nor American chefs ever understood the ultimate impossibility of exporting the true nouvelle cuisine from its native France, but he came to believe as strongly as he had ever believed anything that an understanding of the nouvelle cuisine could reanimate French cooking in America, much of which was growing stale, and that it could make the best American cooking better.

Yanou Collart was the one who really got him started. Craig had once written that the finest seafood restaurant in Paris was La Marée.[25] But when he was in Paris in June 1974—right before his great cure in Italy— Yanou had said to him, "Oh, *non non non non non.* The finest by far is Le Duc. You must dine there, you must have the *poisson cru*"—the raw fish. "I will arrange."[26] He was wowed.

That August, by the arrangement of Yanou, the owner and the chef of Le Duc, the brothers Jean and Paul Minchelli, visited America. They were going to cook lunch at The Four Seasons for a week, and dinner, alas, at the totally bogus Forum of the Twelve Caesars. Yanou arranged for Craig to accompany Jean (and her, as translator) to the Fulton Fish Market at four o'clock one pitch-dark morning. "Mr. Mincielli"—Craig misspelled Minchelli throughout his piece—"led the way to the docks where a boat, the *Felicia,* was unloading a fresh load of ocean scallops." The *Felicia,* it developed, had been at sea for eleven days, and had fifteen thousand pounds of scallops aboard. *Eleven days?* Minchelli, contemplating the age of the scallops in the bottom of the hold, was almost sick. "Here you don't have the small boats that go out in the morning and come back at night," he said. "In Paris I can get these overnight."[27]

Freshness like this was impossible in the States for almost every kind of seafood. Truly fresh fruits and vegetables came only from farm stands or a few select wholesalers that supplied only the handful of restaurants that paid top dollar, as Le Pavillon under Pierre used to do and Lutèce still did. The quality of food in the supermarkets was abysmal, and nobody knew any better. Even Julia Child insisted that perfectly good French food could be made with ordinary ingredients from the corner store.

On the West Coast, the three-year-old restaurant Chez Panisse and a few other practitioners of what was just becoming known as California cuisine were horrified by complacency such as Child's. The laziness of the East Coast's purveyors—especially the fish markets—to them was an outrage. Taking their values from the demanding young chefs of Europe—the Minchelli brothers being perfect examples—California chefs were establishing direct relationships with farmers and fishermen and accepting from them only the freshest and most pristine ingredients.

Yanou Collart and Craig agreed that America needed to know about her clients and the nouvelle cuisine. Yanou would be Craig's guide. He put himself in her hands, and she introduced him to all the great new chefs of France. Like the Minchellis, almost all of them were eager to come to America and show off their *chefs d'oeuvre* in the famous Long Island kitchen of the food editor of the *New York Times*.

"Craig was in love with Paul Bocuse," Collart remembers. "Bocuse did not reciprocate."

Craig called Bocuse "almost indisputably the most famous chef in the world," though almost nobody in the United States except the dedicated travel-to-eaters really knew who he was. Among those in the know, however, Bocuse was known as *le roi Paul,* a title he accepted without false modesty. Craig was flattered that Bocuse would come all the way from New York to his kitchen in East Hampton to make his acclaimed *poulet au vinaigre* and a *navarin* of Long Island lobster. Most grandly, Bocuse favored Craig with the truffle soup he had invented for the occasion of his being named a Chevalier of the Légion d'Honneur by the French president Valéry Giscard d'Estaing, on February 25, 1975.[28] But Craig was shocked by the chef's shameless machismo, and felt compelled to quote him flaunting it: "Women," said Bocuse, "lack the instincts for great cooking. It follows in the same sense that there are so few great women architects and orchestra leaders. . . . They have one or two dishes they accomplish very well, but they are not great innovators."

Craig had to admit, nonetheless, that Bocuse's lobster sauce, his sauce for the chicken, and most of all his truffle soup were "impeccable." Bocuse had arrived at Craig's house with a kilogram of black truffles from France for the soup. Because it was June, these had to be either summer truffles, always inferior in quality to the winter ones, or else frozen, or even—*pace* John Hess—canned. There would be sixteen for lunch at 2:30, and Jacques Pépin and Pierre were there as sous-chefs to chop vegetables, make stock, and roll out puff pastry. Craig's recipe in the *Times* called for store-bought puff pastry and canned truffles. At the bottom of the piece Craig appended a note, perhaps even with Hess in mind: "It almost goes without saying that a soup as costly as this is only for a once-in-a-lifetime occasion."[29]

And this broad-shouldered, hawk-nosed, arrogant misogynist was the king of the nouvelle cuisine? Craig got over his crush pretty quickly. But he did love the food.

In France the nouvelle cuisine was a cultural earthquake. French society was defined by rules, French cuisine by rules. As Pierre Franey had learned in his long apprenticeship and as Craig had learned at L'École Hôtelière de Lausanne, *Sole à l'Adrienne* was to be poached, napped with a *sauce Polignac* (a *velouté* based on fish stock, to which minced mushrooms and a *julienne* of truffles have been added); it was to be garnished with poached lettuce, tartlets containing a *salpicon* of crayfish tails in sauce Nantua, and a couple of nice *fleurons* (puff pastry crescents). There were 366 other standard preparations of sole prescribed in the classic repertoire, each equally strictly defined.[30]

This is why the French have revolutions.

Gastronomic France was ruled by the *Guide Michelin*, which told you about restaurants only in its own obscure code. Let's see, three forks means "very comfortable restaurant." But if they're red, it also means "pleasant restaurant." Four red forks means "pleasant top-class restaurant." One star—actually it doesn't look like a star, it looks like a macaroon, and *macaron* was what the Michelin people for years insisted you call them—one macaroon means "a good restaurant in its class." So three red forks and a macaroon or star means "a pleasant very comfortable restaurant, good in its class." Now, "15/35." That means "Lowest 15 [francs] and highest 35 for set meals served at normal hours (noon to 1:30 p.m. and 7:30 to 9:00 p.m.)," except the small type on the "15" means it is not served on Sundays or holidays. "R carte 25 à 50" is for à la carte meals. "The first figure is for a plain meal and includes light entrée, main dish of the day with vegetables, and dessert. The second figure is for a fuller meal (with 'spécialité') and includes hors d'oeuvre, 2 main courses, cheese, dessert."[31] It goes on, and gets more complicated. The Michelin was, and remains, a very useful guidebook, and its integrity is irreproachable, but its judgment has always been opaque, its rulings handed down from on high.

Most users of the *Guide Michelin* contented themselves with the basics. If you had to drive an extra ten kilometers for a one-star restaurant, all other things being equal, you would. If two hotels were rated the same but one was cheaper, you'd probably go for the cheaper. But if you enjoyed riddling out Talmudic mysteries, the Michelin had plenty of those as well. In 1974, in the Eighth Arrondissement of Paris, Maxim's restaurant had three stars but was ranked below Ledoyen, which had only two stars; the only possible explanation was that Ledoyen's five forks were red and Maxim's five were black, making their official definitions (Ledoyen) "pleasant luxury restaurant, table worth a detour" versus (Maxim's) "luxury restaurant, table worth a special journey." Even less comprehensible was Taillevent, with five black forks and three stars, which was ranked *below* the restaurant of the Hôtel Régence Plaza—also five black forks but only *one* star! The French have a gesture, an expression, and a saying which in combination suit the Michelin Gordian knot to a T: Shrug your shoulders with palms forward, purse your lips, and say, "Figurez-vous!"*

May 1968 shattered whatever rigid decorum remained of the old French system of discipline and hierarchy. Student strikes paralyzed the nation. The issues were both vague and comprehensive—the strikers, millions of them, were opposed to Gaullist conformity and repression, against the American war in Vietnam, against government and corporate establishments of every stripe; they were in favor of sexual liberation, rock and roll, student control of university curricula, and "revolution," in whatever form you personally envisioned it that day. There was a lot of intense, incomprehensible political philosophy. There was also a lot of crazy, anarchic fun that any young American of the same era would have recognized instantly.

* Translation: Go figure!

Enter Henri Gault and Christian Millau. After long experience of writing about travel and restaurants for editors who cramped their style, they realized after the events of May 1968 that the French were "en train de découvrir le farniente, les week-ends, les loisirs"[32]—i.e., in the midst of discovering the pleasure of doing nothing, weekends, leisure. On a shoestring, in 1969, Gault and Millau founded *Le Nouveau Guide—The New Guide*—setting themselves up immediately in contradistinction to the Michelin. They began to prowl the country in search of originality, daring, and fun, and they wrote about it in fierce, overheated prose.

In addition to their proclivity for manning barricades and setting piles of furniture on fire, the French are natural philosophers. Gault and Millau were not satisfied with finding good food that the Michelin had missed: They were in search of underlying principles, something to distinguish their hot passion from the old, stolid, emotionless gray— as they saw it—of Escoffier's world, to which only the privileged and respectable were admitted.

In their own telling it doesn't sound very revolutionary, at least to an American ear:

Les deux compères découvrent ce qui va devenir la nouvelle cuisine, chez Paul Bocuse. Subjugés par une simple salade de haricots verts accompagnés de tomates, pour eux la nouveauté se trouve dans leurs assiettes. Puis ils rencontrent les frères Troisgros à Roanne, qui leur servent des grenouilles aux herbes. Rien n'était préparé la veille, tout était fait "à la minute." Des saveurs oubliées, simplicité et légèreté, la nouvelle cuisine est née. Un concept innovant qu'ils vont largement médiatiser dans leurs pages et en développer le succès.[33]

The two friends discover what will become the nouvelle cuisine, at the restaurant of Paul Bocuse. Stunned by a simple salad of green beans with tomatoes, the novelty for them is on their plates. Then they meet the Troisgros brothers in Roanne, who serve them frog's legs with herbs. Nothing had been prepared the night before, everything was done "à la minute." Forgotten flavors, simplicity and lightness, the nouvelle cuisine is born. An innovative concept that they will publicize widely in their pages and whose success they themselves will amplify.*

* Translation by the author.

191

The big deal? That the food was so simple and yet so good. That's really what the nouvelle cuisine came down to. It's no wonder Craig liked the idea—his first reference to it had been in his dithyramb on Taillevent, in which he singled out the "kidneys in a light vinegar sauce" as a triumph of "what is called 'la nouvelle cuisine'"[34]—but it's also no wonder that it wasn't the earth-shaking transformation to him that it was to the French; he and Pierre, at least from time to time, had been cooking like this for years. What's more, Craig was by no means ready to send their old patron saints Carême and Escoffier to the guillotine.

As French philosophers, Gault and Millau followed a familiar French pattern: They systematized the nouvelle cuisine, and you got the feeling that they would rather have thrown a turkey galantine or a plate of *Sole à l'Adrienne* to a pack of dogs than contemplate the making of such an elaborate, old-fashioned dish. As French revolutionaries, Gault and Millau followed another French pattern, an attempted overthrow of authority—in this case that of the Michelin—and a concomitant assertion of one's own. And how better to express one's philosophy and to claim one's power—in one stroke—than by laying down *rules*? Still better, how about *commandments*? In 1973—the egalitarian fever of 1968 conveniently forgotten—Henri Gault and Christian Millau published in *Le Nouveau Guide* their *Dix Commandements de la Nouvelle Cuisine:*

1. *Tu ne cuiras pas trop:* Thou shalt not overcook.
2. *Tu utiliseras des produits frais et de qualité:* Thou shalt utilize fresh, high-quality ingredients.
3. *Tu allégeras ta carte:* Thou shalt lighten thy menu.
4. *Tu ne seras pas systématiquement moderniste:* Thou shalt not be inflexibly modernist.
5. *Tu rechercheras cependant ce que t'apportent les nouvelles technologies:* Thou shalt nevertheless explore new techniques.
6. *Tu éviteras marinades, faisandages et fermentations, etc.:* Thou shalt avoid marinades, the hanging of game, fermentation, etc.
7. *Tu élimineras sauces brunes et blanches:* Thou shalt eliminate traditional brown sauces and white sauces.*

---

* That is to say, sauces thickened with a *roux*.

8. *Tu n'ignoreras pas la diététique:* Thou shalt not ignore nutrition.
9. *Tu ne truqueras pas tes présentations:* Thou shalt not gussy up thy presentations.
10. *Tu seras inventif:* Thou shalt be inventive.[35]

Julia Child had this to say about the nouvelle cuisine: "Humph! . . . All this beating of poor old Escoffier over the head."[36]

As usual, Craig had the right idea: Embrace the new, keep the best of the old. The nouvelle cuisine was fun. At its best it was delicious. It was nearly always great to look at, and in an entirely new way: Instead of sending out a glistening roast fowl to be presented by the captain and then carved tableside, and by then not looking so great, the new chefs were composing their plates in the kitchen. The waiters rushed them to the individual diners hot, and the meticulously arranged dishes were often quite beautiful. If these chefs were going to be competitive, they had to develop a talent for visual art—a skill that had fallen out of the repertoire since the long-ago days of *pièces montées* and giant ice sculptures. These new dishes didn't trade in Victorian opulence, of course; they looked more like Mirós, Man Rays, Kandinskys.

Some of the instant classics of the nouvelle cuisine were actually revivals. Paul Bocuse was, and is, especially fond of rediscoveries. Alongside such innovations of his own as frog soup with watercress, raw salmon in a Scandinavian marinade, and a sort of napoleon of pigeon meat with young cabbage, Bocuse's menu today lists duck foie gras in a Sauternes aspic in the style of Antonin Carême, sole with noodles as served by Bocuse's mentor, the late Fernand Point (under whom he apprenticed for eight years[37]), and even *filet de boeuf Rossini,* as classical a dish as the haute cuisine ever hatched—the beef sautéed in clarified butter, served on a trimmed round of toast, and topped with a thick disc of foie gras, a fat slice from a big truffle, and Madeira sauce.[38]

Another thing Bocuse liked about the nouvelle cuisine and its ubiquitous promoters Gault and Millau was this: "We used to be servants," he told the grandees gathered for his investiture in the Legion of Honor at the Élysée Palace, "but now we are proprietors. It is a big advance."[39] And how: These chefs got rich fast and then got richer. In 1974 a full-course meal at Bocuse, according to the *Guide Michelin,* would cost you about 150 francs, the equivalent of $130 today—minus anything to drink. Today, a bowl of that truffle soup that Bocuse created for the Legion of Honor will set you back 80 euros ($112 U.S. at the current rate of exchange). The marinated salmon appetizer is €38, the filet Rossini €54—and as three-star restaurants in France go these days, that's cheap. (You may find some comfort in the fact that taxes and service are included, and even in a fancy place like Bocuse, if the French leave something extra, it's unlikely to be very much. The mandatory 15 percent of a $500 lunch for two is a pretty darn good tip.)

Other great dishes from the seminal period of the nouvelle cuisine were variations on earlier dishes—usually simpler and lighter than their forebears. Sorrel sauce was not unknown as an accompaniment to cold poached salmon, but the Troisgros brothers reduced the sauce to a sweet-and-sour green essence, and sautéed the salmon in such thin slices that they seemed scarcely to touch the pan before being rushed to the dining room, their translucence barely beginning to cloud as the plate arrived.

Roger Vergé, at his Moulin de Mougins on the Riviera, sought to reduce the ancient cuisine of the Midi to its elements. One of his best-known dishes was the nearly naked "carpaccio" of zucchini. His idea started with one of old Provençal cooking's most ordinary dishes, sautéed zucchini. Vergé served the vegetable raw, sliced paper-thin, with a grating of Parmigiano Reggiano and Arbosana olive oil[40]—familiar, but a transformation. It hardly needs saying that the squash, the cheese, and olive oil had to be of the very finest quality. Vergé made a terrine in which anglerfish and tomatoes were substituted for pork and pork liver, glazed it with a gelée of the fish and tomato juices, and sauced it with a purée of roasted red peppers.[41] On the inspiration of an old-fashioned, heavy, high-calorie dish he had fashioned something new, light, and bright.

Alain Chapel, at Mionnay, made an ethereally light mousse of pale blond chicken livers and bone marrow, and dressed it with the red-legged crayfish native to the nearby river Saône; the sauce was Hollandaise enriched with crayfish butter. As had become typical of the nouvelle cuisine, Chapel gave the dish a long, literal, yet still poetic name: *gâteau de foies blonds de poulardes de Bresse baigné d'une sauce aux queues d'écrevisses à la Lucien Tendret*.[42] Tendret was a famous lawyer and gastronome of the nineteenth century, and although surely Chapel's version was lighter than its forebears, the dish had been occasionally in the repertory of the haute cuisine for many decades.

It was in its pure inventiveness that the nouvelle cuisine reached its heights—and courted the twin dangers of mockery and inept imitation, for these were tricks only master magicians could pull off. Alain Chapel's *filet de bar au vinaigre et au poivre, jeune poivrons et courgettes à la fleur*[43] is a dazzler of a dish, and somewhat baffling as well, in which a sauce containing crushed black pepper, garlic, tomatoes, mustard, and vinegar must not overpower the delicate flesh of a sea bass. With a sauce potentially so over-potent and an accompaniment of pattypan squash, baby peppers, and zucchini with flowers attached, all stuffed with strong mixed herbs, this is a dish that a clumsy imitator could easily turn into a calamity.

The most radical of the nouvelle cuisine's pioneers was Michel Guérard. When his tiny, very plain but always mobbed Le Pot-au-Feu in Paris was demolished for the widening of the road it was on, he abandoned the big city, and, soon thereafter, he married an heiress named Christine Barthélémy. One of her family's properties was a somewhat rundown spa in southwestern France that had originally been built as a summer palace for Napoléon III's empress Eugénie. There, after extensive renovations, the newlyweds opened a unique hotel and restaurant, Les Prés et les Sources d'Eugénie—the meadows and springs of Eugénie—which comprised two resorts in one. The first offered simple sybaritic luxury and Michel's already famous lightened and simplified takes on old grandma-style classics, of which the pot-au-feu, everything-in-a-pot, was the epitome. The other was a place to come and live and eat like royalty while *losing weight at the same time*—and between the long, lovely, very light meals, whiling away the days soaking in the hot springs, getting massages and pedicures and facials, playing ping pong, miniature golf, or tennis, even riding a horse if you still had the strength.

The secret of Les Prés et Les Sources was Michel Guérard's invention, La Cuisine Minceur—slimming cuisine. It was something of a miracle, food unbelievably low in calories and yet, truly, very good to eat. "Guérard is talking about gâteau d'herbes (a confection of sorrel, spinach, chard, cabbage, greens, and herbs)," wrote Gael Greene, "fish cooked in seaweed, consommé in crayfish jelly, salmon with lemon and green peppercorns, veal à la vapeur, and meats grilled on vine branches with a sauce 'zero calories'—it's thickened with a purée of vegetables instead of egg yolks or flour."[44] Butter and cream were banned.

Greene was so fascinated that she felt compelled to go in person to take the Guérards' luxurious cure and see if this most curious of cuisines actually tasted like food. It did:

> Lunch is, quite frankly, breathtaking: a perfect poached egg crowned with tomato coulis, snips of chive, and bits of minced chicken, riding a crisp "al dente" artichoke heart in a cool, pale green sea of subtle cucumber purée—a concerto of texture, color, and taste. What a glorious lunch. But wait. There is more. A second giant plate appears, a serious statement in beige: thinnest slices of duck in a rich pepper-studded sauce (nothing but white cheese—"zero calorie," as Guérard puts it—duck stock, and water whirred in a blender) with petals of apples. . . . Dessert is another still life: a trembling fluted mound of delicate coffee custard capped with a crunch of espresso ice, ribboned with candied orange peel and a punctuation of ripe currants. The menu posted at the head of the stairs is reassuring: all these sense-beguiling delicacies total precisely 445 calories.[45]

One of the favorite, indeed the imperishable, fantasy-beliefs of Americans is in losing weight while eating all you want. Now here it was—and unfortunately it was Guérard's cuisine minceur that seemed first to take shape as most Americans' idea of the nouvelle cuisine as a whole. If any of them had actually looked at a menu of any of the real nouvelle cuisine's standard-bearers—Bocuse, Troisgros, Vergé, Chapel, and, yes, the non-dieting side of Guérard—they might not have seen much roux, but of butter and cream there was plenty. But really they didn't want to know. Cuisine minceur had all the right words for Americans. Pared-down. Less rich. Fresh. Best of all—the magic word—it was *light*.

You hear the same bullshit to this day. Lightly steamed. Lightly sautéed. What *is* that?

—What's light on this menu?

—Oh, the tilapia is very light.

(Waiters have to play this game. Don't tell 'em about the four tablespoons of butter in its light little sauce, or the two more on the lightly steamed vegetables.)

Gael Greene stayed ten days in the spell of Les Prés et Les Sources d'Eugénie, and Michel Guérard's cuisine minceur was, day after day, nothing short of miraculous:

> Every day brings a series of new tastes, new still lifes, remarkable innovations: chicken poached in paper, a tiny leg of milk-fed lamb baked in meadow grass, slices of goose quick-sautéed rare and tender in one of Michel's low-calorie miracle sauces, remarkable soups—tart sorrel, earthy mushroom, all herbed, lightly salted, but peppered with deliberation.

In her ten days Gael Greene lost nine pounds. Four days later she had regained five.[46]

When *Michel Guérard's Cuisine Minceur* was published in English, Americans newly fascinated with the nouvelle cuisine rushed in droves to buy it. Then you tried to make the stuff. Hours, and hours, later, you served it, you ate it. Hm.

Maybe you had to be Michel Guérard. Maybe you had to have a large professional French kitchen crew simmering duck stock, candying orange peel, sculpting your cucumbers. And where were you going to find that "tiny leg of milk-fed lamb"?

This was where Craig Claiborne rode in to the rescue, bearing gifts of butter and cream. And, as ever, good sense.

Certainly the nouvelle cuisine had turned Craig's attention back to French food, and it excited him. At the same time he was well aware that the intense excitement the nouvelle cuisine was evoking in France derived from the fact that the world of French food had been a small and restricted one, in which the relatively modest and mostly evolutionary innovations of the nouvelle cuisine truly were a big deal. But the United States—thanks in great part to Craig Claiborne—was already open to a food world nearly as big as the planet.

An almost offhand project of his shows how wide his range of interest had become, and therefore how vast the range of opportunity for his readers. In mid-1975, he published the first of his four volumes of *Craig Claiborne's Favorites from the New York Times*. In general he did work hard, but never had he had easier work than this: "This volume," he wrote in the foreword, "is a collection of nearly all the columns that appeared under my byline during the year 1974."[47] The reason he gave for collecting them is that he had "been asked hundreds of times by readers to devise some painless and failsafe method of keeping newspaper recipes intact." He couldn't very well write that he was deep in debt to the New York Times Company and that this was his first installment toward paying it down. He did do some new work, having thrown in "certain personal and anecdotal reflections," including a rather bowdlerized account of his sojourn at Montecatini. But never mind how facile the means of production may have been. You can get too used to Craig Claiborne and start taking him for granted, and then a book like this comes along and you realize that in the course of this one little year his interests had ranged from Ninth Avenue to Bahía, from Port-au-Prince to Bali, from *carciofi all giudea* to the perfect cheesecake, from lox to *bangan bartha*. He had reported from Paris, Amsterdam, Montecatini, Tokyo, Osaka, Bali, Singapore, and Vietnam in one year.

Many of the dishes he was bringing to his readers were drastically different from anything they had known before. In that context he believed that while the more curious and worldly among them *ought* to be pleased to learn about the new cooking from France, he didn't expect Americans in general to go as crazy over it as the French were going.

An American reading Gault and Millau in English, or an American who understood enough French to read them in the original, would quickly bump up against a cultural wall. Peek through it and you wanted to say, What are these guys so worked up about?

The answer to that question illuminates a moral difference between Gault-Millau and Craig Claiborne, and the clue to it is the rather slippery French verb *développer*. In their history of themselves Gault and Millau say outright (as quoted above, on page 191) that they publicized the concept of a nouvelle cuisine and "developed" its success, but the English word doesn't accurately express what they meant. They were building a market for their magazine and their annual guidebook while at the same time creating a sensation called the nouvelle cuisine of which they were the arbiters and grand panjandrums. They made a defined, select few chefs famous and rich—Bocuse and his confrères— and that confraternity's fame and wealth in turn made Gault-Millau's publications necessary to its adherents. You had to know who deserved your adulation and your cash, and only Gault and Millau could tell you.

198

They were so close to their chosen chefs that they called one another by the familiar *tu*.[48] This sort of circular arrangement would have been anathema to Craig.

But he did love the food! It really was pure and clear and precise. It was *thought through*. It took him back to his first falling in love with food.

This time he knew more, however. His ardor for the nouvelle cuisine was deeper, and more nuanced, than his young romance with *choucroûte à l'alsacienne* and *pommes de terre soufflées,* than his mad infatuation with *turbotin à l'infante.* His ripened passion for the new French cuisine would draw him on to what some thought the glorious peak of his professional life, others the shameful nadir.

14

The Feast

Craig loved Henry Creel, but the idea of their living together did not
appeal to him in the slightest. They rarely even spent the night. In Craig's
columns as in all the press, unaccompanied men were customarily identified as "bachelors," and a bachelor was what Craig truly was. Craig
helped Henry adapt a selection of his, Craig's, favorite recipes, and ghost-
wrote much of the text as well, for Henry's book *Cooking for One Is Fun.*

Those words too could have been Craig's own. An evening at home
alone was something he cherished. As much as he did enjoy his whirl-
wind social life, and the ceaseless flow of new and often fascinating people he met in his work, there was still inside him the shy little Mississippi
boy who had to coach himself (his mother speaking silently within) to
stand up straight, look his interlocutor in the eye, remember his manners, turn on the charm, maintain his reserve, smile and keep smiling,
never forget who you are, never forget that you are a *Craig.* This was
work. There was the additional burden, most of the time, of trying not
to look or sound too—gay.

"I enjoy cooking for myself," he told a reporter for *People* magazine.[1]
"I set a place for myself, I light candles. People say, 'What kind of fool
are you?' But I like being alone. I revel in being alone."

Some favorite music on the stereo. A Scotch and soda or two, or
three. Something splendid from the cellar. Ingredients measured,
chopped, sifted, and set out; knives clean and sharp; bowls and dishes
as required; pots and pans at the ready; serving pieces in order; butter
softened; silver polished; crystal spotless; candlewicks trimmed; plates

in the warmer. The voice of Lausanne far away but still clear: *Une place pour chaque chose, chaque chose à sa place.* A simple but never less than elegant dinner.

"I situate the place mat with precision and on it I place a knife and fork (silver by Christofle) and a clear wine goblet (crystal by Baccarat). To the left of the fork is a crisply starched linen napkin. . . . There is no illumination in my dining area other than candles."[2] A first course, a second, dessert. And when the table is clear, the dishes done, the kitchen and dining room immaculate once more, he can sink into his favorite chair with a generous stinger and watch who cares what on the tube. Bliss.

One night in June 1975 it is the middle of Pledge Week on Channel 13 (WNET, New York City's public television station). Most people who hit the tireless, droning importunities of Pledge Week tend to change the channel pronto, but Craig just sits there, half watching, half drowsing. They're auctioning stuff to raise funds. American Express has donated dinner for two, at any restaurant that takes the card, anywhere, no dollar limit.

Anywhere? No dollar limit? They have Craig's full attention now.

The phone number scrolls across the screen. He dials. Bids three hundred dollars. A lot of money for Craig. What the hell, it's deductible.

At the end of the hour, the winning bids are displayed. American Express, meal for two: $300. No! Yes.[3]

§

He called Pierre, who was sure at first that Craig was yanking his chain. Craig insisted it was for real, come over. They pulled down an avalanche of restaurant guidebooks from the shelves. The kids with the sweetest sweet tooth in the world were loose in the world's biggest candy store. It couldn't be farther than Europe, he'd have to pay their air fare, he didn't want the *Times* to know, they'd reimburse him after the story. Soon they had a list of about forty possibilities. But ouch, the restaurant had to take American Express cards—so cross off Taillevent, cross off the sublime Auberge de l'Ill in Alsace.

Carl Sontheimer, the guy who imported Cuisinarts, a real *feinschmecker,* told him about a tiny joint in Paris called Chez Denis. Not in the Michelin—they didn't give stars to places with plastic flowers on the tables. Ridiculously expensive. Ridiculously good. The *patron* was sort of—nuts.

Craig knew whom to consult: Yanou Collart. She knew everything, everyone. "You must come yourself and taste, *mon cher* Craig! You will taste Denis's *chiffonade de homard!* His *ortolans!* And I know you and your *andouillettes*—the lowest things, he serves them *aux truffes!*" Craig and Pierre flew to Paris to audition Denis.

The verdict: "exultation and well-being, if not to say euphoria."

Yanou: "You see?"[4]

Craig explained to Denis—that is, lied—that his fiftieth birthday had just passed, and that a wealthy American friend wished to treat him to "the most expensive meal that can be created on the continent of Europe."

Picture the eyes of the madman Denis shooting out on springs, coming back to rest in their parent sockets, and at last closing in beatific contemplation of this folly of all follies. Who but an American.

Denis began to dream with his eyes open; also his mouth. Craig asked for a letter of proposal. It arrived. The price: 17,600 francs—$4,000. And a deposit of $2,000, please, in good faith. Cash. As between friends.

He didn't have two thousand dollars! And if he asked American Express, it could queer the whole deal. He knew what you do at a moment like this—you call Yanou.

—*Mon cher* Craig, she purred. Do not trouble yourself. I will arrange.

§

Five months later, on Page One of the *New York Times* of November 14, 1975, came the harvest:

JUST A QUIET DINNER FOR 2 IN PARIS:
31 DISHES, 9 WINES, A $4,000 CHECK
By Craig Claiborne

If one were offered dinner for two at any price, to be eaten in any restaurant anywhere in the world, what would the choice be? And in these days of ever-higher prices, what would the cost be?

By submitting the highest bid on Channel 13's fund-raising auction last June, we found ourselves in a position earlier this week to answer these questions. The place: Chez Denis in Paris. The cost: $4,000.

Our winning bid was $300. One factor in the selection of the restaurant should be noted quickly: The donor of the dinner that Channel 13 auctioned was American Express, which set forth as its only condition the requirement that the establishment be one that accepts its credit card.

In turn, when American Express ultimately learned what we had done, its reaction went from mild astonishment to being cheerful about the outcome. "Four thousand—was that francs or dollars?" . . .

At any rate, the selection of the restaurant dominated our fantasies for weeks as in our minds, we dined on a hundred meals or more. . . . We considered Rome, Tokyo and Hong Kong. Copenhagen and Stockholm, Brussels and London. . . .

In addition to excluding those that did not recognize the credit card of the donor, we dismissed from our potential list of restaurants several celebrated places, simply, perhaps, because of their celebrity.

In time we considered Chez Denis, which is a great favorite among several food writers . . . but is nonetheless not well known. It is a tiny place on the Rue Gustave Flaubert, not far from the Arc de Triomphe.

We visited Chez Denis in a party of three to reconnoiter. . . .

There was a chiffonade of lobster (a salad of cold lobster, cubed foie gras, a touch of cognac and, we suspect, cayenne, and a tarragon mayonnaise flavored with tomato, tossed with lettuce).

In addition, there was fresh foie gras with aspic, braised sweetbreads with a light truffle sauce, roast quail and those delectable tiny birds from the Landes region of France, ortolans. There was also a great personal favorite, andouillettes served with an outstanding sorrel sauce. The wine was a fine Pommard.

The meal having passed the test, we were able to ignore the few plastic boughs and plastic flowers tucked in beams here and there. . . .

A Crucial Question, Seriously Answered

After dinner, we asked Mr. Denis*, offhandedly, how much he would charge for the most lavish dinner for two that he and his chef could

* Craig knew that the man's name was Denis *Lahana*; why he insisted on referring to him as M. Denis, rather than properly as M. Lahana, is inexplicable—most likely just an error of his memory.

prepare . . . We told him that we were about to celebrate a birthday and that money was no obstacle. . . . Mr. Denis, with little hesitation, pulled up a chair and sat down. . . .

We asked him to consider the matter at his convenience and write to us with his proposal. When he did, his letter stated: ". . . I propose to organize for you a prestigious dinner. In the land of my birth, the region of Bordeaux, one speaks of a repas de vins, a meal during the course of which a number of wines of great prestige are served. . . .

"I am suggesting nine such wines, to be served in the course of a dinner à la Française in the classic tradition. To dine properly in this style, many dishes are offered and served to the guests, chosen with the sole thought that each dish be on the same high level as the wines and those most likely to give pleasure as the wines are tasted."

He suggested a dinner of 31 dishes that would start with an hors d'oeuvre and go on to three "services," the first consisting of soups, savory, an assortment of substantial main dishes, and ices or sherbets to clear the palate.

This would be followed by the second service: hot roasts or baked dishes, vegetables, cold, light, meaty dishes in aspic and desserts.

And then the third service: decorated confections, petits fours and fruits.

The youngest wine would be a six-year-old white Burgundy, the oldest a 140-year-old Madeira.

Mr. Denis set a price of $4,000. This, we must hasten to add, included service and taxes. We accepted.

The proprietor suggested that the meal be served to four persons— all for the same price—because the food had to be prepared in a certain quantity and would be enough to serve as many as 10 persons, while the wines were enough for four.

We declined, because the rules set by American Express called for dinner for two. The dinner party would be made up of me and my colleague, Pierre Franey. Anything left over, we knew, would not go to waste.

Mr. Denis noted that it was not required that all foods be sampled and that the quantity of the food served would depend on the guest's appetite.

Beluga Caviar
In Crystal

And so, we sat down to our $4,000 dinner.

The hors d'oeuvre was presented: fresh Beluga caviar in crystal, enclosed in shaved ice, with toast. The wine was a superb 1966 Champagne Comtesse Marie de France.

Then came the first service, which started with three soups. There was consommé Denis, an inordinately good, rich, full-bodied, clear consommé of wild duck with shreds of fine crêpes and herbs. It was clarified with raw duck and duck bones and then lightly thickened as many classic soups are, with fine tapioca.

The second soup (still of the first service) was a crème Andalouse, an outstanding cream of tomato soup with shreds of sweet pimento and fines herbes, including fresh chives and chervil.

The first two soups were superb but the third, cold Germiny (a cream of sorrel), seemed bland and anticlimactic. One spoonful of that sufficed. The only wine served at this point was a touch of Champagne. The soups having been disposed of, we moved on to a spectacularly delicate parfait of sweetbreads, an equally compelling mousse of quail in a small tarte, and a somewhat salty, almost abrasive but highly complementary tarte of Italian ham, mushrooms, and a border of truffles.

1918 Château Latour,
The Best Bordeaux

The wine was a 1918 Château Latour, and it was perhaps the best Bordeaux we had ever known. It was very much alive, with the least trace of tannin.

The next segment of the first service included a fascinating dish that the proprietor said he had created, Belon oysters broiled quickly in the shell and served with a pure beurre blanc, the creamy, lightly thickened butter sauce.

Also in this segment were a lobster in a creamy, cardinal-red sauce that was heavily laden with chopped truffles and, after that, another startling but excellent dish, a sort of Provençale pie made with red mullet and baked with tomato, black olives and herbs, including fennel or anise seed, rosemary, sage and thyme.

The accompanying wine was a 1969 Montrachet Baron Thénard, which was extraordinary (to our taste, all first-rate Montrachet whites are extraordinary).

The final part of the first service consisted of what was termed filets et sots l'y laissent de poulard de Bresse, sauce suprême aux cèpes (the so-called "fillet" strips of chicken plus the "oysters" found in the after-backbone of chicken blended in a cream sauce containing sliced wild mushrooms).

Chartreuse of Partridge
And Cooked Cabbage

There followed another curious but oddly appealing dish, a classic chartreuse of partridge, the pieces of roasted game nested in a bed of cooked cabbage and baked in a mosaic pattern, intricately styled, of carrot and turnip cut into fancy shapes.

And a tender rare-roasted fillet of Limousin beef with a rich truffle sauce.

The wine with the meat and game was a 1928 Château Mouton Rothschild. It was ageless and beautiful. The first service finally ended with sherbets in three flavors—raspberry, orange and lemon. The purpose of this was to revive the palate for the second service, and it did. We were two hours into the meal and going at the food, it seemed, at a devilish pace.

The second service included the ortolans en brochette, an element of the dinner to be anticipated with a relish almost equal to that of the caviar or the foie gras.

The small birds, which dine on berries through their brief lives, are cooked whole, with the head on, and without cleaning except for removing the feathers. They are as fat as butter and an absolute joy to bite into because of the succulence of the flesh. Even the bones, except for the tiny leg bones, are chewed and swallowed. There is one bird to one bite.

The second service also included fillets of wild duck en salmis in a rich brown game sauce. The final dish in this segment was a rognonnade de veau, or roasted boned loin of veal wrapped in puff pastry with fresh black truffles about the size of golf balls.

The vegetables served were pommes Anna—the potatoes cut into small rounds and baked in butter—and a purée Rachel, a purée of artichokes.

Foie Gras,
Woodcock and Pheasant

Then came the cold meat delicacies. There was butter-rich fresh foie gras in clear aspic, breast meat of woodcocks that was cooked until rare and served with a natural chaud-froid, another aspic and cold pheasant with fresh hazelnuts.

The wines for this segment consisted of a 1917 Château Lafite Rothschild, a 1961 Château Pétrus, and the most magnificent wine of the evening, a 1929 Romanée Conti.

The dinner drew near an end with three sweets—a cold glazed charlotte with strawberries, an île flottante and poires Alma. The wine for the sweets was a beautiful unctuous 1928 Château d'Yquem, which was quite sweet, yet "dry."

The last service consisted of the pastry confections and fruits, served with an 1835 Madeira. With coffee came a choice of a 100-year-old Calvados or an hors d'âge Cognac.

And for the $4,000, logic asks if it was a perfect meal in all respects? The answer is no.

The crystal was Baccarat and the silver was family sterling, but the presentation of the dishes, particularly the cold dishes such as the sweetbread parfait and quail mousse tarte, was mundane.

The foods were elegant to look at, but the over-all display was undistinguished, if not to say shabby.

The chartreuse of pheasant, which can he displayed stunningly, was presented on a most ordinary dish.

The food itself was generally exemplary, although there were regrettable lapses there, too. The lobster in the gratin was chewy and even the sauce could not compensate for that. The oysters, of necessity, had to be cooked as briefly as possible to prevent toughening, but the beurre blanc should have been very hot. The dish was almost lukewarm when it reached the table, and so was the chartreuse of pheasant.

We've spent many hours reckoning the cost of the meal and find that we cannot break it down. We have decided this: We feel we could not have made a better choice, given the circumstance of time and place.

Mr. Denis declined to apply a cost to each of the wines, explaining that they contributed greatly to the total cost of the meal because it was necessary to open three bottles of the 1918 Latour in order to find one in proper condition.

Over all, it was an unforgettable evening and we have high praise for Claude Mornay, the 37-year-old genius behind the meal.

We reminded ourselves of one thing during the course of that evening: If you were Henry VIII, Lucullus, Gargantua and Bacchus, all rolled into one, you cannot possibly sustain, start to finish, a state of ecstasy while dining on a series of 31 dishes.

Wines, illusion or not, became increasingly interesting, although we were laudably sober at the end of the meal.

§

Craig's piece appeared precisely sixteen days after this headline in the New York *Daily News*: "Ford to City: Drop Dead."

New York City was on the verge of financial collapse, and desperate for a federal bridge loan so that it could reorganize its debts. Those weren't President Gerald Ford's actual words, but they might as well have been: "The people of this country will not be stampeded," he said. "They will not panic when a few desperate New York officials and bankers try to scare New York's mortgage payments out of them."[5] Default was imminent.

Crime was bad. Unemployment was bad. Inflation was bad, and yet there was a recession on. The price of oil was out of control. Saigon had fallen to the Communists in such ignominy that even the fieriest opponents of the war were mortified. Among the most popular recording artists were Neil Diamond, Tony Orlando, Freddy Fender, Helen Reddy, and Barry Manilow. It was a bad time.

Never had the *New York Times* been inundated with so much outrage. "Of the more than 250 letters received by yesterday [November 19, five days after Craig's piece was published], virtually all were condemnatory." A few excerpts:

I thought it was one of the most disgusting things recently published in a news organ. . . .

It strikes me as simply incredible in the face of daily reminders of millions struggling against hunger and disease that today's *Times* should make front-page news of a piece so frivolous, evanescent and unredeeming. . . .

Today I find it impossible to read without amazement and mounting indignation. . . . How can anyone reconcile this smugly decadent story and almost daily reports of worldwide hunger and starvation?

It is almost unbelievable that the *New York Times,* the employer of Mr. Claiborne, saw fit to publicize this vulgarity at length on its front page. . . . Is the *Times* reduced to pandering to the tastes of those who thrive on tales of extravagance, wasteful luxury and extreme frivolity?[6]

There was more, plenty more, but you get the picture. As for Craig Claiborne, was he repentant? Guilt-stricken? Perhaps at least troubled? Guess. A little slice of his reply:

I would like to ask those who were not amused if they seriously believe that as a result of that evening I have deprived one human being of one mouthful of food. . . . I do not think it represents contempt for world hunger any more than if I had won the Mercedes-Benz that was put up for auction.[7]

§

The letters didn't stop. By another week later, the *Times* had received more than 475 of them, "with those criticizing the dinner holding a margin of more than 4 to 1." *Le Tout* New York was talking about it as well, and now a few *Claibornistes* were daring to stick their heads out of their bunkers. Excerpts from the next wave:

Oh, good grief! Where's our sense of humor? Where's our perspective? Where's our *joie de vivre*?. . . . Just how much are star quarterbacks paid while day care centers remain closed? While New York totters on the verge of disaster?

At a time when the gap between the haves and have-nots is so painfully wide (when hasn't it been?), it is simply in poor taste to promote such a glaring example of conspicuous consumption. (I'll bet, though, that few of us would have turned down an invitation to join Mr. Claiborne.)

I was appalled at the degree of appalledness indicated by the letters you ran.

Begone, ye doomsayers. Better lobsters stuffed with truffles than shirts stuffed with piety.[8]

By the time the contumely was beginning to wind down, there had been over a thousand letters. Craig claimed, though no source seems to be findable, that his feast had been condemned by the Vatican.[9] American Express had certainly had more than four thousand dollars' worth of publicity, and the value to Craig's celebrity (or notoriety) was incalculable. Did it matter if half the people who heard about the Chez Denis dinner thought it, and him, reprehensible? That depends on where you come down on the old saw about there being no bad publicity.

§

On January 7, 1976, Julia Child wrote to Craig from her beloved little house La Pitchoune, which she and her husband, Paul, had built on Simca Beck's Domaine de Bramafam, near Châteauneuf de Grasse. In the midst of a considerably longer letter on a wide variety of subjects, she also had a few comments on the still-notorious $4,000 dinner:[10]

Thanks so much for your follow-up on the great dinner chez Denis. . . . What a to-do, really, and I can see no reason for all that indignant uproar—does anyone object when some rich-bitch buys a $4,000 mink coat, or a $35,000 Rolls Royce? . . .

You must come over here and do some more on the Bocuse group—it seems to me they are taking over far too much and, it is rumored, they or somebody are terrible about restaurants they don't like—boycotting them, and even calling up and making all kinds of reservations ficticiously [*sic*] (spell that word?), and not showing up. I wonder if all of that is true? What about Gault and Millau? I must say I do enjoy their magazine "Le Nouveau Guide," but what is their influence, and what are their connections and tie-ins (if any)? How about the Guide Mich, that seems to keep stars where they no longer belong (Baumanière, Tour d'Argent), or give them recklessly (Oasis and Vivarois)? Is the Guide now part of the French Tourist Bureau? Well, I would like to read you on all of this, and hope you will do more on France—your articles on Bocuse and Guérard were very good indeed, I thought.

Enough for now, and here's wishing you a happy New Year. Fond wishes to Pierre, and to yourself,

Julia[11]

15

Pre-Emeritus

Mimi Sheraton, the new restaurant critic, blew into the *Times* like a hurricane. Save the brief aberrancy of Hess's poison-pen interregnum, the job till now had remained true to Craig Claiborne's code of gentility. Raymond Sokolov and John Canaday each had personified the blend of authority and decency that was the mark of the paper's *beau idéal* of a critic.

Sokolov had begun reviewing restaurants even before Craig had left to start the *Craig Claiborne Journal,* and he became full-fledged food editor in his absence. In Sokolov's first-ever review, bestowing four stars on the eccentric Mr. and Mrs. Foster's Place, he wrote that Mrs. Foster "goes to obsessive lengths to buy flawless materials and then works even harder at such deceptively simple tasks as making a pea soup taste like fresh peas"[1]—deceptively simple writing that read like fresh English. A *summa cum laude* graduate of Harvard, a Fulbright fellow at Oxford, a Harvard ABD (All But Dissertation) in classics, Sokolov brought a scholar's love of detail and history to such arcana as the intricacies of Sichuanese and Hunanese cooking, in his day all but unknown in America. He had been the first to write in English about the French nouvelle cuisine.[2] He loved food the way a scientist loves the structures and mechanisms of nature—passionately, while also seeking to understand it.

John Canaday, who had succeeded Hess and preceded Sheraton, never claimed any great gastronomic expertise, and that very lack democratized his perspective and made for an earthy charm you didn't expect

213

from a scholar of art history. Craig obviously didn't mind Canaday's amateurism—he named Canaday to the critic's post the moment he, Craig, was back from his newsletter exile. From Canaday's first review, of the old-shoe East Side hangout Gino's: "Half the pleasure of eating out in New York has to come from the fact that you are in New York, enjoying phenomena that make the city what it is. Food in a New York restaurant bears the same relationship that a band bears to dancing: It is imperative, and how good it is makes a big difference, but it isn't everything."[3]

Casual urbanity like that was had precisely the ring of suavity that for Craig in his days on Kwajalein and in Lausanne was the tone of New York at its best. Having put Sokolov and Canaday in place as his successors was live proof of his having achieved the same dash and urbanity. He knew he was better at the writing than they were—Craig would never have committed Canaday's syntactic solecism ("Food in a New York restaurant bears the same relationship" to *what*?)—but that was all right, a tradition of candid polish and insouciant wit was in place now. He thought.

Canaday had many detractors. He was quite conservative as an art critic at a time when what had been the avant garde had become enshrined as the new classicism. His very first column for the *Times* had assailed what had become the ultimate in painterly seriousness, the New York School of abstract expressionism. Canaday held that many of its practitioners were little more than hangers-on—"the freaks, the charlatans and the misled who surround [a] handful of serious and talented artists"—and asserted that "the nature of abstract expressionism allows exceptional tolerance for incompetence and deception."[4] That position had made him unpopular with the other critics on the *Times* staff and with much of the rest of New York's intellectual establishment. When he went over to his new job, his lack of technical understanding of cooking and the restaurant business infuriated the professionals and sophisticates of the New York food world. But Craig liked Canaday's old-fashioned gentlemanly style.

Then this: Mimi Sheraton. At the moment of her arrival, Sheraton wrote in a memoir, "I already had a chip on my shoulder."[5] When Craig had left the paper in 1972, she said, "Neither I nor any other female food writer I knew was given an interview for his job." Thus snubbed, she had gone running to the National Organization for Women, which was not sufficiently moved to take action. She wrote "highly intemperate letters to several editors as well as the publisher . . . [and t]he letter I got back from the managing editor . . . told me in essence that the attitude expressed in my letters indicated that I could never be employable at the *Times*." When, three years later, the executive editor, A. M. Rosenthal, hired her anyhow, you might have thought that Sheraton's suspicion of the *Times* as a bastion of exclusion would be eased, but her mental picture of the staff she would be joining, as she recalled it, was still "a bunch of elite snobs."[6]

Sheraton's attitude and voice—radical and loud, respectively—were decidedly not in the Craig Claiborne tradition. As far as she was concerned, there was entirely too much bullshit being slung in the restaurants of New York, and she was there on behalf of The People to detect and expose it—though she herself never used the word, and her prim employer, in any case, would never have allowed it.

(The word *bullshit* is used here in a couple of the senses defined by the philosopher Harry G. Frankfurt: "humbug" as "deceptive misrepresentation, short of lying, especially by pretentious word or deed"; and "[talking] without knowing what [one] is talking about."[7])

Sheraton would be the nemesis of the food world's multitudinous bullshitters. Tyrants? She would lay them low. Deception? She would eviscerate its practitioners. Rip-offs? Those she would take particular pleasure in bringing to light. She was much less an esthete than a consumer advocate, and as such she redefined the rating system; for the first time it would include value:[8] "four stars to none, based on the author's reaction to cuisine, atmosphere *and price** in relation to comparable establishments."[9] (When she published a restaurant guide in book form some years later, she wrote: "I have sometimes been accused of having a 'consumerist' approach to restaurant reviewing. No accusation could be more welcome."[10])

Somewhat to her surprise, it did not take long for Sheraton to discover that despite her proletarian dread, she actually liked her colleagues at the paper.[11] Which did not mean, however, that she felt the slightest need to kowtow to their traditions.

The very type of New York mystique that John Canaday celebrated, Mimi Sheraton might have been expected to consider the rankest

---

* Emphasis added.

bullshit. It was, one might think, epitomized in the old sawdust-floored steakhouse technically titled just Palm* but called by everybody *the* Palm. The Palm had no menu. The coat check guy was always reading the racing form, you had to get his attention. Most of the customers were regulars, and they almost always ordered the same things. There were caricatures of many of them on the walls, just short of disrespectful. Your waiter often as not was Italian-born, but if you x-rayed his thorax, you'd see a New York subway map. If you were new to the place, or a regular feeling adventurous, and you asked him what they had, he'd say, "We got steaks, chops, lobster, fish, anything you want." The lobsters were unbelievable—four, five pounds, more if you wanted, grilled under the hottest salamanders in the City of New York, the legs and swimmers charred. Very expensive—you didn't ask how they calculated the price.

Craig Claiborne had never reviewed the Palm. It was *really* not his kind of place.

—Do you have pasta?

—Yeah, we got pasta.

—Linguine with clams?

—We got that.

—Canelloni.

—We don't got that. (There is often a sort of Chico-Marxian rhythm to these conversations.)

—Veal?

—We got veal.

—How prepared?

—Whatever you like.

—What about fish?

—We got swordfish.

—Striped bass?

—We got striped bass.

A friend may have told you about a dish of sliced steak with roasted red peppers and onions on top of soggy toast, insanely delicious, called Steak à la Stone. All you had to do was ask for it.

---

* The name was a corruption, by a typical New York bureaucrat, of the founders' attempt, in 1926, to license the new venture under the name of the capital of Emilia, their *paese*—Parma.

—How you want it cooked?

But then you might see a dish go by and ask,

—What was that?

—That's something we make for Mr. Dalessandro.

—But what is it?

—It's just something we make for Mr. Dalessandro.

So order the Steak à la Stone already.

Craig was still officially food editor, but in his empyrean he existed so far above West Forty-third Street that he had nothing to do with Mimi Sheraton's hiring. For *her* first-ever restaurant review for the *Times,* somehow she had spied out the Palm's menu, and she published it. Everything. With prices.

—Monday Night Salad. Who knew? Did you know they made something called Monday Night Salad?

—Never in my life.

—Maybe that's what they only made for Mr. Dalessandro.

(In fact, it was. Dalessandro always came in with some pals on *Monday Night Football* nights and then they'd go get a hotel room and watch the game together. Dalessandro commanded this particular ungodly salad for himself and his guys—blue cheese dressing, beefsteak tomatoes, radishes, peppers, onions, a linebacker's portion of anchovies.[12] Nobody else ever wanted it.)

So was Mimi Sheraton's review a take-down, a proto-Naderian fussbudget scolding, a hellfire sermon damning the Palm's shameless cholesterol, waste, and make-believe? Nope. She gave the joint four stars.

The food was that good, and so was the theater.

It is said of a great city that if you are delivered there unconscious and magically awoken in its midst, you will immediately know where you are. You may wake in Los Angeles, you may wake in Frankfurt, you may wake in Milan, and be—you don't know where. But when the fairy's wand flutters your eyelids open anywhere in Paris, anywhere in Rome, anywhere in New York, you just know. You could be led blindfolded into the Palm and it was the same. There was no singling out what made that so: It was some indefinable compound of the murmur and clatter and laughing, the thousand aromas, the deadpan nod of the waiter, the heaviness and hand-fit of your Old Fashioned glass, the crust on your hash browns, the naked geometry of your cheesecake slice, the tilt of the bartender's voice mock-grieving "*Tell* me abouddit," the sense of permanence and age, the air of comprehensive confidence, the beef—don't forget the beef—and who knew what hundred other elements too subtle to name.

Mimi Sheraton evidently knew that she would be in a far stronger position to call out and damn the bullshitters of the New York restaurant world if first she showed that she knew what was good. She did know food, and in understanding the Palm she showed that she knew New York style, too. What's more, this bristly feminist had picked a place that could hardly have been more masculine. As an opening gambit it defied attack from any direction, flicking her predictability aside like the flimsiest of pawns. She knew what she was doing.

Sheraton's expertise, however, in Craig Claiborne's system of values, could never be enough. Canaday's lack of technical expertise had mattered much less to Craig than his sensibility, his sense of fineness and grace. To Craig, everything about Sheraton reeked of fineness's opposite. She weighed over two hundred pounds.[13] David Kamp, in *The United States of Arugula,* writes that she did not "seek out friendships with chefs, as Claiborne did. . . . She wasn't going to mince words or cuddle up to maître d's."[14] Craig had prided himself on being so self-effacing as to be naturally unidentifiable; Sheraton reveled in outlandish disguises to preserve her anonymity:

> I believe I was the first restaurant critic to collect a wardrobe of wigs. One was an auburn pageboy affair with straight bangs that I dubbed the Greenwich Village Lady Poet. A second, the Five Towns Macher,* was done up as a silver-blond bouffant cascading over one eye. The third was a long, loose, comb-down of black hair that partially obscured my face in the style of an anguished activist. . . .[15]

You can *feel* Craig shuddering. Sheraton may not have given herself away as the *Times* restaurant critic, but she sure as hell was going to draw attention to herself in a restaurant, and not favorable attention

---

* The Five Towns are nearby suburbs on the South Shore of Long Island, by using which term Sheraton meant to denote middle-middle-classness and absolute non-Manhattanness. Leo Rosten, in *The Joys of Yiddish,* defines the word *macher* as "a big wheel; an 'operator.'"

either. Craig had always believed that you owed dignity and respect to a restaurant, in your deportment and your appearance. Playing an anguished activist or, God help us, a Five Towns macher, was a thumb in the eye of any self-respecting Midtown maître d'hôtel. Never mind— imagine—the weeping ghost of Henri Soulé.

> My only regret about my experience at the *Times* was Craig Claiborne's falling out with me. Craig did more to bring the word of good food to this country than any other writer, and he wrote stories about famous chefs from various restaurants in his well-outfitted test kitchen in the Hamptons. Several times, quite coincidentally, I gave negative reviews to some of those chefs shortly before or after his stories appeared. Craig stopped speaking to me entirely, accusing me of putting down his taste. I was distressed that he believed that, as I did not think he was necessarily wrong to praise the chefs I'd criticized. In his own kitchen, they'd undoubtedly cooked superbly, while giving short shrift to unknowns in their restaurants.[16]

Gael Greene recalls: "Craig had called me looking for someone qualified to be the new restaurant critic. I recommended Mimi as a thoroughgoing professional because she was encroaching on my job as restaurant critic at *New York* magazine—to get rid of her. She knows everything one could possibly know about cottage cheese, I told him. At first he was thrilled to have her. He called to thank me. Then he called moaning and groaning that she was destroying every restaurant he liked."[17]

David Kamp quotes Arthur Gelb, characteristically blunt: "Craig hated Mimi Sheraton, and she hated him."[18]

What at first seems odd about this is that Craig should have let something so trivial get under his skin. But he had never not been touchy on matters of social class, and he had worked hard to elevate the position of restaurant critic at the *Times* to one that not only the ghost of his mother but also his peers on the staff considered worthy of respect. Not for nothing had he started his very first column with that euphonious and knowing "ripple and marble striation . . . of free-form glass from the Adriatic shores." What did this Sheraton know of Venetian glass? Or of sauces, *pâte à choux*, proper service—for that matter, euphony?—or good manners?

In fact, look around. Here was a world of his making. Vast and: his own? People said so. Everybody said he was the king of the food world. But the fact was, and he knew it, it was too big for one king now. It had already splintered into duchies, enclaves, warring city-states, with barbarians at the wildland fringes—barbarians even now making urban incursions, in many a city where civilization had still not planted its flag. Most of the time this was all fine with Craig; he told himself he had never wanted to be a king.

When people wanted him to go on television, he usually said no. He wasn't like Julia; he didn't have her gift for the camera, or the urge either. He was too shy. He would have to drink to calm his nerves, and then he would show up drunk, and that didn't do at all. Word got around rather quickly about that. This was a turning point in his life, though he didn't know that it was. Oh, television, oh, hell. Julia was wonderful at it. Wonderful person, too. They were from different planets, they could never be intimate friends, but he loved her. Sometimes he thought he had made her. Always he was proud of her, in that Southern way that almost means you're unselfishly glad for somebody but is ever so slightly ambiguous.

So Craig Claiborne was absolutely the top person in American food, but he didn't wish, though thank you very much indeed, to perform the public role. And really and truly he was grateful. Royally ensconced in East Hampton, or in his first-class seat on the way to somewhere marvelous, and of his own choosing, he was free to be as elitist as he wished when he wished, as populist when he wished that. The best thing would be to choose to be really, truly glad about all these *marvelous* things going on in the food world that he had created, and that is what he made every effort to do. He was almost never photographed without a beatific smile.

But he wasn't quite sure about how this whole thing—the food world, the mania—was spreading out. Remember his first "Restaurants Under Review"? A hundred words apiece. Now not only Sheraton but Gael Greene, and who knows who else, everybody was writing these long personal essays under the guise of restaurant reviews. And Arthur— Arthur Gelb seemed to be turning the *New York Times* into a "lifestyle" magazine. What a word. In his memoir, *City Room,* recalling his planning of the new Friday Living section, Gelb wrote:

The section would combine sophisticated articles about wine and food, as well as such subjects as the science of the palate, celebrity cooks in their own kitchens, service columns on health and medicine and off-beat pieces about where to buy the best corned-beef sandwich or the tastiest ice cream cone. The weekly columns preceding the culture report would be written by two of the best stylists on the staff. John Leonard, our literary critic, would write "Private Lives," an intimate essay, sometimes ironic, sometimes poignant, about the world around him, and Charlotte Curtis would write "New Yorkers, etc.," an irreverent sketch about life behind the scenes in what remained of Manhattan's high society.

Although the emphasis was on food, I tried to keep original non-food ideas flowing. There was to be a column by Al Krebs called "Notes on People" (celebrated people, of course); a column, "Metropolitan Diary," by Tom Buckley, consisting mainly of short anecdotes and verse contributed by readers ... a column, "Living Abroad," informal jottings by our own foreign correspondents (the first contributed by our London bureau chief, Robert Semple). . . .

But to guarantee the section's success, I knew I needed to enlist Craig Claiborne.[19]

The Living Section made its sprawling debut in November 1976. Craig and Pierre had traveled to Crissier, Switzerland—near Lausanne—to acquaint themselves with the restaurant of Frédy Girardet. Girardet, Craig wrote, was "said to be the most illustrious thing to come along since Mrs. Escoffier gave birth to Georges Auguste 130 years ago." The reputation of his relatively new and relatively modest establishment was as "conceivably the greatest French restaurant on the European continent." Once he and Pierre had feasted there—"the meal was bliss . . . not a dish to be faulted"—Craig's own opinion was that Frédy Girardet had, "solely on his own native talent, become one of the greatest creative forces in the world of chefs today, second neither to Bocuse, Guérard, Vergnes, or any of the other titans on the European scene.

"His cooking," Craig added, "is also universally conceded to fit the mold of the much publicized nouvelle cuisine of France."[20]

Pierre was as excited about Girardet's food as Craig, and the Living Section gave generous play to Pierre's adaptations of it for home cooks.

No home cook in America, however, could ever hope to duplicate the taste of Girardet's dishes, because nobody in America could find ingredients to compare with Girardet's Bresse chickens, his duck livers from the Vendée, his butter from the mountains of the Jura, or his Mediterranean *loup de mer,* which had been flopping in a fisherman's net no more than twenty-four hours before turning stiff and barely opaque in the oven at Crissier. Craig delighted in praising Long Island ingredients and any other realistic possibilities, but he deprecated all invidious comparisons; it would not have been polite.

In this same first Living Section Pierre Franey also began a solo career, as The 60-Minute Gourmet—each column to furnish recipes for much or most of a meal makeable in less than an hour. His first was "concerned with improvisation: I was challenged by a friend who likes to serve margaritas before dinner"—guess who—"to concoct a dish with the same ingredients as that potent Mexican libation."[21] *That potent Mexican libation?* Parlez-vous Claibornais? Evidently the francophone writer of record was getting a little ghosting from his anglophone margaritaphile friend.

Crevettes Margarita is a great dish. You marinate the shrimp briefly in lime juice, salt, and pepper, sauté the shrimp in butter for two minutes, add shallots, deglaze the pan with tequila, add cream and reduce it, toss in avocado slices just to heat, and sprinkle with cilantro ("available in markets that specialize in Chinese, Spanish, or Mexican greens"). The editing of Pierre's first 60-Minute Gourmet left a bit to be desired, however. In the little introductory essay comes the priceless sentence "Guava shells are available in cans," when nowhere else in the column is there any mention of guava.

Pierre's shrimp dish was pure nouvelle cuisine—what Frédy Girardet called "spontaneous cuisine." *La Cuisine Spontanée* was in fact the title of Girardet's cookbook in French.* In the very shadow of the École Professionelle de la Société Suisse des Hôteliers, where Craig had learned that every dish and every procedure in French cooking had one proper way and one only, and under the eyes of a chef (Pierre) who had trained in the equally classical school of Henri Soulé, Frédy Girardet was mak-

---

* Girardet's U.S. publisher dumbed the title of the American edition down to *The Cuisine of Fredy Girardet.* They even tossed out the *accent aigu* in his first name.

ing it up as he went along every day. Girardet served a dinner to Gael Greene that was at once so multifaceted and so delicious that it left her, of all people, speechless. "Come for a week," Girardet told her. "I'll cook you ten different dishes every day."[22]

§

Craig was enthralled by the nouvelle cuisine—more excited even than he had been by his work on Chinese cooking with Virginia Lee half a decade ago—but he couldn't sustain a career and a life as America's foremost food authority on that one rarefied thing. He felt certain that in time the nouvelle cuisine would have a profound influence on serious cooking in America, but as it was presently constituted in Europe, it was simply too difficult for nearly all American chefs. They didn't have the precision, they didn't have ingredients of sufficient quality, they didn't have the essential sense of restraint. As for American home cooks, forget it, the real thing was virtually impossible. So he found himself without much to say of real interest even to himself.

All around him were people looking up to him; and wherever he searched for something to interest him, he found himself almost always gazing into the past. The Craig Claiborne these people were looking up to was not who he was now but who he used to be.

His own newspaper wrote about him as a celebrity, his dinner parties as legend. "The Claiborne-Franey establishment richly merits a three-star rating (the most Michelin accords any restaurant),"[23] ran the adulatory feature, which somehow made his life seem frozen in time. The piece had come about at the instigation of the writer's wife, Joan Whitman, a dear friend of Craig's, but the fact remained that Alden Whitman was, as Craig would later recall, "the distinguished obituary writer for the *Times.*"[24]

He was constantly referred to as a restaurant critic—"undoubtedly the best-known and perhaps the most influential of a growing number of critics who keep diners informed and restaurateurs on their toes," the *Wall Street Journal* called him[25]—but he hadn't actually been one for years. That may have been why he began to feel the occasional need to justify himself, as when, with unaccustomed rancor, he took on Milan's old and renowned Ristorante-Caffè Savini: "The food, generally, is above average. But the haughtiness, the smug, holier-than-thou attitude of the service staff is stifling. It is, in brief, rude, curt, and borders on the dis-courteous, top to bottom."

One thing about reviewing that Craig did love was getting letters from outraged restaurateurs, like the *cri de coeur* he'd gotten in 1967 from Soulé's successor at Le Pavillon, the blighted Philippe. This one, dated August 27, 1977, had been written not to him but to the news-paper *Il Giorno*, by the president of Savini S.p.A., Angelo Pozzi. Pozzi made sure that Craig got a copy, and translated it himself. An excerpt:

The sincere and unconditional esteem of the very select Savini's custom-ers, Italians and people of all over the world . . . cannot and could not be discussed by Mr. Claiborne, a very esteemed critic and journalist.

What amazes me, on the contrary, is the inadmissible ease by which Mr. Claiborne "shoots" his inapellable "ipse dixit" about complained (by him) shortcomings and rudeness of the service staff.

Pozzi went on to assert that Mr. Claiborne had surely not been well. He supposed that he also had not had the attention of the full complement of the dining room staff.

This is enough to prove that the emeritus critic and journalist passed, maybe, his hurried and heavy judgement basing it, perhaps, exclusively on some waiter who was serving him but unpleasant to him.

This is a stroke of bad luck which can happen to every customer of "Savini" or of every other restaurant, very famous and esteemed in the world.[26]

Cheap fun, amusing oneself at an Italian's bad English. How, after all, does one's own pathetic Italian strike an Italian? Who cares, it's fun anyway. No doubt Craig thought so—why else would he have saved the letter?

Life, otherwise, was—dull. In what ought to have been the prime of it, Craig was getting to be, sort of, *emeritus*. Even old Pozzi from Savini had called him that.

Channel 13, for its next fund-raising auction after Craig and Pierre had skinned American Express alive, persuaded them to donate a dinner at King's Hill Road. The winning bid, a thousand bucks, came from a Maurice Segall, president of the credit card division of—American Express.[27]

There seemed to be no end to the controversy over that $4,000 dinner. Over a year afterward, none other than the former president of the Culinary Institute of America was writing in its quarterly journal that the meal had been "in execrable taste . . . reprehensible gluttony . . . a disservice to gastronomy and the restaurant profession . . . [a] desecration of great wine and food."[28]

Not to be outdone, a restaurateur and bar owner from Queens named Peter Cipolla, to celebrate his forty-second birthday, dined at Manhattan's supreme temple of Rabelaisian excess, the Palace Restaurant, on December 14, 1977, with Craig and Pierre's threshold clearly in mind. Before the evening was out, Cipolla and his girlfriend had run up a bill of $5,004.20. (The Cristal, Bollinger, and Dom Pérignon had flowed freely to a no doubt elated staff.) On a personal income of about $40,000 a year, and with no subsidy from American Express, the *New York Times,* or anyone else, Cipolla paid the tab of five large out of his pocket. His girlfriend said the food had been "reasonably good but not the best I've had."[29]

Craig was still defending the $4,000 dinner in 1978—three years after the fact. In an interview with the Chicago *Tribune,* you could tell he had had it about up to here, and he did himself no favor in spitting out, "People wrote in from all over the country complaining about the poor people. Why? Poor people wouldn't have liked that dinner anyway."[30]

Again and again his life seemed to settle to a center of gravity in time gone by. He went to Brussels for the fiftieth anniversary of the restaurant Comme Chez Soi, at which a number of the greatest chefs and restaurateurs of Europe foregathered, many of them now old friends of his— Jean-Claude Vrinat of Taillevent, Pierre Haeberlin of the Auberge de l'Ill, Pierre Troisgros, Roger Vergé, Paul Bocuse—and he wrote it all up for the paper, reporting that they had dined on "dishes we have remembered from years past."[31]

Invited to address a graduating class of the Culinary Institute of America in Hyde Park, New York, Craig made clear, however, that he had no unblinkered love of the old days:

You have lived in an age of phenomenal changes, when all of the old, conventional, established, deeply entrenched values were brought into question. To my generation, the world almost overnight became topsy-turvy. . . . You grew up in an age of rethinking what is right and what is wrong, and what has emerged from that revolution is, to my mind, nothing short of magnificent. . . . It was a time when we said to our parents, to our lovers, to our wives, husbands and friends, "You cannot con me any longer. Don't try."

And suddenly we find ourselves in a world that has rid itself of so much hypocrisy, so much sham. And yes, so much shame.

A young member of the faculty, William Primavera, steered the speaker through the crowd toward a reception. "My God," said Craig, "I need a drink the very moment we get there."[32]

In the fall of 1977, there was a sudden burst of flame in Craig's heart—his skipper from Korea, John Smits. Had it been too long? Not at all. The years fell away. Would he like to spend Christmas with Craig on St. Barts? Without Ann, perhaps? Just the two of us? Craig held his breath.

Smits said yes.

A brown envelope, tied with string, is among the things Craig kept in a bundle of souvenirs from the trip. Written on the envelope, in a neat, formal hand, were the words "Capt. C. J. Smits of U.S.S. *Naifeh*, Korean Conflict." Inside were snapshots, faded to silver—all of them, the whole crew! Shirtless, skinny, grinning, with the dear old *Naifeh* hove to in the background.[33] Craig kept the photographs, the room receipt, some restaurant checks, and various other small mementoes to the end of his days in an envelope of his stiff, thick, elegant personal stationery, which you could tell had been opened quite a number of times.

Craig also saved the travel documents prepared for the trip by his usual travel agent, Bollinger Davis, reserving "one villa with double bedroom" at the Village St. Jean at the rate of $70 per day, plus 10 percent service charge.[34]

That same fall, Craig and Pierre had polished off the final touches on *Veal Cookery*, surely as dull an undertaking as they could possibly have hatched. Published late in the year, it did not set the world of gastronomy on fire.

Also in the fall of 1977—precisely when Craig and Pierre were visiting Girardet in Switzerland—Mimi Sheraton set out on a "one-month *tour de gueule*" of France. Her trip was "then the most lavish the *Times* had ever commissioned, at the height of the nouvelle cuisine craze."[35] Her reporting on the trip, for reasons unknown, did not appear until the following summer.

Sheraton then reported that she had had a lunch and a dinner at ten of France's eighteen Michelin three-stars. She liked Guérard, Chapel, Pic, and the Auberge de l'Ill—if she hadn't, she'd have been nuts—but she hated the sacrosanct Pyramide, now in the hands of Fernand Point's widow Mado, for whom all the French critics made sentimental allowance. She hated Alain Senderens's arch-nouvelle Archestrate in Paris, and the truly phony-baloney Vivarois, whose three stars were one of those continuing mysteries that exegetes of the *Guide Michelin* puzzled over each year. (You will recall that Julia Child agreed that Vivarois had no business with three stars.) She reviled L'Oustau de Baumanière in Les Baux, which had been in decline for years and which the Michelin, with its own unique syndrome of separation anxiety, had still been unable to downgrade to the one star it might be said to deserve if it cut its prices by three-quarters.

So far, according to current food world orthodoxy, Sheraton was on solid ground. But when she insulted the humble, saintly brothers Troisgros, that was going too far. And to take on that Légionnaire d'Honneur, *le roi Paul,* the highest Himalaya of humbug in France, and to say that she—a *woman*—"found the decor vulgar, the duck breast tough and salty, and the *gâteau de foies de volailles* tasting as though it had been made of beef liver, instead of the delicate blond livers of Bresse chickens"? Bocuse's response was that something must have been wrong with the critic's sex life. She was all over the papers, and not only in France: Munich's *Süddeutsche Zeitung* ran a headline that translates as "Atlantic Battle Concerning Culinary Paradise."

France being France, you knew there had to be a philosophical discussion on television. Teamed up against the teammateless Mimi Sheraton on the bleakly intellectual program *Dossiers de l'Écran,* or "Screen Files,"[36] were Christian Millau of Gault and Millau's *Nouveau Guide*; Jean Didier of the *Guide Kléber*; the unattacked chefs André Daguin of the two-star and very nouvelle Hôtel de France in Auch; Léa Bidaut of Lyon's venerable Chez Léa; the aggrieved Pierre Troisgros; and, seething, Paul Bocuse. Sheraton, by now a public figure and therefore in need of professional anonymity, was supplied with a wig and a mask. The show—France being France—was three hours long. Not to be intimidated, Sheraton chided Paul Bocuse for so rarely being actually present at his restaurant, and suggested that he fly a flag when he was in residence, like the Queen of England.

When the show was over, Bocuse, in a towering rage, charged at Sheraton and tried to rip her mask off. His first attempt failed. On his second go, Sheraton gave him a shove, and *le roi Paul* went stumbling over the TV cables.[37]

"I'm sorry I didn't hit him in the face," she told *People* magazine.[38]

Now substitute Craig Claiborne for Mimi Sheraton in this scene. Can't do it?

§

And maybe she was right about Bocuse's food. Maybe even poor Mado Point. And Baumanière, yes, you had to grant she was right about Baumanière. But Troisgros? *Non non non non.* Craig was beside himself. Mimi Sheraton did not *get* the nouvelle cuisine. Yes, most of it was very hard to execute, it was not for duffers, it was not for these ham-handed kids coming out of the CIA with knife skills but no taste. You *could* do something like the French originals with American ingredients, but they had to be sparkling fresh, and your technique had to be near perfect. Old-fashioned sauces could cloak a host of errors, but the nouvelle cuisine was almost nude. If everything weren't cooked to just the right degree of doneness, the dish wouldn't work. It was all about balance and grace. In the hands of the few masters in France, it could be poetry. In the hands of their many clumsy imitators, even supposedly well-trained French professionals, the results were likely to be mystifying at best: Four waiters, four dishes, they'd lift the four silver domes all at once with a flourish, you'd admire the artfully composed plates, you'd taste, and then you'd say, *This is it?* By the time it reached American shores, what dozens of restaurants were now calling nouvelle cuisine was often far worse—psychotic clashes of ingredients, a bad joke. Jacques Pépin wrote:

In succumbing to the temptations of overexperimenting, many novice chefs felt they were applying the tenets of nouvelle cuisine. But these very excesses caused nouvelle cuisine to become misunderstood as a cuisine of small portions and high prices, pretentious overdecoration, weird mixtures, and miniature vegetables. Although invention and creativity were among its dogmas, it was never intended to shock the diner with esoteric ingredients or strange presentations.

Imagination, the "mistress of error" in the words of Pascal, can be truly dangerous in a kitchen if the cook has little knowledge of technique and poor taste buds. Adding more and more ingredients ... does not produce a coherent dish. . . . What used to be called, ironically, *cuisine de palace* (hotel food) in France . . . was replaced by bad nouvelle cuisine: paper-thin slices of meat fanned out in the middle of an oversized plate and surrounded by eight types of undercooked baby vegetables and three different overreduced sauces, finished with butter, with a slice of exotic fruit or a few raspberries on top. That is not simplification; it is complication.

Yet when nouvelle cuisine is properly understood and controlled by a thorough knowledge of basic techniques and, more than anything else, by a healthy dose of good common sense, its standards still apply: Use the freshest possible food, be innovative, use new ingredients, seek variety in the kitchen, and insist on lightness in sauces.[39]

What Alice Waters and her first great chef, Jeremiah Tower, were doing at Chez Panisse in Berkeley, California, did resemble the nouvelle cuisine in that it was impossible without superb ingredients and technique, but Waters and Tower would have howled in revolt if you had called what they did nouvelle cuisine. For one thing, the food at Chez Panisse was much simpler, more modest, more rustic, and more old-fashioned. Waters loved the *cuisine grand'mère* of rural France, and while a Michel Guérard or Alain Chapel might have enjoyed, even admired, a meal at Chez Panisse, and probably would have found it superior to almost any other food he had eaten in America, he would not have envied it.

Gourmet magazine had first brought Chez Panisse to national attention with a review of intense enthusiasm in 1975,[40] but it was Craig who introduced her techniques and cooking philosophy to American home cooks in the East. When his "discovery" of Waters was published, the restaurant was already ten years old, but New Yorkers—as was typical of their wariness of anything with its genesis in California—were just starting to catch on. From Craig's piece:

> Where American gastronomy is concerned, there is one commodity that is rarer than locally grown black truffles or homemade foie gras. That is a chef of international repute who was born in the United States. Even rarer is such a celebrated chef who is a woman.
>
> There is, however, one here in Berkeley who could justifiably deserve such renown. Her name may not be a household word from Maine to California, but many culinary experts, both here and abroad, sing her praises without reservation.
>
> Alice Waters is chef-proprietor of Chez Panisse, a cunningly designed, somewhat raffish establishment with a noteworthy menu and kitchen. . . .[41]

It took a few years, but a sort of New American Cuisine did start to take shape in New York. William Grimes—restaurant critic for the *Times* from 1999 to 2003—writes that "the free license granted by nouvelle cuisine gained traction among a cluster of chefs strongly influenced by James Beard and the possibilities of applying French techniques to American ingredients and dishes."[42] Larry Forgione turned out distinctly American food with the precision and delicacy of nouvelle cuisine at the River Café. Alfred Portale at the Gotham Bar and Grill, Barry and Susan Wine at the Quilted Giraffe (though not at first; only as it matured), and, most significantly, David and Karen Waltuck at Chanterelle created dishes of refinement and originality in settings much less formal than any in which food of such quality had ever been seen in the city: The River Café was on a barge moored on the Brooklyn side of the East River, the Gotham in Greenwich Village, Chanterelle on a dark corner in SoHo; only the Quilted Giraffe was in Midtown.

None of the young French masters, surely, would have wished to be forced to express an opinion of any of these comparatively amateurish undertakings. Nor would the American chefs or owners who were struggling to emulate the French masters of the nouvelle cuisine have wished to know their opinions. The Americans' day would come, but not soon.

The 1980s would see an explosion of creativity in New York restaurants, and many of the chefs would be getting a grip on technique as well.

Quite a bit of this change took place only at the edge of Craig's awareness, if in it at all. In a declining industrial district below SoHo, Drew Nieporent opened Montrachet, featuring a wine list of extraordinary Burgundies (many of them at very good prices) and the cooking of a superb French-trained American chef, David Bouley. As the neighborhood grew around Montrachet, it came to be known as the Triangle Below Canal, or TriBeCa; it is now among the more fashionable districts of Manhattan, and the internal capitalization has been dropped. The Parisian brother and sister Gilbert and Maguy le Coze opened a New York branch of their Paris seafood bistro Le Bernardin, and the New York establishment, more luxurious and more ambitious than its French cousin, was such a spectacular success that the Le Cozes closed their Paris location. Le Bernardin was a fish and seafood restaurant of a quality never before even approached in New York, and it now carries three Michelin stars. Tony May's Palio and San Domenico brought an unprecedented level of luxury to Italian dining; Palio featured an extravagant, and immense, mural by Sandro Chia of the famous Tuscan horse race Il Palio di Siena.

Regions whose traditions were previously absent from the New York scene, or at best underrepresented, had proud exemplars. Arizona 206 took the traditional cooking of the American Southwest as a point of departure for experiments that were both highly creative and recognizably true to their origins. Aquavit presented Scandinavian food of the highest order in a former Rockefeller townhouse in Midtown; Aquavit would grow still more interesting under the chefship of Ethiopian-born, Swedish-raised Marcus Samuelsson. Indochine, across from the Public Theater on Lafayette Street, was perhaps only notionally Vietnamese-Cambodian, but it was the first Asian restaurant to which the downtown, trendsetting set flocked for late-night self-display and surprisingly good Asian-something hybrid food. Da Silvano's cooking was as close to pure Florentine as New York could get. Provence was perhaps not quite as Provençal, but it was close, and *très sympa*. Dawat, the creation of the glamorous Claiborne "discovery" Madhur Jaffrey—who was already a movie star when Craig made her a food star—served Indian food of great sophistication. On a lonely block of the south Village, a casual bistro named Rakel turned out astonishingly delicious food under two cooks who would later be rather better known—Thomas Keller and his sous-chef Tom Colicchio.

Mimi Sheraton liked Chanterelle, finding the dining room "romantically beautiful," the food "as delicate and graceful as the setting."[43] She hated the River Café—"a limited menu . . . but not limited enough"[44]— though that was pre-Forgione, and the place was really still all about its sensational view of Manhattan. Sheraton's review of the Quilted Giraffe showed both how badly this ambitious New York restaurant in its immaturity could misinterpret the nouvelle cuisine and with what ferocity Mimi Sheraton hated that kitchen's mangling of it:

> The Quilted Giraffe . . . is the city's newest bastion of the nouvelle cuisine—the lighter, more natural and all too often overly sweet and contrived "new cooking" . . . If you forget that fact, don't worry about it; the captain is sure to remind you. On our first visit he said "nouvelle cuisine" seven times. . . ."
>
> Combining beautifully fresh chunks of lobster and the white-fleshed fish lotte in a cream sauce with cantaloupe balls and raspberries is just a little too much gastronomic fun for us. . . .
>
> The green mint ice cream tastes like cold toothpaste and the vodka ice cream tastes like nothing at all. . . .
>
> Pretentious, self-conscious service . . . culinary travesties . . .[45]

Wham-o. One measly star. Okay, a vulgarian, *provocatrice*, whatever. Say what you like, Mimi Sheraton was standing up for the customer, even if the customer didn't shop at Bergdorf's or Brooks Brothers. And the early Quilted Giraffe really was awful. Eventually the food got good, sometimes fantastic—Barry and Susan Wine, the proprietors, came to recognize that Barry was a better impresario than chef, and they hired serious kitchen talent, which made all the difference—but the restaurant stayed a paragon of 1980s excess, a magnet for Wall Street self-parodies who bought wine by the price (the higher the better) and were so blasted on coke they couldn't taste it anyway. For all its eventual culinary virtues, in style and attitude the Quilted Giraffe was the archetype of New York affectation that Mimi Sheraton was put on this earth to call to account.*

---

* On August 21, 1981, Sheraton would find the Quilted Giraffe sufficiently improved to raise it to two stars. On January 20, 1984, Marian Burros, Sheraton's successor, gave it four.

Still she did have her blind spots, big ones, usually involving issues of social class—kind of like Craig. What really irritated her was what she took to be pretentious grandeur, where Craig would have seen simply formality, as at, for example, La Caravelle. (In her restaurant guide published in 1981, she would call Craig's friend Roger Fessaguet, the chef and co-owner of La Caravelle, "graceless and unwelcoming."[46] On the Soulé principle of composing the crowd to look like an Impressionist painting—which would definitely not have required an Anguished Activist—he probably *was* graceless and unwelcoming.) Her social-class issues were the obverse of Craig's, however: So what if she was blind to fine distinctions? She didn't give a damn. She was just barging on through life, relentless, excited, immune to embarrassment, full of beans.

The contrast was painful. Craig couldn't seem to get excited about much of anything. People? No. Henry—he took Henry to mainland China in the fall of 1978, the first sixteen days being an official gastronomic tour, Craig's first exposure to culinary life behind the Iron Curtain, but Henry went home, and the whole trip went sort of flat. Equally flat was the life Craig returned to. On August 10, 1978, the Newspaper Printing Pressmen's Union called a strike against not only the *New York Times* but also the *Post* and the *Daily News*. All the other unions but one (which had a no-strike contract) backed the pressmen, including the Newspaper Guild, of which Craig was a member.[47] Talks dragged on for almost three months, and for almost three months New York was without a daily newspaper and Craig was without a job.[48]

Craig's friends were worried about him, especially Ed Giobbi and Jacques Pépin, his closest—but more and more often their concern only irritated him. Now that he had finally arranged for Pierre and himself to be working together on an equal footing, or almost, Pierre, with his own column, and a salary of his own at last—no, he loved Pierre, Betty, the kids, he did, stop complaining. Boys? No, too ridiculous. All right, once in a while he'd cruise the Hamptons, find someone, get drunk, give pleasure; too drunk for pleasure of his own. The gay life, tra la.

Finally, on December 31, 1978, he published a quite long piece in the Sunday magazine headed "Dining Out in the New China." He was back in classic wry form:

Visitors are advised never to give gifts of substantial monetary value to a Chinese. (An outright gift of money is unthinkable. And insulting.) One publication I consulted suggested: "A few Frisbees, pictures your kids painted, old-fashioned real-ink pens and pictures of your hometown." I went to China empty-handed. I would not insult a child with a Frisbee; I don't have kids who paint; the only old-fashioned real-ink pens I know of are made by Parker and cost $50, and I was certain that no Chinese in his right mind would care to see a picture of Sunflower, Miss.

It was more a travel piece than a culinary one, and a highly idiosyncratic travel piece at that ("I managed very nicely . . . with several loose-fitting shirts"). There were no recipes, and his references to food were more often jocular, or simply peculiar, than explanatory ("a deep-fried fish that looked like a porcupine," "cold duck liver stuffed with a pigeon egg"). He recommended several restaurants that he had enjoyed and a few that he had not even seen the inside of, including "the Snake Restaurant, where live snakes are brought to the table before being cooked." That was the last that Craig's readers were to hear about his long trip to China.

A return of ennui had awaited Craig at home. In early 1979, he decided that a new house in East Hampton would surely stir his blood. He found a perfect bayfront lot on Clamshell Avenue, still in East Hampton and in fact not far from King's Point Road and with as good a view. He met a contractor at a party and seemed to have the idea that the man was an architect, which he wasn't; in any case he awarded the project to him without a second thought. A few sketches later, the house began to rise. Ed Giobbi drove out to see it under construction and nearly fainted at the sight. He went running to Craig in alarm. "Craig," he cried, "you can't even see the God-damned water from the thing. The guy is an idiot! You've got to stop him and get a real architect."

Craig just smiled his serene little rock-headed smile and said it was all going to be fine.

"Craig had this thing," says Giobbi. "Once he got attached to somebody like this, some service person, or—we'll talk about the doctor later—he just wouldn't let go, no matter what sort of incompetent or even crook the person was. He wouldn't change his mind. And so that was the house he got. It was dreadful. Made no sense at all. It was incredibly badly built, you could never heat it properly. Had a huge kitchen, to accommodate TV crews, lights, all that. Complete restaurant equipment, of course. It had an Indian tandoor, which he never used. Maybe once. It was not a comfortable kitchen, like the one on King's Point Road, it was just big. Everybody, all his friends, when they first saw this house, they were mystified. Nobody could believe—there it was, right on the beach and you couldn't see Gardiners Bay. Most of them didn't say anything to Craig. He thought it was great."

Coincident with his move to Clamshell Avenue, in September 1979, Craig gathered an immense trove of letters, photographs, clippings, travel documents, hotel bills, receipts, miscellaneous memorabilia, and what most people, though never the omnivorous archivist Howard Gotlieb, would consider junk, and Gotlieb sent his secretary, Vita Widershien, down from Boston University, to help Craig pack it all up. Gotlieb, who rightly valued telltale stuff-you-might-consider-junk over boilerplate honorific citations and pictures of grinning honorees in tuxedos, not only thanked Craig effusively but also, in the same letter, wrote, "As you know, I wish to document your life and career as fully as possible . . . so I do hope that you will continue to save everything."

Perhaps it started with this random boxing-up of these mementoes, or some other aspect of his so often looking backward. Encouraged by his fellow Mississippian and drinking buddy Willie Morris, the former editor of *Harper's Magazine*, Craig had begun to think of writing a memoir. He did not begin his work on it as a narrative: It was more a gathering of scraps, with the idea that he would eventually patch them together in some sort of order and hope that a story would emerge. In only one part of his labors at this time did he pursue a goal in an orderly fashion, and that was one that ultimately did not find its way into *A Feast Made for Laughter* at all, greatly to his and its benefit. That was his revival of the bitter one-sided genealogical war that his mother had waged against his father's side of the family in the long-shadowed past.

Seeking, in retaliation, to establish the Claibornes' social superiority over the Craigs, Craig dug deep into his father's family history. Somewhere he found a privately printed book containing a great, spreading family tree, its cover stamped in gold:

The kitchen was designed with the media in mind.

Claiborne Family Reunion
Jamestown Expo
June 18, 1907
Norfolk, Virginia
1621–1907

It was always good to establish that your people had been here a long time, and this accomplished that. Over months in various libraries he found extracts from the *Virginia Land Patents* of the colonial era showing that one William Claiborne had been born in England in 1587, had come to Virginia about 1621, had been named secretary of state in 1625, had led a campaign against the Indians in 1629, and for that leadership had been awarded a grant of five thousand acres by the crown. Somewhere he dug up an invitation to the wedding of Rosa Marie Pourciau ("of pure French [La.] heritage") and Louis B. Claiborne at the Église Ste-Marie in New Roads, Louisiana, on February 23, 1870.

Amidst Craig's heap of genealogical treasures was also an amazingly bogus family history purporting to show that the Claibornes were "lineal descendands [*sic*] of the de Toenys, standard bearers of Norway, who descended from Niord, King of Sweden 40 B.C. and through him from Odin, King of Escardia, who with an army of Goths, conquered Northern Europe, settled Sweden, and reigned and died there."[49]

§

Throughout this time he was also doing his real job, publishing his De Gustibus column weekly and his collaborative pieces with Pierre in the magazine at least twice a month, and assembling the 751-page *New New York Times Cook Book* as well, for publication in 1979. The title was a problem—people didn't seem to see that extra "new"—but Craig didn't care, as far as he was concerned they should pay better attention; and at Times Books and for that matter at the *New York Times* in general Craig Claiborne was like Lola in the song from *Damn Yankees*—whatever Claiborne wants, Claiborne gets.

Not much about *The New New York Times Cook Book* was new. Indeed it was decidedly backward-looking. "One of the happiest thoughts to cross my mind within recent years," Craig writes in the introduction,

237

itself titled "De Gustibus," "is that as food editor of the *New York Times*, I, along with Pierre Franey, have played some small role in what has often been referred to as the gastronomic revolution in America." Accompanying a collection of nostalgic photographs, many of them taken in his East Hampton kitchen and featuring such luminary visitors as Marcella Hazan, Diana Kennedy, Jean Troisgros, and Paul Bocuse, is a long pastiche of memories of Craig's past twenty years. "Call it sentiment or the approach of senility," he writes, "but I find pleasure in whiling away an afternoon in my own reflection of things past." There are short pieces, all previously published in some form, condemning cigars, iceberg lettuce, and people who try to help with the dishes. He quotes letters from readers with suggestions for adding cottage cheese to chili, letting corn stand in hot water in its shucks for seventeen hours, and thawing turkeys in the dishwasher.

There is also a story—reprinted word for word from a De Gustibus column[50]—about a woman who serves a questionably old salmon mousse to a dinner party and her kitten; sees the kitten after dinner lying unmoving on the kitchen floor; assumes therefore that she has poisoned her guests; rushes them and herself all to the hospital to have their stomachs pumped; and once home learns from a neighbor that he had run over the kitten but didn't want to disturb her dinner party by telling her in the midst of it. This Craig thought was funny.

The most significant passage in the introduction is the one in which Craig pointedly defends his diet, which was rich in fats but which he always consumed in small portions. As far as Craig was concerned, that was all he needed to know. "My weight remains generally at 158 pounds in the morning, 162 pounds before retiring, and my health is good."[51] That last statement could be disputed. He got virtually no exercise of any kind, he salted all his food extraordinarily heavily, and his alcohol consumption was literally stupefying. He did a lot of his drinking, in those days, at home, alone.

His typical intake, he actually *said* to *People* magazine, was "six margaritas before dinner (with salt-encrusted glass) and six glasses of wine during it."[52] There followed, as we know, however many stingers he needed until, like Tennessee Williams's Brick, he got "that click in my head that makes me feel peaceful . . . that turns the hot light off and the cool one on."[53]

§

One day in May of 1979, Craig was walking across Fifty-seventh Street, near his apartment in the Osborne, when he "felt some disorientation." His "balance was off and the sun suddenly seemed unbearably bright."[54]

What Craig was undergoing was a cerebral vasospasm. This means that he had already been walking around with a hemorrhaging cerebral aneurysm for probably at least a couple of weeks. A cerebral aneurysm is a thinning and ballooning of a blood vessel in the brain. Cerebral aneurysms subject to high blood pressure not uncommonly rupture and bleed, and these ruptures often eventuate in strokes.[55] By the time Craig made it to a doctor, his blood pressure was 186/112.[56] For a man his age—fifty-nine—the upper limit of normal is 140/80. He was at risk of dying of a stroke at any moment.[57]

Love and Remembrance

From 1980 to 1988 the person Craig Claiborne and the public figure known as Craig Claiborne diverged and diverged, until they met again in a sudden, horrible crash.

In the same period, two men changed everything for Craig the human being. The first was the doctor to whom he had gone, in terror, with the hemorrhage in his brain. Joseph Rechtschaffen, an internist at Doctors Hospital, was the personal physician of Craig's longtime friend Michael Tong, the owner of Shun Lee Palace. Craig told Rechtschaffen about his "bizarre appetite for salt"—so extreme that his idea of a nice soft drink was a glass of sauerkraut juice—and the doctor "frowned in a paternal sort of way and gave me the details of a diet. . . . [which] included, in addition to no salt, modified fat and modified sugar. I was to lose twenty pounds and he strongly advocated exercise. . . .

"To ease my fears that such a diet would be the equivalent of placing me in a gastronomic strait jacket, he added that I might drink alcohol in temperate amounts and that I could on occasion . . . indulge myself."[1]

Rechtschaffen then added, "But always within reason." It was too late for that, though. The doctor had left an opening wide enough for Craig to drive a truckload of salt-free margaritas through.

In the introduction to *The New New York Times Cook Book,* published in 1979, Craig had reported his weight as fluctuating between 158 and 162 pounds. Rechtschaffen's diet seemed to Craig something of a miracle. He swore off salt, and his blood pressure plunged. Barely a year after his brush with death, *Craig Claiborne's Gourmet Diet* hit the bookstores. In the introduction, Craig reported that he had in fact lost the prescribed twenty pounds, and his weight was now 150. Once again the magic of Craig's memory had achieved an outcome conceivably of greater worth than one measurable by mere arithmetic—unquenchable optimism. He'd never liked arithmetic anyway.

Among a great many other strenuous claims in the introduction to *Gourmet Diet,* Craig wrote, "I have totally eliminated margaritas and stingers from my list of acceptable alcoholic potables."[2]

"Oh, right, oh sure," groans Ed Giobbi, who remembers Craig's personal gourmet diet vividly. "What he wrote in that book and the way he lived his life were completely different things. That doctor just wanted to get into Craig's social life, and naturally Craig wanted to please him. All of a sudden that guy and his wife were out in East Hampton all the time. Craig was good about the salt, that's true, but as far as he was concerned, he could drink all he wanted."[3]

"He wasn't hiding it," Craig's Long Island friend Vivian Bucher remembers. "The doctor and his wife would go out to dinner with Craig. They would drink together."[4]

"And he was starting to get nasty to everybody, including me," Giobbi recalls. "And Ellie."

It must be understood that Ed Giobbi was one of the three closest friends Craig had in the world. The others were Pierre Franey and Jacques Pépin. His relationship with Pierre had begun to fray, and would eventually tear apart, but Giobbi and Pépin would stand by Craig until the end of his days. Craig did not make it easy for them. In his autobiography Pépin writes:

> I first noticed the change in Craig one night when he, Pierre, and I joined another friend, Ann Seranne* . . . to see about finding a kennel to house the championship Yorkshire terriers Ann owned. Ann was a beautiful, sensitive woman, and for no reason at all, Craig began ranting at her, somehow interpreting her desire to have a first-class home for her dogs as a severe character flaw.

* The reader will recall that it was Seranne who gave Craig his first job in New York when she was editor of *Gourmet,* and who was the first to publish his work, in the same magazine.

"You're a consummate control freak, Ann," he said. "Everything has to be just perfect for you, doesn't it. You have to be right all the time. Well, people are getting tired of you. . . . "

Several times, I tried to interrupt, but Craig raised his voice and continued his tirade. By then, Ann was crying. If anything, that spurred Craig to greater heights of insult.

This turned out not to be an isolated incident. Everywhere I went in New York, I heard stories of Craig's erratic behavior when drunk. . . .[5]

So much for Craig's professed belief that he would never knowingly humiliate anybody.

"That was when he started treating Henry Creel so badly," adds Elinor Giobbi. "Who knows why. Henry was always so nice, such a gentleman, and Craig would just snarl at him over nothing.

"And me too. We were talking about our therapy as usual. He'd just gotten a new therapist. He was always changing therapists, though he also always wanted to be friends with them—he'd invite them out for the weekend."[6]

"Remember the crazy one?" Ed puts in. "He had this one shrink who would act out Mickey Mouse and Donald Duck at parties. There was another one who beat his wife."[7]

"All Craig ever wanted was for them to make him feel better," Elinor recalls. "Anyway, it was early in the morning, and Craig was very hungover. I was teasing him about his drinking. He went after me so hard, it was terrifying, he was boring into me. I couldn't stand it, I went to our bedroom. Finally he came down and apologized profusely, but it was terrible. I felt at the time that he thought I was like his mother in some way.

"And he started bullying Pierre. That was intolerable. They'd loved each other for so long. Craig started trying to control everything Pierre did. This was after Pierre had his column, and he was a little independent, and Craig was jealous. Jacques Pépin was always the diplomat, he'd try to cool Craig off, but pretty soon he'd be back at it. Pierre was very patient, but Betty Franey was furious. She was already very tired of losing Pierre every weekend of the world. She came to the dinner parties sometimes, but she didn't really enjoy them, and when Craig started drinking so much, she *really* didn't like that, and she *really* didn't want her children to be around it."

"By that time," wrote Pépin, "Pierre's column . . . had become a popular fixture; he was writing books with other collaborators such as Bryan Miller;* and he was branching out into television, working for PBS. Essentially, he was becoming more successful than Craig, and that created a serious strain on their friendship."[8]

"Pierre wrote that book—*The Sixty-minute Gourmet*—without even telling Craig," says Florence Aaron.[9]

§

Craig's alienation of those closest to him set the stage for the entrance of the second man, also a physician. Fifty-seventh Street is one of New York's great stages, and it seems to have been especially so for Craig. It was, of course, his home address—the Osborne stood at the corner of Fifty-seventh Street and Seventh Avenue. Fifty-seventh Street had been the setting for his near-death moment the previous spring. Now it was the scene of another life-changing drama. It was July 3, 1980. Craig was walking east, and Dr. James Dinneen was walking west, and their eyes met.[10]

Sometimes it is that simple. You don't need theories of pheromones or "gay-dar" or the intervention of the gods. For an infinitesimal instant Craig and Jim looked into each other's souls.

Craig being Craig, it was going to be simple for about that long. To start with, Jim Dinneen was married—to the heiress of a major fortune. He lived far away, in Florida. He had six kids, and an arrow-straight life in which he was deeply embedded. Dinneen was now retired from the practice of medicine; he had been the medical director of the Charles Pfizer Company. He was now president of a real estate holding company, Eastern Diversified Inc., which had developed industrial parks, shopping centers, and Merritt Island, the home of NASA's Kennedy Space Center. He was also: president of the investment firm Sunstand Inc.; founding director of the Trust Company of Florida; a trustee of Winter Park Memorial Hospital; a trustee of Holiday Hospital; vice president of the Florida Symphony; a trustee of Trinity Preparatory School; a mem-

---

* Bryan Miller was a food writer and restaurant critic for the *Times*; he became the chief restaurant critic in October 1984.

ber of the board of the Orange County, Florida, YMCA; a member of the board of the Salvation Army; a member of the President's Council of Rollins College; a member of the board of directors of the United Children's Fund; a founding member of the Committee of 200, "dedicated to the orderly development of Central Florida"; vice president of the Central Florida Development Committee; a charter member of the Central Florida Tennis Confederation; a founder of the Orlando Racquet and Tennis Club; active in Republican politics,[11] and a generous donor to Republican candidates.[12]

Craig did not yet know any of these things about Jim Dinneen save that he was married; many he would never know. It seems very likely that none of the people in these organizations knew anything of Dinneen's secret life. His wife and at least one son did know, or did come to know.

Craig in a way *liked* the fact that Jim was married. He had always prided himself on his talent for luring men across the divide. "He thought he was the first man ever to have seduced Dinneen," Florence Aaron recalls. "I thought that seemed—doubtful."

This was no mere seduction, however. This was love. It was love that Craig had never before known more than the first few feet of the infinite depth of. It took him out of himself, and had the additional benefit of getting him away from his pesky friends. Because their rendezvous were necessarily secret, Craig and Jim nearly always met somewhere besides New York or East Hampton. Jim's money provided first-class tickets for getaways to Martinique, Guadeloupe, San Francisco, the luxurious Golden Door spa in the California desert (where Craig actually did give up drinking for a week).

Craig spent Christmas of 1980 in St. Barts as usual, and with Henry Creel, but now he and Henry were in separate bungalows.[13] By March of 1981, Craig was entering Jim's name in his pocket calendar as "*Dinneen!*" The entry for July 24, 1981, is DINEEN'S B'DAY [*sic,* misspelled], circled five times.

His relationship with Jim seemed to embolden Craig in many ways. He told the gay news magazine *The Advocate* that he was "involved with a man his own age, and they both believe things will work out for them in the long run." Craig added a brave prophecy: "We've already planned that New Year's Eve at the advent of 2000 we'll be at Windows on the

World celebrating with Champagne. And we'll be spending the rest of the evening *very close*."[14]

Craig was already at work on his memoir when he met Jim, and in it he was going to declare his homosexuality to the world; perhaps more important, he was going to declare it to Mississippi.

He started devoting more of his columns to Southern food—Paul Prudhomme's nouveau Cajun,[15] a reprinted 1942 Southern cookbook by Marjorie Kinnan Rawlings,[16] even his mother's beaten biscuits.[17] He was in rapture over one Savannah bachelor's deviled crab, chicken pilau, hoppin' john, and chess pie. On the same day[18] he published another piece on Mrs. Wilkes's Boarding House, also in Savannah, of which he declared, "There is something warm and congenial about a Southern boarding house (I should know; I grew up in one)." He delighted in her okra casserole, Brunswick stew, black-eyed peas, collard greens, sweet potatoes flavored with orange, cornbread, biscuits, sweet iced tea, banana pudding, and butterscotch pie. It was not hard to feel a certain maternal magnetism at work, and soon he had also been drawn to a family reunion in Tennessee.

Now he was prepared to take on Mississippi itself. In 1981 catfish farming was the first good new agricultural idea the Delta had seen in a long, long time, and it was booming, nowhere more so than right around Craig's birthplace of Sunflower and his hometown of Indianola. (In the early 1980s, Mississippi was producing 150 million pounds of catfish a year.[19] By 1990, it would be 400 million.[20] Today, thanks largely to competition from Vietnam, a good many of those ponds are derelict mudholes.[21]) Invited to have a look, Craig saw three appealing angles right away: an idea for a column, a chance to visit with his sister Augusta, and the prospect of finding out what it would feel like to breathe that sultry, haunted Delta air again.

He returned to East Hampton with thirty pounds of frozen fillets, where in addition to good ol' fried catfish and hushpuppies he and Pierre worked up recipes for catfish *meunière*, catfish *au vin blanc*, and catfish *Grenobloise*.[22] More important, he brought back the redolence of sin, shame, and anger that would fuel what he was then planning to call *A Matter of Taste . . . and Distaste*. He was by God ready to tell those people in the Delta not just that he was gay. He was going to unfold some tales of Chicago that would harrow up their souls, freeze their

246

Back in Indianola, at the corner
of Craig and Claiborne.

old blood, make their eyes start from their spheres. He was going to tell them how he groped his own daddy.

In the finished book he details a memory of a sort of quasi-sexual encounter with his father in language so opaque as to call the incident's very existence into question. He writes that they were occupying the same bed when young Craig—age unstated—"discovered his [father's] fingers enfolded around the throttle of his lust," the result of which was, in Craig, "an all-engulfing gushing of adrenalin, the likes of which I have never known before or since. It was as though all of my being were inundated with warm waves of ecstasy, the sensation of drowning and awakening shaken on a safe but hitherto unexplored island. . . . I continued to lie with him for countless nights that ensued. And when I would hear

Craig with his sister, Augusta Claiborne Barnwell,
at the house they grew up in, in Indianola.

the breathing that indicated sleep on his part, I would begin an exploration of his body. The affair was never consummated and he never once
acknowledged his awareness of my encroachments."[23]

Okay, but what *happened*? Beyond these purple abstractions, he never
said. Before publishing the story in his memoir, he seems never to have
told a living soul one word about any sort of sexual relationship with his
father. The sheer implausibility—his father *sleeping* through this groping
night after night?—plus the story's placement close to the beginning of
the book, may suggest that this memory was more nightmare than fact.

It should also be remembered that Craig loved to shock people. There
was a sort of jolting binary oscillation in his self-presentation. Most of
the time he was the composed and courtly gentleman, perfectly dressed
and groomed, almost prim in manner, then suddenly he'd be grabbing
some poor dinner guest by the balls and cackling like a maniac. Did
these lurches in behavior correspond to some sudden interior shifts in
identity? One of his several psychotherapists might have had some idea,
but for anyone else it can be only speculation.

So-called gay liberation wasn't making life particularly easier. You didn't get not-mixed-up overnight. Here was Jim, the straight Republican family man, sending him greeting cards with unbelievably obscene photographs.[24] What was Craig supposed to make of that? And now just when everybody was coming out of the closet, just when it finally seemed safe to come out, AIDS was rampaging through gay communities. People were *angry*. Craig was angry, dejected, disoriented. What was he angry at? He himself didn't seem to know.

Maybe the memoir would help. He kept jabbing at it. Sometimes he would photocopy stuff from his columns and literally paste it into the manuscript. He made little attempt at anything like a flowing narrative. On one page he scribbled, "Give description of her here taken from her obit." He would sit at the typewriter and hammer out single paragraphs, not knowing where they might fit. Some he did not use but still thought worth keeping for the BU archive:

It may be a minor or moot point, but almost every food and/or restaurant critic about whose sex life I am familiar, is dedicated to the pleasures of oral sex.

To my innocent mind, Chicago might have been Sodom and Gomorrah, and I lived it up with innocent abandon. Of the favorite sayings in those days was "Never put off until Gomorrah what you can do in sodomy." When I heard that phrase I would break up with laughter. . . . Lest anyone take me literally, let me hasten to add that while I then did have the morals of a billy goat (some people say I still do), sodomy did and does not count among my pleasures.

I had no more control over the shape of my life than a man in the moon, to choose one of my mother's precise phrases. . . . It is not that I have not been faced with and made choices. I have. . . . But the essential me, in its formation, I have had very little to do with. That began long ago in my cradle in an alien land called Mississippi.[25]

The published book retained a decided patchwork pattern. The text occupied only 227 of its 400-odd pages; the rest was bulked up with "My Recommended Cookbook Library"— his own first and then, accompanied by brief prose sketches, 114 more, including Henry's *Cooking for One Is Fun*—and then "My One Hundred Favorite Recipes." The memoir proper contained just enough shocking confession to horrify his family. The really grim stuff, like the scenes with his father, have such a dream-like quality that it is not unreasonable to attribute them to fantasy, to Craig's notoriously unreliable memory, or even to the sort of "recovered memory" that at that time was being "discovered"—falsely—in adults who believed they had been sexually abused as children. (Sometimes they had been, sometimes they hadn't, but the "memories" frequently turned out to have been generated in their unconscious minds.[26])

Craig drew the title he had ultimately chosen, *A Feast Made for Laughter*, from Ecclesiastes 10:19. The whole of the verse reverberates perplexingly: "A feast is made for laughter, and wine maketh merry; but money answereth all things." What was he thinking? Arthur Gelb says, "Money was very important for Craig, and he never thought the *Times* paid him enough"[27]—but Craig says nothing in the book about money, one way or another. The simplest answer is that he liked the first half of the verse and didn't worry his head about the rest; but he did, after all, quote the whole thing as the book's epigraph. It's a conundrum.

§

To launch *A Feast Made for Laughter*, Craig staged a spectacular blowout at the house on Clamshell Avenue, and his newspaper covered it as a major event. CBS and ABC television did, too.[28]

It was September 4, 1982, Craig's sixty-second birthday—and just a few days short of the twenty-fifth anniversary of his first published piece in the *New York Times*. There were thirty-six chefs all cooking at once. The Clamshell kitchen was huge, but nowhere near big enough. Neighbors and friends had volunteered kitchens of their own, guest rooms, cottages, tables and chairs. Two hundred guests were invited and four hundred showed up.

Pierre, nominally, was in charge. "There are just too many people here," he said.

Craig said, "I stopped saying no days ago, and I figured if the food runs out, too bad; if the Champagne runs out, too bad."[29]

Ed Giobbi roasted a lamb on a spit. Jacques Pépin made ceviche and stuffed it into watermelons carved in his antic signature style. Also cheffing were Roger Fessaguet, Jean Vergnes, Alice Waters, Maida Heatter, and Madhur Jaffrey. Diana Kennedy flew in from Mexico, Roger Vergé from the south of France. Paul Prudhomme drove all the way from New Orleans hauling a house trailer converted into a restaurant kitchen; he brought two hundred pounds of redfish to blacken.

The menu was wildly various: coconuts stuffed with clams and green chiles, sole *Dugléré*, fried catfish and hushpuppies, bouillabaisse, clams in blini, "Chinese ratatouille," tortellini, lasagna, Peking noodles, turkey mole poblano, smoked chicken, *rôti de veau*, Brazilian *churrasco*, Indonesian beef, English trifle, twenty cakes, seven hundred cookies, ten loaves of bread overnighted from Poilâne in Paris with "Craig Claiborne" baked into the crusts. Sam Aaron brought four thousand dollars' worth of wine. Music was supplied by the Sometimes Swing Band under the leadership of a local painter by the name of Larry Rivers.[30]

If only the reception of *A Feast Made for Laughter* could have lived up to its launch party's glory.

"Craig Claiborne should have stuck to cookbooks," read a not unrepresentative review, in *Newsday*. "The private matters aired in public and the rambling long-windedness could perhaps be forgiven. But the uncharitable reader will distrust some of the experiences Claiborne describes, as well."[31]

Eliot Fremont-Smith—long a distinguished book critic for none other than the *New York Times*—wrote, "You ingest *A Feast Made for Laughter* smiling, if at all, in deep embarrassment."[32]

Craig and Pierre entertained the writer for *Time* in East Hampton, and gave him of their best, doubtless including a fine vintage or two. "So light and joyous is his touch when he writes about food, and so much of the praise redirected toward his talented colleague, French chef Pierre Franey, that his self-beguilement seems no more than just," their well-oiled admirer wrote. "Claiborne's present happiness is infectious, and this makes his book, on balance, a rare pleasure to read."[33] Note how "self-beguilement" sort of slips in there.

When one of its own published a book, the daily *Times* always assigned an outside writer to review it. For *Feast* they chose the movie critic Rex Reed, who apparently had never written anything about food in his life, or anything else having anything to do with anything in Craig

Claiborne's world. Reed allowed that "Some of the book's revelations must have hurt the author . . . [but it is] the only autobiography I have ever read that made me hungry."[34]

In the *New York Times Book Review,* the eminently well-qualified Betty Fussell wrote, rather strangely, that Craig "confesses [that] he owes his fame and fortune as our foremost gastronome, restaurant critic and progenitor of America's post–World War II revolution in food to the fact that he is a yokel and a gooney bird." She also, however, provided a readily clippable blurb: "It's a funny and touching and fascinating story of a loner who miraculously finds a home."[35]

The author must have found some comfort in that one, at least. But Craig was accustomed to selling a lot of books. *The New York Times Cook Book,* for example, after twenty-one years in print, had earned him $32,000 in the first quarter of 1982 alone. In the same three months, royalties from his *Menu Cook Book* of 1966 were $3,000, from the 1971 *International* $13,000. *Craig Claiborne's Gourmet Diet* was on its way toward a quarter of a million copies. Even poor little *Cooking with Herbs and Spices,* now nineteen years old, was still good for three or four thousand bucks a year. In that quarter alone, Craig's total earnings had been $267,000. And now, just before Christmas of 1982, he learned that the sales of *A Feast Made for Laughter* amounted to all of 31,142 copies.[36]

§

For some time now Craig had found that speaking at charity events suited him very nicely, and in these years he increased the pace. He liked how he looked in black tie, he had a whole line of patter that suited any occasion, and wherever he spoke, his standing as the undisputed premier of the food world was sparklingly reinforced. Often he would act as a judge of some sort of cooking contest as part of the affair. Often there'd be an interview in the local paper.

> He is an impeccable figure of a man. His posture is steeled, the cut of his tuxedo perfect. His body is lean and trim. . . . He is told how he looks with his much-publicized weight loss. But he shakes the comment off, confiding, "I'm tired, very, very tired. I stayed up too late last night and drank too much."[37]

Sometimes the public man's artful candor would slip from his grasp in an interview, and the private Craig stand embarrassingly exposed:

"If I'm in a crowd, I tend to drink too much because of my insecurity, which still persists, though to a lesser degree. People respect the fact that I can't go out, and so they don't invite me anymore."[38]

Which wasn't true, but was a window into the man's dark interior.

Craig adopted the March of Dimes as his main charity, though he liked Citymeals-on-Wheels as well, and Colonial Williamsburg, and the Fund for Animals. The New York Public Library was very grand, supported by the city's oldest, richest families. Guild Hall of East Hampton was grand in its own way, and they were neighbors. Obviously he couldn't turn them down. And the New York–Madrid Sister Committee—who knows how he got into that?[39] He also became a popular and passionate speaker on behalf of the Gay Men's Health Crisis organization.

Craig liked the microphone, but not the camera.

Craig loved to perform before a crowd, but he was terrified of the television camera. Thanks to her consistently amusing and genuinely useful series *The French Chef* and *Julia Child & Company,* Julia Child had been much more famous than Craig Claiborne for some years, and now Pierre and Jacques had both taken to the medium with ease. Craig wrote to the lawyer and all-round promoter and connector Mort Janklow, who was trying to lend him a hand: "I do not feel an aggressive desire to become involved in any TV project that would require special planning and preparation, complicated procedures and long hours. At my age and my emotional fatigue, real or imagined, I simply cannot become involved."[40]

Yet he had to get involved in television in some way, and he knew it. The public Craig Claiborne respected obligation—the good Southern boy inside him trying to hew to duty. Pierre, as ever all discipline, was equally stalwart. Putting their differences aside, therefore, Craig and Pierre buckled down and jointly produced a step-by-step guide to the preparation of four complete menus, for the first time in two media: a lavishly illustrated book and, yes, a video. The food shows zero influence of the nouvelle cuisine. The first dish, a fish mousse, requires two cups of heavy cream. Its *sauce bonne femme*—six tablespoons of butter, four tablespoons of flour, and thick enough, if flung, to slide down a wall very slowly—calls for an additional cup of cream. That's for four servings

The video quality barely rises to the level of amateurish. Craig, every word apparently scripted, sounds like a school kid reading a book report. When he's behind the typewriter or there's action on the counter, the clattering of the keys or the cookware drowns out his voice. Pierre, too far from the microphone, doesn't have much to say but when he does, he shouts. Neither of them ever cracks a smile. Neither of them ever looks at the other, or at the camera. It is absolutely terrible.

Any professional TV producer, anybody period, especially if thinking about the contrast of Julia Child on screen—booming, laughing, having the time of her life—would have said it was hopeless, Craig, do please go back to books. But a couple of years later, sans Pierre, sans companion book, Video Craig was back, with East Hampton scenery, tables set, a more or less relaxed informal interview in which he reminisced about Sunflower and his mother, and a soundtrack of corny canned music. The result was the really not so terrible *Craig Claiborne's Video Cookbook.*

Craig was a trouper, and so was Pierre. Whatever their private friction may have been, they remained united in their admiration of the nouvelle cuisine and in their belief that its principles had much to offer American home cooks. Their excellent *Cooking with Craig Claiborne and Pierre Franey*, published in 1983, offered "the nouvelle cuisine recipes of such distinguished European chefs as Roger Vergé of the Moulin de Mougins above Cannes; Eckart Witzigmann of the Aubergine in Munich; Alain Senderens of L'Archestrate in Paris; and Gérard Boyer of Chez Boyer in Reims."[41] Senderens's *homard à la vanille* (lobster roasted with a vanilla-scented cream sauce), undeniably a masterpiece, was wonderfully described by Craig as "a triumph of taste over logic."[42]

Most of the dishes also continued Craig's adherence to low salt, and the recipes were also "not wholly without butter and cream . . . but we have cut down the amount of these ingredients to a more reasonable degree." The book also featured "a keener appreciation of the American regional heritage."[43]

These were the days of the Reagan regime, and Americanism was in the air. When the United States was to play host to the Ninth Assembly of World Industrialized Powers—known as the G8—on Memorial Day weekend of 1983 in Williamsburg, Virginia, the White House asked Craig to plan all-American menus for the whole three-day meeting:

> How, I wondered, will Prime Minister Yasuhiro Nakasone of Japan feel about shoo-fly pie? Would President François Mitterrand of France stand still for pork barbecue?
>
> I invited to assist in this adventure [Paul] Prudhomme, chef-owner of K-Paul's Restaurant in New Orleans and one of the foremost authorities on Creole and Cajun cooking; [Zarela] Martinez, a highly respected Tex-Mex cook from El Paso; [Wolfgang] Puck, the young Los Angeles chef whose innovations with American fare are widely admired; Maida Heatter, an expert on desserts; Wayne Monk of Lexington, N.C., referred to by many as the barbecue king of North Carolina; Tom Slough of Jackson, Miss., a businessman whom I consider the best catfish cook in the country, and Leo Steiner, owner of the Carnegie Delicatessen in Manhattan.[44]

At the end of what had been a touchy and contentious summit, the *New York Times* Quotation of the Day, from the president's deputy chief of staff, Michael K. Deaver, was, "They loved the gumbo."[45]

Bringing American food to these sophisticated foreigners was one thing. Translating the nouvelle cuisine into the American vernacular was another, and teaching Americans to get it right—to exclude the froufrou and fraud that seemed to dog its every step—was hardest of all, but Craig was determined to do it. His first great difficulty was that it was already so widely bastardized and therefore so widely misunderstood. He addressed the problem in a passionate essay prompted by a conversation in a sauna with a stranger who had asked him, "What do you think's going to happen to cooking over the next ten years?"

Craig's answer had been prompt: "Nouvelle cuisine."

The piece was one of his best. "I feel strongly obliged to take issue with any and all of my colleagues—and they are legion—who tend to disparage, damn, and belittle the whole notion of nouvelle cuisine," he wrote. "I simply do not understand the naïveté of those supposed professionals who maintain that 'traditional' cuisine remains the true and unalterable genius of French (and therefore the supreme) cooking."

He went on to deprecate the "book-bound and straightjacketed" haute cuisine that had been handed down nearly unaltered from Escoffier, and remained the same, whether in "Burgundy, Provence, Paris, or the so-called French kitchens of Manhattan, Fort Wayne, Ind.,* or Singapore." He did believe that a grounding in the classics was essential, also that the nouvelle cuisine, in skilled hands, could allow chefs "to be innovative to the limits of their imagination."

Craig recognized the distortions and misunderstandings that the nouvelle cuisine was so vulnerable to. But he believed that in an age of declining formality, of increasing individual freedom, of greater health-consciousness, the nouvelle cuisine "liberate[s] all of us from a monstrous thou-shalt-not way of thinking, and that . . . it will be increasingly innovative, endless in its possibilities. . . ."[46]

§

---

* What was it with Craig and Fort Wayne? This may remain a mystery for the ages.

When you get to the actual contents of the book supposed to body forth Craig's passion for the nouvelle cuisine—the aforementioned *Cooking with Craig Claiborne and Pierre Franey*—the nouvelle cuisine is there, intermittently, but Craig's habitual pan-global eclecticism easily trumps any thematic focus. *Dindonneau en demi-deuil* swims, truffled cream and all, in the same great ocean as chicken gumbo, tandoori chicken, *gai yang,* and chickens *cacciatore, paprikash,* and fricassee. Alongside the truly nouvelle *filets de poissons au beurre blanc, filets de sole enrobés de laitues,* and Taillevent's seafood sausage are deep-fried catfish, deep-fried crab-and-pork balls, and a po' boy sandwich requiring twenty-four deep-fried oysters to serve two.

Craig seemed to be having another of his second winds. Perhaps it was love that had energized him—meaning Jim. Perhaps it was his low-salt diet, which had even cleared up the red blotches that had formerly appeared on his face in times of stress; they had embarrassed him for years. It was not that he was drinking any less. Perhaps it was just that he had taken command of himself again, and that was what had made those other good things possible.

Then one day suddenly the light was too bright, he reeled, he was falling, no, just kneeling, just to catch a breath, just to catch his balance. He awoke, no, he half-awoke, sedated, in Doctors Hospital.

It was just a passing thing, Rechtschaffen said.

All right. He let it pass, and went on.

The one hundredth Gourmet Gala of the March of Dimes Birth Defects Foundation was another all-star multi-chef tribute to Craig Claiborne. Craig could hardly believe that he'd done almost fifty of them—judging amateur cooks, smiling, smiling, giving his talk again and again, town after town. Raised a hell of a lot of money. Still, this was sensational, more than he deserved. He had to struggle not to cry.

There really was no end to Pierre's generosity—he put the whole thing together. And Warner LeRoy—Warner gave up a whole night's revenue at Tavern on the Green. And so many of the chefs Craig loved—Roger Fessaguet of course, Michael Tong of course, Jean-Jacques Rachou from La Côte Basque, André Soltner from Lutèce, Christian Delouvrier from Maurice, Alain Sailhac from Le Cirque, Seppi Renggli from The Four Seasons, Barry Wine from the Quilted Giraffe, Michel Fitoussi from 24 Fifth, Zarela Martinez from her new place, Georges Perrier from Le Bec-

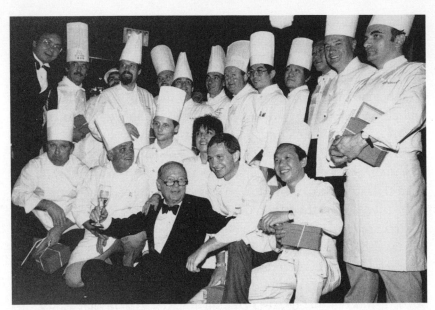

Craig loved chefs and they loved him.

Fin in Philadelphia, Jean Banchet from Le Français outside Chicago. Sweet Paul Prudhomme had come all the way up from New Orleans again. Seven courses, six wines, Cognac, and framboise from dear Sam Aaron, bless his heart.

And the crowd—this was it, the best of New York, all he had dreamed for himself. A violinist and an off-key tenor serenaded him, so loud he couldn't hear a word his tablemate Beverly Sills was saying. There were mimes in silly costumes, narrow-beaked Knickerbocker grandees, helmet-haired society dames double-air-kissing, Lauren Bacall and Pauline Trigère, Carroll O'Connor and the Sarnoffs, Mayor Ed Koch, ex-Mayor John Lindsay. Sydney Gruson was the chairman of the whole shebang and also happened to be chairman of the New York Times Company.

They called it "The Great Chefs Honor Craig Claiborne: A Personal Remembrance." *Remembrance?* I'm not but sixty-four years old, how come this is all like I'm already dead?

Well, memories. Memories were his stock in trade now. *Craig Claiborne's Memorable Meals* was beautifully published in 1985 not by the

Ed Giobbi.

skinflint New York Times Company but by E. P. Dutton, with a wine-red linen cover, thick, soft paper, and as much color as he wanted. It was illustrated with the lovely watercolors that Jacques Pépin and Ed Giobbi had painted in his leather-bound memory books. Each menu recalled a particular, truly memorable meal. One was an elaborate *dîner à deux* with Seppi Renggli when a blizzard had blacked out Craig's power and none of the guests could make it through the snow. Another had been a clambake for fifty to benefit George McGovern's campaign for the presidency and end the God-damned Vietnam War. There was the Christmas Day feast he had improvised for people he'd barely met on St. Barts, for which somehow he'd managed to find and serve fresh oysters, pâtés, terrines, prosciutto, *boudins créoles, poussins rôtis, salade niçoise,* French cheeses, good bread, an authentic *bûche de Noël,* fine Burgundies and Bordeaux; he had required each guest, regardless of age, to bring a bottle of Champagne. And how could he omit his giddy dance to the "Jet Song" from *West Side Story* and subsequent headfirst (and head-splitting) descent of the spiral stairs?

In May 1986 Craig got a little job for big bucks giving talks on an S.S. *Norway* cruise. Among his numerous inexplicable but eloquent donations to the archive at Boston University are his bar bills from that voyage. On May 17th he had five drinks at the ship's bar; May 18th, seven; May 19th, seven; May 20th, seven; May 21st, seven. With his meals there was also wine. He saved the note a steward had slipped under his stateroom door the first night: "Dear Passenger, We Sincerely Regret That Your Luggage Has Been Lost."

§

The day after Craig's return home from the S.S. *Norway* cruise, on May 23, 1986, a car struck and killed Henry Creel. Henry left Craig everything he owned.

§

Craig went on.

"It is my belief that we have reached a plateau in our culinary borrowings,[47] he wrote. "Restaurants that serve so-called back-to-basics fare—some call it mom-and-pop food—are proliferating."[48]

In *The United States of Arugula,* David Kamp quotes Bryan Miller, who had become the *Times*'s chief restaurant critic in 1984: "His writing deteriorated terribly. It got so bad that the desk wrote it. It was like staccato notes."[49]

It wasn't only the quality of his work that declined, it was the quantity. Throughout his career at the *New York Times* up through the 1970s, Craig had published between two and three pieces a week, week after week, sometimes long ones, as well as sixteen cookbooks. In 1980 he had had 128 pieces in the paper. Suddenly, in 1981, the number fell to sixty. He continued at just over an article a week until 1986, when he had only forty-three.

On January 25, 1987, Craig was admitted to Doctors Hospital on East End Avenue. On January 26, his pocket calendar records "surgery," but no other record seems to survive. In the light of later events, it is possible that he had suffered some sort of cardiac event, perhaps a heart attack, and required the surgery to repair a lesion or unblock an artery. By February 3, Craig had moved to the hospital at Southampton, Long Island. A month later, on March 2, 1987, his calendar notes "physical therapy." There are no other records.

On April 23, 1987, his calendar notes for the first time ever that he had a "meeting" at the *New York Times*. Through April and May and the first half of June, many pages of the calendar are blank. The entry for June 14 is "Vacation Ends Tomorrow."

A letter on the stationery of Galef and Jacobs, Attorneys, dated June 15, 1987, states that as of June 3, 1987, Claiborne-Franey Productions was dissolved. Thenceforward Craig Claiborne would have one company and Pierre Franey another, each to receive one-half of any joint book royalties, etc.

Craig's calendar entry for July 29, 1987, is "Tuinal / Dalmane." Tuinal is a combination of two barbiturates, used as a sedative and sleep aid;[50] it "promotes physical and psychological dependency and carries a high risk of overdose."[51] Dalmane is a benzodiazepine (in the same family as Valium), also used as a sleep aid.[52] Craig was getting his prescription medications from Dr. Joseph Rechtschaffen.

"Jim was giving him drugs, too," says Ed Giobbi. "Including cocaine. Craig told me so himself."[53]

On June 30, 1987, Craig was called to another meeting at the *Times*.

Calendar, August 3, 1987: "Rechtschaffen Halcion, Tuinal, Dalmane." Halcion is another benzodiazepine.[54]

On August 12, 1987, *Craig Claiborne's Southern Cooking* was published. "Nothing rekindles my spirits, gives comfort to my heart and mind, more than a visit to Mississippi," he wrote in the introduction. He went on to remember his childhood with unalloyed fondness, his mother in particular. Transformed from the monster she always used to be, she now had a "fantastic palate." "Where Southern food is concerned," he wrote, "I lived in the best of all possible worlds." As he had done before, he referred to Miss Kathleen as "aristocratic," though this time he enclosed the word in quotation marks. The men in that faraway fairyland "wore white linen suits" and the ladies "carried parasols to guard their skin against that burning Mississippi sun." And now "Perhaps the most prized possession in my reference library . . . is the manuscript notebook compiled for me by my mother when I returned from the Navy. . . . "[55]

Craig's appointment calendar for 1987 contains these entries as well:

August 26: "Bile Test."
October 22: "meeting NYT."
October 23: "meeting NYT."
December 12: "to Mexico."

From December 18 to December 26, 1987, Craig's adored former destroyer escort captain, John Smits, this time accompanied by his wife, joined Craig at the Garza Blanca Beach Club in Puerto Vallarta to share his two-bedroom villa for the Christmas holiday.

On December 28, 1987, Craig was back in New York in time to fly to Paris with Jim Dinneen, where they had a suite at the Hôtel San Régis, in the Eighth Arrondissement. They stayed there three nights, for which the bill was 6,275 francs—2,123 of today's U.S. dollars, including 875 francs (= $295) for items from the *frigobar* in the room. They dined at L'Ami Louis and at Craig's beloved Taillevent. For New Year's Eve they flew to Nice and drove on to Monte Carlo for the nouvelle cuisine of the hottest young chef in France, Alain Ducasse. By January 3 they were back in New York. Their plane tickets had cost $4,623 each, equivalent to $8,754 today.

In the year 1987, Craig Claiborne's byline appeared only twenty-three times in the *New York Times*. Meanwhile, food writers and food publications were proliferating. Every general-interest magazine seemed to carry frequent articles about food. *Gourmet, Food & Wine,* and *Bon Appétit* all had large and growing bases of subscribers. Magazines such as *Travel & Leisure* and *Condé Nast Traveler* more and more frequently focused on gastronomic destinations. Virtually every major newspaper in the United States had not just a restaurant critic but a whole weekly section devoted to cooking, dining out, shopping for food, chefs, farmers, wines and spirits. The writers and editors were often young, and excited, pursuing the latest hot thing. Chefs, while often less skillful than flashy, had become celebrities. Trend-chasers clamored for reservations at the star chefs' restaurants, and, as the stock market boomed, fueled by a mania for new technology, the newly affluent spent more and more

on fashionable food and wine. If Craig had been paying attention, he would have found most of the writing, the attitude, the clamor, and, God knows, the culinary creativity utterly hollow, and he would have been right. But he wasn't paying attention. He was hardly doing anything.

He drank. Time passed.

His editors could hardly not notice. Even Arthur Gelb didn't speak up for him now. Craig Claiborne was one of the most respected members of the staff of the *New York Times,* an eminence, an icon. But he wasn't producing.

Calendar entry, January 14, 1988: "NYT meeting."

Then every so often Craig would rouse himself from his torpor, having realized that something of genuine importance was going on:

> In the late 1940s, it was Fernand Point of La Pyramide in Vienne; in the 50s, Paul Bocuse, who owns the restaurant that bears his name in Lyons; in the 60s, Michel Guérard, installed at his restaurant in Eugénie-les-Bains, and in the 70s, Frédy Girardet, the owner and chef of the restaurant named for him in Crissier, Switzerland.
>
> Today, connoisseurs of fine food are trumpeting the name of Alain Ducasse, the 31-year-old chef at the Louis XV restaurant in the magnificent Hôtel de Paris in Monte Carlo.[56]

That is an excerpt from the only piece that Craig published in January 1988. He would publish another in February, one each in March and April, and two in May. His appointment calendar entries for 1988 are infrequent as well.

> February 11: "NYT meeting."
> March 28: "Pierre."
> March 29: "Jim."
> April 6: "Jim."
> April 7, 8, 9: "to SF."
> April 13: "meeting?"
> May 1: "Giobbi—marriage—Open House."

"I was married to Kevin Bone on May 1, 1988, at the house in Katonah," Eugenia Bone remembers. "Craig was there. A whole bunch from

Craig's cheffy crowd cooked. My mother and father planned the whole thing. It was wonderful."[57]

Later in May 1988—the date is unrecorded—Arthur Gelb, the managing editor of the *New York Times* and for many years Craig's protector and defender, called him in for a meeting. Gelb told him that it was time for him to go.

17

Fate

What was he now? The person and the public figure seemed, to Craig, both to have been destroyed.

Naturally there had to be yet another multi-chef gala dinner, this one truly a farewell, "to honor Craig Claiborne, who recently announced his retirement as food editor of the *New York Times*." Was he dead? Maybe not quite. "Mr. Claiborne, who is widely credited with pioneering serious restaurant criticism in American newspapers, was asked to choose an all-star squad of chefs. . . . He did so with élan."[1] But in a way he *was* dead. Thenceforward the public Craig Claiborne would exist only in memory, in his books, in the thousands and thousands of delicious things he had taught his readers to make and to love, in the vastness of the world he had created. Wasn't that enough?

The agony for the man Craig was that the public figure Craig Claiborne was now irrevocably severed from himself. He could not expect *maîtres d'hôtel* to fawn as once had been reflexive. A great many "friends" had silently floated away. The telephone posed its implacable demand: He would have to stop and think before he spoke. He was no longer Craig Claiborne of the *New York Times*.

What could he be, then? He would be the partner, for life, of Jim Dinneen. "It's the clearest thing in the world," he told a young journalist named Dan Perlman.* "I'm totally faithful to him, and he is to me. It's

* On July 6, 1991, Craig met Perlman at a bus stop on Long Island, and what Craig must have hoped was going to be a casual tryst turned into a formal taped interview for a magazine called *Genre* (although the piece was never published).

James Dinneen.

been an incredible relationship. All I ever wanted. He's the kindest, gentlest, most thoughtful, considerate man." Craig's old, true friends knew that Jim's affection for Craig was genuine, but only so deep. Jim was never going to leave his family. Craig believed that he would, however, and then they both would be new men. Craig was sixty-eight, Jim sixty-five, yet why should it be too late? Alone in the watches of the night, Craig drank his dread away.

"What do you see in the future for you?" Perlman asked. "What's next?"

"Death," Craig answered. "That's the only thing left for me." But then he laughed, and said, "No, I don't know. Well, having Jim for a friend. That's what I live for. To be with him."

In the first couple of years of Craig's unemployment, Jim found a lot of time for Craig. They went to Florence, to Puerto Vallarta, to Casablanca, to Paris, always flying first class, always staying in the best hotels, dining at the best restaurants. They spent several weekends at what had become their own special refuge, the ultra-epicurean, decorated-to-a-fare-thee-well Inn at Little Washington in Washington, Virginia.[2]

In Craig's pocket calendar for December 28, 1989, dinner at Le Cirque: "Jim!" It had been nine and a half years, and the name still called for an exclamation point. But Jim did have his other life; he could not be with Craig all the time.

Defendant in custody: from 8:45 PM February 9, 1990 To 0:00 AM
    February 10, 1990
LOCAL CRIMINAL COURT
TOWN OF EAST HAMPTON
THE PEOPLE OF THE STATE OF NEW YORK
AGAINST
(1) CRAIG CLAIBORNE (69)

... COUNT # 1 DRIVING WHILE INTOXICATED ...
.10 OF ONE PERCENTUM OR MORE BY WEIGHT OF ALCOHOL IN HIS
    BLOOD, TO WIT: .13% ...

... The defendant's breath smelled of an alcoholic beverage, his eyes were bloodshot, speech was slurred, and he was unsteady on his feet while walking, and/or standing.[3]

From: Craig Claiborne
To: [his Alcoholics Anonymous sponsor]
    ... [On] the evening of February 9 of the current year [1990] ... I had gone to dinner at O'Mally's restaurant in East Hampton and on arrival, I drank a glass of vodka with soda. When I left the bar, an old friend asked to buy me a drink. I joined him for a second glass and went to my table. I ordered a hamburger and a glass of red wine. I paid my bill and left to drive home. A few blocks away (in front of Il Monastero Restaurant on Main Street), I drove through a yellow light which is quite unaccustomed for me. I studiously observe traffic signals. A parked car on my right drove away from the curb into the center lane and I struck the car which would be called in common parlance, a fender-bender. Within second[s] three police cars

arrived and an officer gave me a breathalyzer. I barely flunked and he took me to the police station. I was put in jail and spent the night awake. I was arraigned the following morning. Shortly thereafter I reported for seven weeks to drinking drivers' classes at Riverhead and was then assigned for consultation at Catholic Charities in Bridgehampton. [My counselor] then proposed that I go to weekly sessions to Alcoholics Anonymous meetings which I have done for the past several months.

My opinion, for what [it] is worth, is this: I think Alcoholics Anonymous is one of the greatest, most positive forces ever created in America. It has been a life-saving institution for countless thousands. But I do not feel that I belong there. The primary thing it has convinced me of is that I am not an alcoholic.[4]

Two weeks after his arrest, Craig was in Jacksonville, Florida, to judge a "Healthy Heart Cooking Contest." Dr. David Hess of the Jacksonville Cardiovascular Clinic offered Craig a free PET scan, and Craig accepted. In a letter dated February 26, 1990, thanking Craig for officiating at the contest, Dr. Hess wrote that a colleague, presumably a cardiologist, had already spoken with Craig's physicians (plural), and that he (Hess) had forwarded Craig's test results to Rechtschaffen. "Although we did not expect to find a problem in the blood flow pattern of your heart," Hess's letter continued, "we hope that perhaps by finding the problem we may have 'headed off' a heart attack that might have been lurking in your near future."[5]

Ed Giobbi isn't certain whether or not Craig even discussed the results of the PET scan with Rechtschaffen, but he is certain that Craig took no action whatever, and continued drinking at his usual pace.

Not quite a month later—on March 24, 1990, at ten o'clock at night— Craig was in the emergency room at Roosevelt Hospital, having been mowed down by a New York City taxi. The hospital report lists multiple bruises, a broken fibula (the smaller bone of the lower leg), and some sort of head injury.

The doctors sent Craig home with a form stating, "You have suffered a head injury,"[6] and advising him to see his own physician promptly. It is to be hoped, but is not known, that he did so.

For Craig's seventieth birthday, Yanou Collart arranged the most spectacular tribute dinner yet—three days of lucullan feast under the

Save the date !

Craig Claiborne's
Seventieth Birthday

Tuesday, September 4, 1990

at Louis XV
Hôtel de Paris - Monte-Carlo

Yanou Collart   Alain Ducasse

Invitation to Craig's seventieth-birthday party.

direction of Alain Ducasse at his three-star restaurant Le Louis XV, in Monte Carlo's Hôtel de Paris. (By coincidence, this was the very kitchen that had furnished the chef for the French Pavilion restaurant at the 1939 World's Fair—which had evolved into Craig's beloved Le Pavillon.) The list of chefs for the 1990 gala was the most stellar yet:

Juan Mari Arzak, Restaurante Arzak, San Sebastián
Paul Bocuse, Restaurant Paul Bocuse, Collonges-au-Mont-d'Or
Daniel Boulud, Le Cirque, New York
Frédy Girardet, Girardet, Crissier, Switzerland
Marcella and Victor Hazan, Venice
David Keh, David K's, New York
Diana Kennedy, Zitacuaro, Mexico
Gualtiero Marchesi, Ristorante Gualtiero Marchesi, Milan
Zarela Martinez, Zarela, New York
Robert McGrath, The Four Seasons, Houston
Mark Miller, Coyote Café, Santa Fe, New Mexico

Patrick O'Connell, The Inn at Little Washington, Washington,
    Virginia
Jean-Louis Palladin, Jean-Louis at the Watergate, Washington, D.C.
Georges Perrier, Le Bec-Fin, Philadelphia
Alfred Portale, Gotham Bar and Grill, New York
Paul Prudhomme, K-Paul's, New Orleans
Seppi Renggli, The Sea Grill, New York
Maurizio Santin, Antica Osteria del Ponte, Milan
Jimmy Schmidt, the Rattlesnake Club, Detroit
Jacques Thorel, L'Auberge Bretonne, La Roche-Bernard
Antoine Westermann, Buerehiesel, Strasbourg
Jasper White, Jasper's, Boston
Eckart Witzigmann, Aubergine, Munich
Pierre Wynants, Comme Chez Soi, Brussels

Considering that they all had to pay their own way there, the guests were a pretty considerable crew as well. Jim Nassikas had come all the way from San Francisco. Craig's old skipper John Smits was there with his wife. From Long Island and New York had come the songwriters Betty Comden and Adolph Green, Joseph Heller, Sam and Florence Aaron, Michael Tong, the cookware dragon Fred Bridge, Craig's former secretary Velma Cannon, the Giobbis, Pierre, and—wouldn't miss a party like this for the world—Dr. and Mrs. Joseph Rechtschaffen. A couple of dozen restaurateurs and noncooking chefs were also in attendance. Collart had put together more than forty sponsors, including the Hôtel de Paris, Mumm Champagne, and trusty old American Express. Craig and Jim flew to Paris on the Concorde, and arrived in Monte Carlo by helicopter.

The festivities—all covered by the *Times,* to be sure[7]—kicked off with a cocktail reception and a sort of Trader Vic's–ish dinner at a restaurant on the beach. For the next day, stepping up a few notches, Collart had organized a little garden party, at the nine-garden Villa Éphrussi de Rothschild in St.-Jean-Cap-Ferrat, with regional specialties from all the chefs and a hundred-odd cheeses. Then came the big event, dinner at Le Louis XV. The menu included

a heady bouillon perfumed with truffles and garnished with tiny, gossamer gnocchi . . . a warm salad composed of langoustines, cuttlefish, clams, lobster and octopus . . . seared hake on a bed of buttery fresh white beans and sweet red peppers, sharpened with a touch of chili and a splash of aged vinegar and garnished with fried parsley and garlic . . . spit-roasted Pauillac lamb rubbed with sage, with simmered kidneys and sautéed baby vegetables . . . wild strawberries in a warm strawberry juice with Mr. Ducasse's famous mascarpone sorbet. A layered frozen confection of chocolate mousse, coffee ice and mocha mousse was Mr. Ducasse's version of birthday cake. Ten wines accompanied the dinner, beginning and ending with Champagnes and including a 1983 Château Guiraud Sauternes poured from imperials, which are the equivalent of eight bottles.[8]

§

In February 1991, Craig was diagnosed with an aneurysm of the abdominal aorta—a ballooning of the primary vessel carrying blood from the heart to the abdomen and legs. Dr. Simon Whitney, a physician and lawyer at Baylor Medical School, has elucidated this and all the subsequent medical events in Craig's life (insofar as they are knowable; the evidence is fragmentary). If an aortic aneurysm ruptures, Whitney explains, there can be massive internal hemorrhage, which usually means rapid death. Craig's cardiologist recommended surgery to repair the aneurysm. After consulting with the cardiologist, Craig met with Joseph Rechtschaffen. After that, Craig chose to postpone the surgery, and he continued to postpone it.

"That doctor of his just let him get away with it," says Ed Giobbi, who consistently refuses to speak Rechtschaffen's name. "Kept on socializing with him, of course. And Craig kept on drinking."

Craig posted a letter to Ferdinand Metz, president of the Culinary Institute of America, on April 9, 1991, to tell Metz that he had decided to change his will. He was no longer going to leave his professional papers and his book collection to Boston University. "My library books number in the thousands," he wrote, "and I think they might make a nice nucleus for your new library when it is finally installed." These would include rare old European cookbooks, first editions of all his own work, and, dearest to him, the leather-bound journals recording and illustrating, in watercolors and drawings, three decades of meals grand and modest at

Craig's table. These were, he had written in *Craig Claiborne's Memorable Meals,* "among the great treasures of my life."[9]

Craig thought he might have one more book in him. Appalled by the barbaric behavior he witnessed every time he went to a restaurant, by "a society that seems to believe that manners have no place in the order of things," he set his hand to a spare, stern little volume to be called *Elements of Etiquette: A Guide to Table Manners in an Imperfect World.*

> It is small wonder that people of the present generation do not know what is expected of them. In fact, for the multitudes in the age of greed, punk music, and the ME generation, nothing is expected. . . . There is no longer a widely accepted standard for public behavior. Nowhere is this loss more acutely felt than at table, for it is here that insecurity, insincerity, and insubordination rule.[10]

"It was going to be a fairly nice book," he said in his July 1991 interview with Dan Perlman. "The publisher had given me an advance for it. So I sent them the manuscript, and they didn't like it."

A rejection? Nothing like this had ever happened to Craig Claiborne.

"They wanted about twenty thousand more words. And I can't rewrite. I never have, in all my life. If I write anything once, it comes out like that. For the *New York Times* I never rewrote an article. I'm just not emotionally equipped to do it. . . . So I paid a young man who works for the local newspaper out here about $7,000 for a rewrite job. He did a very nice job. I sent that back. They didn't accept it. So I said screw it."

In fact, however, in his own good time he beat it into shape. He didn't add twenty thousand words. He kept it strict, austere, fastidious, quite consciously in the spirit of his mentor Conrad Tuor and the École Professionelle de la Société Suisse des Hôteliers. It is an exquisite little book.

Also in the Perlman interview, Craig turned to one of his favorite sources of false pride, one that now encompassed, most awkwardly, the man he loved: "I have never met someone, a straight guy, who I haven't been to bed with, who I couldn't take. I mean, I don't care how many children they have, you get anybody in the right situation, gain his confidence, and after a couple of drinks, if you're kind, he will—that's all. I mean . . . almost every man I've ever met, if I wanted to, I'd seduce and go to bed with." This was baloney, of course. And not an indication of robust mental health.

Craig's physical health continued to decline as well. He was hospitalized for a kidney infection, and had arthritis in his wrist so bad he couldn't type.[11]

His temperament was faring no better. When the James Beard Foundation chose to give him its highest honor, the Lifetime Achievement Award, Craig told them he had a prior engagement. "Naturally, we are all terribly disappointed that you will be unable to attend the ceremony to accept your award for Lifetime Achievement," the foundation's program director, Melanie Young, wrote him on March 19, 1992. She was apparently hoping for a change of mind: "We will not announce this honor until the evening of May 4."[12] Alice Waters was named Chef of the Year; Chez Panisse was the Restaurant of the Year.[13] Craig's prior engagement was a knife sharpener demonstration at a supermarket.

July 3, 1992, was the twelfth anniversary of Craig and Jim's first meeting. They spent it and the Fourth of July weekend at the Inn at Little Washington, and Craig presented Jim with a personal poem. He had not written it himself, however. He had ordered it from a company called Limerick Lane Poetryworks. "Giving us what we need to create an original poem that is truly 'yours' is easier than you think," their boilerplate ran. "To help you in organizing your thoughts for the poem, we are enclosing our standard Background Information Form, which will take only a few minutes to complete. . . . "[14]

The poem was long. Two of the verses are reproduced here. The first:

> For long months now, I have pondered,
> > And through scores of shops have wandered,
> To find a gift that's strictly "entre nous,"
> > Something great for our reunion,
> That will celebrate our union,
> > 'Til I thought of verse as an ideal thing to do.

And the last:

> Let this weekend of jubilation,
> > Celebrated all throughout the nation,

Honoring the loyalty of men forever free,
    Serve to record with skybursts blazing
Our gift so glorious and amazing,
    The boundless love that's there 'twixt you and me.

Limerick Lane Poetryworks' invoice was for $240, plus $13 in shipping charges.[15]

On February 1, 1993, Ferdinand Metz wrote a letter to Dr. James B. Dinneen—at Craig's address on Clamshell Avenue—which read in part, "On behalf of everyone at the Culinary Institute of America, especially our students, my thanks for your very generous $60,000 donation toward The Craig Claiborne Endowed Scholarship Fund."[16]

§

In late 1992, Craig had begun to find himself short of breath when he was walking. Sometimes two blocks was enough. It got worse and worse until finally, on June 17, 1993, his distress was so severe that he took himself to the emergency room at Beth Israel Hospital.[17] An angiogram (in which an injected dye becomes visible on an x-ray) showed obstruction of the largest artery supplying blood to the left ventricle of his heart—its major pump. A trickle of blood was getting through the lower section of the vessel, but nearer the end it was completely blocked. His heart function was reduced, and the heart muscle itself was weak. The evidence suggests that he had probably already had at least one heart attack.

Craig needed coronary artery bypass surgery. (The procedure is commonly acronymized as CABG. Doctors, in their typically chilling offhand way, pronounce it as "cabbage.") This was too serious to put off. Yet just as he had done two years before, Craig managed to postpone the surgery: Somehow he finagled a delay of three weeks.

Giobbi recalls that Craig's cardiologist told him he had to stop drinking immediately. Craig was also supposed to give some of his own blood to have in reserve during the operation. He did neither.

The night before Craig was to enter the hospital, Pierre Franey just happened to be walking along West Fifty-seventh Street and just happened to see his old partner and friend Craig Claiborne pitch out of the Russian Tea Room stumbling-drunk.[18]

Craig was admitted to Lenox Hill Hospital on July 6, 1993.[19] In his initial interview, he claimed that his daily alcohol intake was six ounces of wine. The doctors apparently knew better: The record of his preoperative diagnoses includes "ETOH," a code for alcohol—a warning to any subsequent doctors to be on the alert for possible alcohol withdrawal.

Craig's condition was much worse than anyone had foreseen. His coronary arteries were severely narrowed, and they were obstructed in numerous places. They showed a great deal of calcification; they were literally hardening into something like stone. These arteries supply blood to the heart itself, and when they close off, your heart muscle dies—you've had a heart attack.

He was desperately ill. Craig's operation would have to be a quadruple bypass.

The highly regarded cardiac surgeon Valavanur Subramanian opened Craig's chest the next day, July 7, 1993, splitting Craig's sternum from his collarbone to its lowest limit. The surgeon rapidly ran tubes between Craig and the Frankensteinian heart-and-lung machine that would oxygenate his blood and pump it through his circulatory system—in other words, keep him alive—during the surgery. Healthy vessels were harvested from elsewhere in Craig's chest and from one of his legs. Craig's body was cooled to about eighty-six degrees Fahrenheit, and his heart was cooled further, with ice-cold saltwater, until it stopped beating. The surgeon could then hold Craig's cool, still heart in his hands. One by one he bypassed the clogged and calcified old arteries. This is fast, exacting work, demanding intense concentration and precise, tiny stitching. In forty-nine minutes, Subramanian had replaced all four of the arteries of Craig's heart, and recoupled them to the severed conduits of his lifeblood.

Craig's body was rewarmed to normal temperature. An electric shock from a defibrillator jolted his heart back to life. His chest was stitched back together. The surgical staff counted their needles and sponges to be sure they had not left any of them inside their patient, and Craig was wheeled off to the intensive care unit in "fair" condition.[20]

When Craig returned to consciousness, he was confused; he could not say where he was or what day it was. The diagnosis was "ICU psychosis," which is not extremely unusual. His blood chemistry was out of balance, and that may have been the cause of his mental dysfunction,

275

or in Craig's case it could have been due to withdrawal from his alcohol habit. It was expected to resolve itself fairly quickly.

A week later, however, on July 14, when he should already have been discharged and on the mend, Craig was still in intensive care. He was beginning to emerge from what was recognized at that point to have been severe alcohol withdrawal; this was an extraordinarily long time for it to have lasted.

Because he continued to be confused and disoriented, a neurologist was called in to examine him. Craig described himself to that specialist as "discombobulated," and said he was missing his Scotch. He had been allowed one glass of wine the previous evening. He had had no tremors, fever, or hallucinations. The doctor reported that Craig knew where he was, and why, and the "approximate" date. His speech was "fluent and appropriate, though a bit slow and thickened." Asked how many nickels there were in a dollar, Craig said a hundred—but he might have said that on any day of his life, so bad was his arithmetic; in any case he quickly corrected himself. The neurologist's diagnosis was "toxic metabolic syndrome," meaning that the blood supply to Craig's brain did not have the appropriate blend of glucose, oxygen, and other substances vital to mental function. He recommended that Craig continue to be observed, that his physical activity be increased (from essentially zero), and that antipsychotic medication be considered.[21] Things were not going well at all.

Five days later, on July 19, Craig was examined by a doctor who was both a neurologist and a psychiatrist. He reported that Craig was "lethargic" and "poorly oriented," and did not know the name of the hospital. His speech was slurred and unclear. He was "mildly depressed." He had "mild but significant" memory problems. His tongue was deviated to the left side of his mouth.[22]

The tongue irregularity was the critical finding, and a very bad one. It could mean only one thing: Something was wrong in Craig's brain. The doctors believed that he almost certainly had one or more cerebral embolisms—pieces of plaque from the walls of his arteries that had broken loose and floated downstream until they blocked blood vessels in his brain, thereby cutting off the supply of oxygen to certain areas of it. Brain tissue deprived of oxygen will cease to function within a minute and a half, and by the time an hour and a half passes, the damage will be irreversible. This is called an embolic stroke.

On July 21, 1993, two days after Craig's neuropsychological examination, a CAT scan revealed "abnormal soft tissue density" in his chest. The radiologist reported to Subramanian that it "could represent a postoperative hematoma or abscess," and recommended a white blood cell count to ascertain whether it was an infection.[23]

Two days later, on July 23, 1993, a CAT scan of Craig's head showed "an area of decreased density in the left lentiform nucleus and right caudate nucleus suggestive of lacunar infarcts"—more strokes, deep in the brain. The report then says, "CONTINUED . . . SEE PAGE 2."

But there is no page 2 in the records supplied by Lenox Hill Hospital, so what happened next cannot be affirmed with absolute certainty. Ed Giobbi, Velma Cannon, and Vivian Bucher all remember that Craig developed a severe staphylococcus infection. A sepsis of that sort can spread quickly through the body and become systemic. Staph will invade the blood, the bones, the lungs, the valves of the heart. It is an extremely dangerous disease.[24]

A patient in Craig's condition at that point would require a second surgery to deal with the infection. His chest would be split wide open once again. The accumulation of pus would be scooped and vacuumed out. The gaping chest wound would then be not closed fully, so that tubes could continue to drain out the poisons. It is major surgery, requiring intensive care and a long and perilous recovery. Ed Giobbi remembers that this was precisely what Craig underwent.

Could the infection have been prevented?

It can be all but impossible to assign blame. Who's going to know, or speak out, if someone failed to give preoperative antibiotics, or if somewhere along the line there was a violation of sterile procedure? You might be able to say that Hospital A has an infection rate of 6 percent and hospital B has one of 2 percent, and so maybe it's three times more likely that an infection at hospital A is somebody's fault. But whose? And maybe it's nobody's. Many accidents are only accidents.

But as recently as April 2011, Tina Rosenberg was reporting in the *New York Times* that "Health care workers fail to wash hands a good percentage of the times they should. Doctors are particularly bad."[25]

But but—if Craig had never had the infection, the strokes alone would probably have been enough to change his life irremediably for the worse. Nobody is to blame for those—at least nobody in the hospital.

For that tragic fate, we have to look to Craig himself, and perhaps also to his personal physician. How much did Craig's high-fat diet have to do with his heart disease? Mightn't it just as easily have been hereditary? He hadn't smoked in thirty years, and when he did, he didn't smoke much. It's true he never exercised worth a damn, and that certainly can't have helped. He wasn't overweight. And even though he hadn't been very faithful to the low-salt diet he had proclaimed a decade earlier to be his salvation, he had been on medication for his blood pressure and that had kept it down. The prime culprit in Craig's behavior was alcohol.

Yes, alcoholism is a disease. But when we look at Craig truly, when we see the power of his will in so many other things, can we deny him the power of decision over his drinking? Wouldn't that be to demean him, to make him smaller and weaker than we know him to have been? If we deny him that strength, do we not deny him also his selfhood?

His heavy drinking had almost certainly contributed to the weakening of his heart muscle. It would have suppressed his immune system, making him more vulnerable to the infection. All those margaritas and vodkas and Scotches and stingers had also made him more reckless, allowed him the denial he needed to postpone and postpone taking care of himself.

Craig's friends say that Rechtschaffen looked the other way, even drank with him. But suppose this. Suppose Craig either told his friends what he wanted them to hear, or—more likely—just heard what *he* wanted to hear from Rechtschaffen. Maybe Rechtschaffen *was* a social climber, and certainly he oughtn't to have hobnobbed with his famous patient, but there's no evidence at all that he would get really drunk with Craig. Craig saved getting *drunk*-drunk for elsewhere.

Ed Giobbi says: "I had to face it. I hated to. But Craig was self-destructive. He did it to himself."

Craig was put on intravenous antibiotics and moved to the Rusk Institute of Rehabilitation Medicine, on First Avenue. He was there for over a month, at times close to death.

Residuum

Through the last six years of his life Craig Claiborne sank slowly into darkness. His heart surgery and the subsequent infection had damaged his body irreparably. Now he began to suffer a series of transient ischemic attacks and "silent strokes." In a TIA, blood supply to a part of the brain is briefly interrupted, most typically by a piece of plaque that has broken loose from an artery or a small blood clot from the heart. Symptoms can include numbness, confusion, slurred speech, and loss of balance, but the effects are usually temporary.[1] A silent stroke is painless and unnoticeable because it does not affect motor function, but it is unlike a TIA in that the blockage of blood supply lasts long enough to cause permanent brain damage; a silent stroke commonly affects mood regulation and cognitive abilities, and doubles the risk of additional strokes and dementia.[2]

As these years passed, Craig's emotions and his thinking were intermittently unstable. The effects on his mood were nearly always bad: He would lash out in unreasonable anger, or weep and not know why. Sometimes he would talk at great length, sometimes he would hardly speak at all. He spent most of his time in his studio apartment in the Osborne.

Friends came to see him, but he was often so unpleasant to them that a number of them quit trying. He was still drinking, and they tended to attribute his slurred speech and his haywire outbursts to that, but what was going on in his heart and brain was the principal story. After all, he had always been drinking, and while doing so he had usually

A visit from Paul Bocuse, Roger Vergé, and Pierre Franey, 1994.

been charming (except with his closest friends, for whom he had always saved his worst). Also: At that time it was not well understood that heart surgery alone quite commonly precipitates major depression or exacerbates existing depression.[3] The depression in turn increases the risk of further cardiac problems, and is often associated with increased alcohol consumption.[4]

Craig was terrible to Ed Giobbi and Jacques Pépin, but they never gave up on him. "He'd be such a son of a bitch," says Giobbi, "and then I'd look at a book on his shelf, and the next week it would be in my mailbox." Jacques arranged for many of New York's best chefs to send him full-course dinners. "But he could be very crabby about that, no matter how good the food was," says Giobbi. "He always wanted to go out, even if it was to some lousy restaurant. He hated staying in."

Uncertain of his balance, Craig often kept to his wheelchair now. "There were these steps down into the street from the lobby of the Osborne," Giobbi recalls, "and it took two men to carry him down to the sidewalk, and usually that would be Jacques and me. Then we could only go to places that we could wheel him straight into. There were no handicap ramps in those days." Sometimes the doorman would pitch in, and Ellie Giobbi would take Craig to a little old-fashioned French restaurant a short way down Fifty-seventh Street.

Gael Greene, who for all her flamboyance was the one restaurant critic who most truly upheld Craig's professional standards, had worshiped him when she was younger and had now grown to love him. She came to see him faithfully in his darkness.

When Velma Cannon, his former secretary, always impeccably dressed, soft of voice, and formal of manner—characteristics Craig always admired—met Craig at a neighborhood restaurant, "He never talked about food. He always wanted to know what was going on at the *Times,*" she remembers, vibrant at the age of ninety-two. "And he said, 'Velma, I told Jim I want him to leave his wife,' and I said 'Craig, you know he's not going to do that. It would be the worst thing for you anyway.' He did love that man so much."[5]

Michael Tong also remained a loyal friend, and Craig relished the food Tong always brought him from Shun Lee. Pierre Franey came to call occasionally, but then, on October 15, 1996, having just performed a cooking demonstration aboard the *Queen Elizabeth II* en route to England, Craig's longtime partner and best friend dropped dead of a stroke.[6]

In September 1996 the *Times* published a long article headed "Etiquette: Is It Back?" The piece included a sort of bibliography that listed Craig's *Elements of Etiquette,* and noted, "This little book is wonderful on the intricacies of eating. But it is out of print and hard to find."[7] It was only four years old, but already forgotten.

Jim Dinneen arranged for nurses to attend on Craig, in the latter years around the clock, and he did visit from time to time, though in the last year or two of Craig's life, in Elinor Giobbi's recollection, Jim "seemed to have disappeared."[8] Michael Tong recalls that Jim himself was ill.[9] He may have provided financial support, and he may have visited more often than Craig's friends realized, but he was not a friend of Craig's friends and so did not confide in those who have survived. Jim Dinneen died in 2008 and left no record of his relationship with Craig.

Craig's financial situation through this time is difficult to know. Some of his friends thought he was broke, and dependent on Jim for not only medical care but his very sustenance. But Craig's brokerage statement from Lehman Brothers of April 30, 1994, showed a balance of $232,866.27,[10] equivalent to about $340,000 today, and in 1986 he had had $355,624 in retirement funds.[11] His residence in East Hampton was worth a great deal more than that, and he could have sold it quickly had he wished to: The house was, as we know, no prize, but the bay-front land was very valuable; he had sold a small piece of it in 1986 for $199,168.20.[12] In 1988 he had inherited $178,909.63 from Henry Creel's estate.[13] His income from book royalties continued to be substantial: In 1989, despite his having nothing current on the market, his adjusted gross income had been $140,643.[14] But what about medical insurance? His illnesses could have drained every last cent from his reserves and his continuing income, especially once he required twenty-four-hour nursing care. What of this, if anything, did Jim pay for? Craig told no one, Jim told no one.

Craig's will left a number of specific gifts to friends—the Soulé watch to Warner LeRoy, two Howard Chandler Christy paintings and a silver tea caddy to Sam and Florence Aaron, five antique French cookbooks to Roger Fessaguet, a set of Charles II dining chairs to the Giobbis, money to Velma Cannon, other things to others dear to him. He bequeathed his remaining books and papers to the Culinary Institute of America. The CIA bequest was meant to include the stack of large leather-bound journals that so beautifully represented the revels and feasts in Craig's East Hampton homes since 1963, comprising "menus, occasional notes about weather conditions, the artwork of friends (mostly watercolors), and the signatures of guests." They had "fill[ed] me with the joy of living a good life in the company of those who have mattered most in my life."[15] In the vulturine snatching and grabbing that were to swarm through the house on Clamshell Avenue in the days after Craig's death, however, those volumes would all disappear. Much, indeed, would find its way into the possession of suddenly once-again devoted—friends.

All else that Craig owned, including the house in East Hampton and his New York apartment, he left to Jim Dinneen. It was Jim's wife who would come to clean out the premises, assisted by one of their sons. Mrs. Dinneen would also oversee the execution of the will, and the sale of the various properties. Because she never spoke of it, whatever all that may have come to remains a black box.

On June 5, 1995, Craig managed to attend a Citymeals-on-Wheels benefit at Rockefeller Center. In the group photograph[16] he was seated next to Julia Child, who was closing in on eighty-three years old but still sprightly; Craig was not in his wheelchair, but he looked half dead.

Gael Greene organized a tribute dinner for November 27 of the same year, at Warner LeRoy's Tavern on the Green in Central Park. The invitations called it "A Hug for Craig." There were over a hundred in attendance—virtually the whole Food Establishment, colleagues from the *Times*, favorite guests from Craig and Pierre's East Hampton weekends, the Sulzberger family (the owners of the *New York Times*), Mayor Edward Koch, all of Craig's best friends. "Craig was wheeled in," wrote Greene in her memoir, *Insatiable*. "He grinned like a spoiled child on Christmas morning as he gazed around the room at the family faces. . . . Many of us stood in turn and told a Craig Claiborne story. Craig couldn't stop smiling."[17]

Elinor Giobbi recalls: "Everybody was ignoring him. He said to me, 'Ellie, I'm very unhappy.'"[18]

During these years Craig did not write at all. Briefly, he had an idea for a book on "new kinds of quiches," which he proposed to cowrite with the Giobbis' daughter, Eugenia Bone. "But then," she says, "I remember he was very red in the face, florid, and he said, 'I just can't, I can't do it.'"[19]

In 1998, Gael Greene and Michael Tong and eight other friends honored Craig at Shun Lee Palace with a Chinese New Year's banquet. "After the fifth course," however, she wrote, "he announced he was ready to go home."[20]

In the spring of 1999, Joe Luppi—one of Craig's favorite bartenders, who had come to be a personal friend—came in from Long Island to take Craig out to dinner. "I folded up his wheelchair and put it in the trunk of a cab, and we went uptown to a place called the Café Crocodile, and we had bouillabaisse and cassoulet, two of his favorite things. He ate maybe four mouthfuls. He wasn't drinking alcohol anymore. He was not quite there—he was in and out. Every so often he would pause and ask, 'How's my old friend Joe Luppi?' Like I was somebody else."[21]

More and more often, Craig couldn't speak clearly, or would become confused. In his undiminished Mississippi Delta pride he didn't like for anyone to see him when he was flustered, visibly unwell, unshaven, or not properly dressed, and would tell the doorman not to let anyone come up to the apartment.

Shortly after New Year's, 2000—when, as he had said seventeen years before, he had planned to be atop the World Trade Center with Jim to celebrate the advent of the millennium and things working out in the long run—Craig was admitted to Roosevelt Hospital, a few blocks west of the Osborne. Velma Cannon came to see him on January 22. "He was in the fetal position. I heard what we in the South call the death rattle. I knew he didn't have but a few minutes."[22]

Darkness closed over him.

CODA

The closest thing Craig got to a tombstone is a bronze plaque that Ed Giobbi designed, and he and Jacques Pépin commissioned, for the French Culinary Institute, on lower Broadway, and hung on the wall there at the closest thing he ever got to a funeral, a modest memorial service four years after his death.

Craig's ashes had been thrown into Gardiners Bay, as he had wished, without ceremony. None of his friends still living remembers who did it, or when.

His monument is in a sense invisible—too big to see: It is the gastronomic landscape he looked out across in the middle of the twentieth century and believed he might transform, and did transform.

§

Invitation to memorial service, April 26, 2004. Watercolor by Ed Giobbi.

Victor Hazan grew up in New York, the son of a furrier, but he was Italian-born, and returned to Italy to find a wife to bring back to Fifty-seventh Street. His bride, Marcella, with a double doctorate in natural sciences and biology,[1] had never cooked anything in her life, but after tasting catchup—"inedible"—and American coffee—"as though I had been served the water used to clean out the pot"—she taught herself Italian cooking.[2] Eventually she got good enough to give lessons in it, and Craig Claiborne got wind of her.

In the *New York Times* of October 15, 1970, he published an account of an "eminently delicious" meal at the Hazans' apartment. Food was just one of Mrs. Hazan's interests—she was also studying Japanese flower arranging and giving classes in ceramics—but from that day on, Italian cooking was going to be her life. Craig's article quickly led to a contract with Harper's Magazine Press, and the outcome, three years later, was *The Classic Italian Cook Book*. But Harper's, in Marcella's opinion, did a poor job of publicity, and now Julia Child stepped in. She urged her own editor, Judith Jones, to bring the book to Alfred A. Knopf and republish it, which, though it took a further three years, Jones did. It was a big hit, Marcella was a star, and four decades later, she still is; and *The Classic Italian Cook Book* remains, for Americans, the classic Italian cookbook.

Marcella Hazan was but one paradigm of Craig's unprecedented innovations: the ennoblement of the home cook. He did it again and again. In his books and in his columns, he respected expertise, no matter who you were. As one Marcella after another found her way to fame through him, American home cooks found self-respect.

It wasn't goofy or effeminate anymore for a man to cook. Cooking was no longer thought of as laborious, either, nor lonely—it could be fun, it could be communal, the heart of a party. People hadn't stood around in the kitchen like this before, laughing, watching, drinking wine, kibitzing. A kitchen like Craig's in East Hampton looked like a fun place to be, and those copper pots, those whisks, the seriously sharp chef's knives— all those things that Craig so casually and so artfully praised in his writing really did making cooking at home an entirely different experience. After the vicarious experience of Craig's big kitchen and professional equipment, people wanted their own.

The nature of dinner parties changed. They were looser, they flowed between kitchen and table. As often as not, like Craig's own in the Sunday magazine, they were *about the food*. Before Craig, in much of polite society food wasn't considered a proper topic for conversation, even while you sat at a table eating it. It was okay to smoke between courses but not to ask what that was in the aspic.

In a majority of American households, garlic had been so daring as to be almost indecent, and fresh ginger unknown. Many an Italian-American or Chinese-American family was embarrassed to serve his ancestral cuisine to guests from outside the cousinry. Craig Claiborne made ethnicity—any ethnicity—a badge of pride. The stink of a kidney or goat cheese to him was perfume. When he explored Ninth Avenue or Saigon in quest of new sensations, thousands, in their hearts, followed. What he brought home to try, they too tried, and often loved.

"Restaurant critic" had not been a job at all before Craig invented it. By the end of the twentieth century hundreds of restaurant critics had full-time (and prestigious) jobs as such, though only a few lived up to the standards he set, well described here by Robert Sietsema in the *Columbia Journalism Review*:

> Claiborne . . . established an ethical and procedural framework for restaurant reviewing [that had never existed before]: Reviews would be done by a single individual. The reviewer would set his own name to the work. He'd visit a restaurant at least three times, and each visit would involve a table of at least three or four diners, with an eye to covering the menu as completely as possible, eating some dishes more than once to test for consistency. The publication would pay for the meals, and no free meals would be accepted. Most important, perhaps, was the stricture that the restaurant critic remain anonymous. Thus, the reservation would be made under a false name, and the critic and his party would do nothing to call attention to the fact that a review was in progress.[3]

The fact that he could make or break a restaurant made him uneasy, but it was a fact, and his readers found something thrilling in the danger he threatened and equally in the prospect of discovery. Not a few would rush out to buy the Friday paper and turn first to Craig's latest review.

The clear result of his critical rigor was a continuous increase in the quality of New York's restaurants and in others across the country. Long past was the day when a serious restaurant in New York might dare to substitute specks of black olive in place of truffles. "Great cuisine in the French tradition and elegant table service"—Craig's words in the piece that made him famous[4]—had *not* "passed from the American scene." The featureless desert that Craig had predicted forty years before his death was precisely what the American gastronomic landscape was *not*, least of all in Craig's adopted hometown—in good measure thanks to him. Menus were *not* "as stereotyped as those of a hamburger haven." Far from it: By the time Craig left the *Times*, New York was teeming with restaurants as varied as the city's clans, cults, allegiances, and heritages. From the Bronx to the Battery were Chinese restaurants galore, many of them specializing in regional traditions, including the fiery Sichuanese that Craig had done so much to popularize. Virtually every corner of Italy was represented. Japanese cuisine of high refinement was easily had. There were Brazilian, Vietnamese, Cuban-Chinese, Swiss, Swedish, and Syrian restaurants. No longer were Greek, Indian, and Mexican food served only in cheap joints: Luxurious iterations of each were thriving. With its modernist design and restrained, unaffectedly elegant food, The Four Seasons had redefined formal American dining. New York's breathtakingly rude French restaurants had had to learn to be polite. Particularly since the opening of Danny Meyer's Union Square Café in 1985, no new restaurant could hope to succeed without genuine, open-hearted hospitality.

In Craig Claiborne's columns Diana Kennedy had shown that Mexican food was infinitely more various and complex than the taco-enchilada-refried-bean routine that was all that most Norteamericanos had known of it. Paul Prudhomme had made the previously all but unknown Cajun repertoire familiar. Edna Lewis's Southern cooking had inspired countless Yankees. The Troisgros brothers' nouvelle cuisine was now accessible to ambitious American home cooks (though still not easy). Wolfgang Puck's unique hybridization of French, Italian, and Oriental techniques no longer seemed strange. When Craig left the scene, Pierre Franey was publishing his own cookbooks and soon would have his own TV series. Julia Child, of course, was still charming millions on hers, and Jacques Pépin, having published at least half a dozen books of his own, would soon be co-starring with Julia. Ed Giobbi had introduced Craig to the dandelion's deep-red Italian cousin *radicchio,* and a good many other first-time-evers, and now he was winding up work on a cookbook, too, *Pleasures of the Good Earth.*

Basil, pine nuts—hence *pesto genovese.* Arugula, balsamic vinegar. Prosciutto di Parma. *Crème fraîche, nuoc mam, epazote.* Cilantro. *Porcini.* Macadamia nuts. The Cuisinart. The *salad spinner,* for heaven's sake. Almost nobody had ever heard of any of these till Craig wrote about them. As for the recipes, he introduced literally thousands to his readers. He had set new standards of clarity and precision in cookbook writing, and for diversity no cookbook writer had ever come near the range of his work. To this day *The New York Times Cook Book* of 1961 remains one of the two or three standard reference works that belong in every home cook's kitchen, and it has never stopped selling strongly.

When new gastronomic possibilities arose, it was Craig Claiborne—and for many years he virtually alone—who brought them before the

American public. Here too he was in the position of arbiter. When the nouvelle cuisine was electrifying France, for example, and soon was invading the United States in often grotesquely distorted form, Craig took on the task of defining and explaining the real thing and attempting to make something resembling it practicable for Americans. The task of discrimination and education that he undertook was particularly difficult because there was so much nonsense flying around at the time, but that was what you knew you could count on him for. You could trust Craig Claiborne. He made cooking daring, an exploration, sometimes rather daunting, but he convinced you that the adventure would be nothing to fear.

If he could plunge into the street markets of Marrakesh, Marseille, and Oaxaca, why not you? When he wrote that the great three-star chefs of France loved nothing better than to be asked in advance to cook what they wished for a naïve young couple who had never before dined in such style, young couples wrote those letters and dined in bliss, coddled by charming waiters, delighted by little extra courses run out steaming from the kitchen by the chef himself. Craig expressed his own pleasure and ease so gently that in situations where uncertainty and trepidation might have been natural to a newcomer, his readers' anxieties floated away.

Craig's legacy has been changing ceaselessly, becoming less recognizably his. The roast *canard Bigarade* that he mastered at Lausanne may have given way to a rare *magret* with a quick Grand Marnier *déglaçage,* which in turn may have given up its place to an artful composition of mosaic, julienne, and bright squiggles, and that dish, now, in Spain, perhaps, or Chicago, may have sublimated to an abstraction, its components deconstructed to smoke, vapor, foam, gel, and a puzzle for the palate—was that a waft of burnt-orange scent, is this fast-melting gelée a decoction of duck? But at each stage of this pell-mell evolution we've been paying close attention. It's second nature for us now to want to know what the critics are saying—certainly the *Times*'s or our local paper's but also the grim invisibles of the Michelin and possibly Yelp as well. Quite a few of us even want to know how the dish is made, though we're as unlikely to try it ourselves as Craig's readers were to make an attempt at his absurdist turkey galantine of 1961.

Our world is full of restaurant critics; we're all restaurant critics. Our world is full of chefs; we're all chefs. Neither of those developments was imaginable before Craig set it in motion.

He probably would find it all a bit amusing now. It's easy to hear him saying: "I really had no *i*-dea this would get so damned *big*."

§

Well, Craig, it is that big. And when something is this big, and this permanent, and evolving all the time, it is no longer a *thing*. The world you transformed, Craig Claiborne, is the world we cook in, dine in, and talk about food in.

Here's to you.

ACKNOWLEDGMENTS

This book could not have been written without the generosity of two people possessed of deep, precise, and vivid memories, whom I must thank above all others. Diane Franey—daughter of Pierre—was only a kid during much of the time she remembers, a fact that makes her recollections all the more remarkable. Ed Giobbi was one of Craig's closest friends but never let friendship blind him to complexity and contradiction. He has an artist's mind, always studying a scene from differing angles, in light and in shade. I could never have known Craig as I believe I came to do without Ed's and Diane's insights.

Ed's wife, Elinor Giobbi; Vivian Collyer Bucher; and Craig's nephew Claiborne Barnwell and his wife, Marion, all illuminated the strange and sometimes shocking dark passages of Craig's life—and showed me plenty of sunshine too—and to them I owe thanks as well.

Marion Dulux and her colleagues at the École Hôtelière de Lausanne led me through that grand institution's present and past with extraordinary grace and hospitality—even to the extent of bringing together some of the now far-flung *professeurs* of Craig's era for me to meet. Jim Nassikas's memories of life at the school were virtually cinematic, and invaluable.

The supremely charming and intelligent Yanou Collart, who introduced Craig to the stars of the nouvelle cuisine and arranged the notorious $4,000 dinner, was a major force in Craig's life, and crucial to this book's understanding of his passion for French food. To dine in a Paris restaurant with Yanou, or just with her introduction, helps one understand even better.

Dorothy Kalins, when she was editor of *Saveur*, first had the idea that I might write about food, which I had never done, and it was her idea that I write this book. My literary agent, and friend, David McCormick, also thought it was a good idea. I wasn't so sure at first; I'm grateful to them both for persisting. David is much more than an agent. He is a guide, a man of balance, a big-picture thinker—especially good to have around if you're a writer who occasionally loses perspective.

When Georgeanna Milam Chapman was at the Center for the Study of Southern Culture at the University of Mississippi, she wrote a master's thesis on Craig Claiborne, and she has let me plunder it to my heart's content, which probably saved me a good year of research. John T. Edge, her major professor at Ole Miss and a fine writer too, put on a celebration of Craig Claiborne's life in New York in June of 2009 that showed what a challenge this elusive subject might be, and his gentle encouragement helped persuade me to take it on.

Emily Loose, my editor, has been patient when I flagged, gently corrective to my rhetorical extravagances, attentive to the most minute details of text and architecture—in short that precious rarity, a real editor. Praise be!

To my wife, Elizabeth, the best reader I've ever had—the only one who has known everything I'm trying to do in my work—I owe gratitude beyond measure.

T.M.

NOTES

Chapter 1: A Sensation

1. *New York Times,* January 6, 1958.
2. *New York Times,* April 28, 1958.
3. *New York Times,* May 10, 1958.
4. *New York Times,* April 3, 1959.
5. Bracken, Peg. *I Hate to Cook Book,* p. 14.
6. Bracken, Peg. *I Hate to Cook Book,* p. 117.
7. Bracken, Peg. *I Hate to Cook Book,*p. 117.
8. *New York Times,* April 13, 1959.

Chapter 2: Beyond the Delta Horizon

1. Claiborne, Craig. *A Feast Made for Laughter,* p. 37. Hereafter cited as *Feast.*
2. Cobb, James C. *The Most Southern Place on Earth,* p. 125.
3. *Feast,* p. 17.
4. *Feast,* p. 24.
5. *Feast,* pp. 35–37.
6. *Feast,* p. 36.
7. *Feast,* pp. 38–39.
8. *Feast,* pp. 49–50.
9. *Feast,* p. 50.
10. Dollard, John. *Caste and Class in a Southern Town,* p. 8.
11. Cobb, James C. *The Most Southern Place on Earth,* p. 175.
12. Dollard, John. *Caste and Class in a Southern Town,* p. 7.
13. *Feast,* pp. 57–58.
14. From the Craig Claiborne collection, Howard Gotlieb Archival Research Center, Boston University. Hereafter cited as "Claiborne archive, Boston University."
15. *Feast,* pp. 58–60.
16. *Feast,* pp. 58–60.

Chapter 3: War and Love

1. http://en.wikipedia.org/wiki/USS_Augusta_%28CA-31%29.
2. http://en.wikipedia.org/wiki/Naval_Battle_of_Casablanca.
3. *Feast*, p. 62.
4. *Feast*, p. 63.
5. http://www.etymonline.com/index.php?term=gay.
6. *Feast*, pp. 62–66.
7. *Feast*, p. 65.
8. Unpublished draft manuscript of *A Feast Made for Laughter* from the Claiborne archive at Boston University. Hereafter cited as "*Feast*, unpublished."
9. *Feast*, p. 70.
10. *Feast*, p. 66.
11. *Feast*, p. 91.
12. Claiborne archive, Boston University.
13. Perlman, Dan. Interview with Craig Claiborne, unedited transcript. Recorded July 6, 1991. Broadcast in edited form on Outlet Radio Network, October 22, 2004. Hereafter cited as "Perlman interview."
14. *Feast*, unpublished.
15. *Feast*, p. 75.
16. *Mississippi State Alumnus Magazine*, 1961.
17. *Feast*, p. 78.
18. *New York Times*, March 18, 1981.
19. *Feast*, p. 89.
20. http://en.wikipedia.org/wiki/USS_Naifeh_%28DE-352%29.
21. *Feast*, p. 82.
22. http://wiki.answers.com/.
23. *Feast*, pp. 93–94.
24. http://en.wikipedia.org/wiki/Marshall_islands#cite_note-14 (*Stephanie Cooke* [2009]. *In Mortal Hands: A Cautionary History of the Nuclear Age*, Black Inc., p. 168.
25. http://en.wikipedia.org/wiki/Kwajalein_Atoll.

Chapter 4: Good at Something

1. *Feast*, p. 98.
2. All: http://www.ehl.edu/eng and interview with Marion Dulux, April 19, 2010.
3. Tuor, Conrad. *Wine and Food Handbook: Aide-Mémoire du Sommelier*, p. 42.
4. Tuor, Conrad. *Wine and Food Handbook: Aide-Mémoire du Sommelier*, p. 51.
5. *Feast*, unpublished.
6. Interviews with James Nassikas, January 11, 2010, and August 13, 2010.
7. *Feast*, p. 101.
8. *Feast*, p. 103.

Chapter 5: Spring Like a Cat

1. *Feast,* p. 123
2. *Feast,* p. 138.
3. New York Public Library menu collection: http://menus.nypl.org/menu_pages/5199.
4. Root, Waverly, and Richard de Rochemont. *Eating in America: A History,* p. 321.
5. http://menus.free.fr/index_fichiers/page1719.htm.
6. New York Public Library menu collection: http://menus.nypl.org/menu_pages/7926.
7. New York Public Library menu collection: http://menus.nypl.org/menu_pages/1843.
8. New York Public Library menu collection: http://menus.nypl.org/menu_pages/23821.
9. Morison, Samuel Eliot. *The Oxford History of the American People,* pp. 789–902.
10. Root, Waverly, and Richard de Rochemont. *Eating in America: A History,* p. 321.
11. *Forbes* magazine, March 1972.
12. *Feast,* p. 139.
13. http://en.wikipedia.org/wiki/Great_Mississippi_Flood_of_1927.
14. http://menus.free.fr/index_fichiers/page716.htm.
15. *Feast,* p. 34.
16. Tyree, Marion Cabell, ed. *Housekeeping in Old Virginia,* p. 186.
17. Tyree, Marion Cabell, ed. *Housekeeping in Old Virginia,* p. 223.
18. Tyree, Marion Cabell, ed. *Housekeeping in Old Virginia,* p. 23.
19. Claiborne archive, Boston University.
20. *Craig Claiborne's Favorites from the New York Times* (volume one), p. xi.
21. *Feast,* p. 121.
22. *Feast,* p.107.
23. Canaday, Margot. "We Colonials: Sodomy Laws in America." *The Nation,* September 3, 2008.
24. *Feast,* p. 73.
25. Claiborne archive, Boston University.
26. Kamp, David. *The United States of Arugula,* p. 98.
27. Pépin, Jacques. *The Apprentice,* p. 257.
28. Bender, Marylin. "Elizabeth Howkins, Editor, Dies; Headed Times's Women's News." *New York Times,* January 12, 1972.
29. Perlman interview.

Chapter 6: Becoming Craig Claiborne

1. *New York Times,* October 14, 1957.
2. http://en.wikipedia.org/wiki/Edward_VII_of_the_United_Kingdom.
3. Tifft, Susan E., and Alex S. Jones. *The Trust,* pp. 384–385.
4. Gelb, Arthur. *City Room,* p. 249.
5. *Feast,* p. 128.

6. *Feast,* p. 130.
7. Perlman interview.
8. *New York Times,* December 7, 1957.
9. *New York Times,* August 21, 1955.
10. *New York Times,* August 26, 1955.
11. *New York Times,* June 22, 1955.
12. Clark, Robert. *James Beard,* p. 157.
13. Clark, Robert. *James Beard,* p. 283.
14. Both: Kamp, David. *The United States of Arugula,* p. 62.
15. Prial, Frank J. "What Was Eating James Beard?" (review of *James Beard: A Biography,* by Robert Clark). *New York Times,* December 26, 1993.
16. *New York Times,* September 19, 1958.
17. Centers for Disease Control and Prevention.
18. *New York Times,* August 20, 1959.
19. *New York Times,* April 2, 1959.
20. *New York Times,* December 7, 1957.
21. *New York Times,* May 29, 1958.
22. *New York Times,* February 25, 1958.
23. *New York Times,* January 6, 1958.
24. *New York Times,* October 19, 1958.
25. *New York Times,* October 28, 1958.
26. *New York Times,* November 16, 1958.
27. *New York Times,* December 1, 1958.
28. *Feast,* p. 132.

Chapter 7: Pierre

1. *Feast,* p. 142.
2. Franey, Pierre, with Richard Flaste and Bryan Miller. *A Chef's Tale,* p. 115.
3. *Feast,* p. 145.
4. *Feast,* p. 141.
5. Interview with Diane Franey, November 22, 2009.
6. *New York Times,* July 16, 1959.
7. *New York Times,* October 2, 1959.
8. *Feast,* p. 188.
9. Claiborne archive, Boston University.
10. *Feast,* unpublished.
11. *Feast,* unpublished.
12. *Feast,* p. 57.
13. *Feast,* p. 73.
14. *Feast,* p. 142.
15. *Feast,* p. 90.
16. *Feast,* p. 104.
17. *Feast,* pp. 103–106.
18. *Mississippi State Alumnus Magazine,* 1961.
19. Interview with Donald Smith, June 25, 2011.

20. *Feast,* p. 106.
21. *Feast,* p. 106.
22. Claiborne archive, Culinary Institute of America, Hyde Park, NY. Henceforth cited as "Claiborne archive, CIA."
23. Franey, Pierre, with Richard Flaste and Bryan Miller. *A Chef's Tale,* p. 60.
24. Claiborne archive, Boston University.
25. Wechsberg, Joseph. *Dining at the Pavillon,* p. 23.
26. Franey, Pierre, with Richard Flaste and Bryan Miller. *A Chef's Tale,* p. 87
27. Franey, Pierre, with Richard Flaste and Bryan Miller. *A Chef's Tale,* p. 88.
28. Franey, Pierre, with Richard Flaste and Bryan Miller. *A Chef's Tale,* p. 88.
29. Wechsberg, Joseph. *Dining at the Pavillon,* p. 203.
30. Wechsberg, Joseph. *Dining at the Pavillon,* p. 51.
31. Wechsberg, Joseph. *Dining at the Pavillon,* p. 46.
32. Wechsberg, Joseph. *Dining at the Pavillon,* p. 67.
33. Franey, Pierre, with Richard Flaste and Bryan Miller. *A Chef's Tale,* p. 94.
34. Franey, Pierre, with Richard Flaste and Bryan Miller. *A Chef's Tale,* p. 93.
35. Wechsberg, Joseph. *Dining at the Pavillon,* pp. 205–206.
36. http://146.142.4.24/cgi-bin/cpicalc.pl?cost1=100&year1=1962&year2=2011.
37. *Town & Country,* March 1963.
38. Franey, Pierre, with Richard Flaste and Bryan Miller. *A Chef's Tale,* pp. 100–105. Additional information from interview with Ed Giobbi, December 19, 2011.
39. Franey, Pierre, with Richard Flaste and Bryan Miller. *A Chef's Tale,* pp. 91–92.
40. Franey, Pierre, with Richard Flaste and Bryan Miller. *A Chef's Tale,* p. 107.
41. Franey, Pierre, with Richard Flaste and Bryan Miller. *A Chef's Tale,* p. 107.
42. Kuh, Patric. *The Last Days of Haute Cuisine,* p. 76.
43. Claiborne archive, Boston University.
44. Franey, letter to Soulé, February 16, 1960. Courtesy of Diane Franey.
45. Pépin, Jacques. *The Apprentice,* pp. 144–145.
46. Claiborne archive, Boston University.
47. Pépin, Jacques. *The Apprentice,* p. 146.

Chapter 8: Authority

1. *Feast,* p. 236.
2. *Feast,* p. 133.
3. *New York Times Cook Book,* p 6.
4. *New York Times Cook Book,* p. 27.
5. *New York Times Cook Book,* p. 17.
6. *New York Times Cook Book,* p . ix.
7. *Feast,* pp. 133–134.
8. *New York Times Cook Book,* p. 77.
9. *New York Times Cook Book,* p. 189.
10. *New York Times Cook Book,* p. 597.
11. *New York Times Cook Book,* p. 112.
12. *New York Times,* January 1, 1960.
13. *New York Times,* March 6, 1961.

14. *New York Times,* April 7, 1961.
15. *Washington Post,* February 3, 2011.
16. http://menus.free.fr/index_fichiers/page2239.htm.
17. *New York Times,* February 5, 2011.
18. *New York Times,* April 7, 1961.
19. *New York Times,* January 25, 1961.
20. *New York Times,* February 18, 1961.
21. *New York Times,* April 10, 1961.
22. *New York Times,* April 15, 1961.
23. *New York Times,* March 28, 1961.
24. *New York Times,* June 6, 1961.
25. Franey, Pierre, with Richard Flaste and Bryan Miller. *A Chef's Tale,* p. 117.
26. *New York Times,* November 26, 1960.
27. Kuh, Patric. *The Last Days of Haute Cuisine,* pp. 93–94.
28. Grimes, William. *Appetite City,* p. 257.
29. Fabricant, Florence. "La Caravelle, a French Legend, Is Closing After 43 Years." *New York Times,* May 12, 2004.
30. *Feast,* p. 132.
31. Jones, Judith. *The Tenth Muse,* p. 61.
32. Jones, Judith. *The Tenth Muse,* p. 68.
33. Jones, Judith. *The Tenth Muse,* p. 69.
34. *New York Times,* August 3, 1961.
35. *New York Times,* October 18, 1961.

Chapter 9: Attention

1. Greene, Gael. "Papa Soulé Loves You." New York *Herald Tribune* Sunday magazine, June 13, 1965.
2. *New York Times,* January 26, 1962.
3. Wechsberg, Joseph. *Dining at the Pavillon,* p. 36.
4. Greene, Gael. "Papa Soulé Loves You."
5. http://en.wikipedia.org/wiki/Happy_Birthday,_Mr._President.
6. *Feast,* p. 164.
7. Interview with Arthur Gelb, November 18, 2009.
8. Whole episode: *Feast,* pp. 134–136.
9. Chapman, Georgeanna Milam. *Craig Claiborne: A Southern Made Man,* p. 79.
10. Appointment calendar, January 7, 1963. Claiborne archive, Boston University.
11. Appointment calendar, February 19, 1963. Claiborne archive, Boston University.
12. Appointment calendar, January 2, 1964. Claiborne archive, Boston University.
13. *Feast,* p. 164.
14. *Feast,* p. 165
15. Interviews with Diane Franey.
16. Interview with Claudia Franey, February 27, 2010.
17. Gelb, Arthur. *City Room,* pp. 363–364.
18. *New York Times,* December 17, 1963.
19. *New York Times,* October 1, 1961.

20. *Chopped,* aired February 14, 2012.
21. *New York Times,* July 11, 1963.
22. The foregoing quotations combine several conversations with Ed and Elinor Giobbi.
23. *New York Times,* September 1, 1963.
24. *New York Times,* October 30, 1964.
25. *New York Times,* May 24, 1963.
26. Claiborne archive, Boston University.
27. *New York Times,* August 17, 1965.
28. *New York Times,* August 21, 1965.
29. *New York Times,* August 24, 1965.
30. *New York Times,* August 28, 1965.
31. All: *New York Times,* August 5, 1965, and *Life* magazine, August 25, 1965.
32. *Feast,* p. 179.

Chapter 10: Olympus

1. *New York Times,* October 25, 1965.
2. *New York Times,* October 25, 1965.
3. Claiborne archive, Boston University.
4. *New York Times,* December 11, 1964.
5. Grimes, William. *Appetite City,* p. 259.
6. Greene, Gael. "Papa Soulé Loves You," New York *Herald Tribune* Sunday magazine, June 13, 1965.
7. *New York Times,* June 29, 1965.
8. Greene, Gael. "Papa Soulé Loves You."
9. "Columnists: Dishing It Up in the Times." *Time,* October 29, 1965.
10. *Esquire,* November 1975. Later a chapter in Capote's unfinished novel *Answered Prayers,* 1987.
11. *New York Times,* December 17, 1965.
12. Franey, Pierre. *A Chef's Tale,* p. 116.
13. Grimes, William. *Appetite City,* p. 258.
14. *New York Times,* January 28, 1966.
15. *New York Times,* March 5, 1964.
16. Erwin, Ray. "Reporter-epicure Knows How to Order." *Editor & Publisher,* December 24, 1966.
17. *New York Times,* January 17, 1967.
18. *New York Times,* March 15, 1966.
19. *Feast,* p. 156.
20. *New York Times,* April 17, 1967.
21. Claiborne archive, Boston University.
22. Claiborne archive, Boston University.
23. *New York Times,* November 6, 1967.
24. Zuber, Amy. "Henri Soulé." *Nation's Restaurant News,* February 1996.
25. *New York Times,* December 8, 1967.
26. *New York Times,* March 2, 1968.

27. *Time.* "Reporting: Search Beyond Sadism." August 16, 1968.
28. Greene, Gael. "The Gourmet's Gourmet." *Look,* August 20, 1968.
29. Ephron, Nora. "Critics in the World of the Rising Soufflé." *New York,* September 30, 1968.
30. *New York Times,* February 19, 1968.
31. Manville, W. H. "That Anonymous Man in the Corner Can Make or Break This Restaurant." *Saturday Evening Post,* December 14, 1968.
32. *Newsweek.* "Waiter!" January 13, 1969.
33. *New York Times,* January 1, 1970.
34. *New York Times,* January 2, 1969.

Chapter 11: Quits

1. *Craig Claiborne's Memorable Meals,* p. 89.
2. http://en.wikipedia.org/wiki/Duff_Cooper.
3. Quoted in *Feast,* p. 165.
4. Claiborne archive, Boston University.
5. Martin, Douglas. "Howard Gotlieb, an Archivist with Persistence, Dies at 79." *New York Times,* December 5, 2005.
6. Claiborne archive, Boston University.
7. Claiborne archive, Boston University.
8. Claiborne archive, Boston University.
9. Interview with Jim Abbott, March 3, 2010.
10. Claiborne archive, Boston University.
11. *Memorable Meals,* p. 89.
12. Quoted in Chapman, Georgeanna Milam. *Craig Claiborne: A Southern Made Man,* p. 92.
13. *Memorable Meals,* p. 89.
14. Interview with Diane Franey, November 22, 2009.
15. *Memorable Meals,* p. x.
16. *New York Times,* January 2, 1969.
17. http://en.wikipedia.org/wiki/The_Osborne.
18. *New York Times,* December 24, 1968.
19. Greene, Gael. "How Not to Be Humiliated in Snob Restaurants." *New York,* April 13, 1970.
20. *New York Times,* May 28, 1970.
21. *Feast,* p. 210.
22. *New York Times,* October 15, 1970.
23. *New York Times,* November 14, 1970.
24. *New York Times,* December 6, 1970.
25. *New York Times,* December 10, 1970.
26. *New York Times,* December 3, 1970.
27. *New York Times,* December 12, 1970.
28. *New York Times,* December 15, 1970.
29. *New York Times,* December 16, 1970.
30. *Feast,* p. 212.

Chapter 12: Prodigal

1. *The Chinese Cookbook,* p. xiv.
2. *The Chinese Cookbook,* p. xxi.
3. *Harper's Bazaar,* June 1972.
4. Claiborne archive, Boston University.
5. *New York Times,* October 29, 1972.
6. *Feast,* p. 213.
7. *Craig Claiborne Journal,* November 1, 1972.
8. *Craig Claiborne Journal,* July 15, 1973.
9. *Craig Claiborne Journal,* May 15, 1973.
10. Kleiman, Dena. "Allons Enfants! Chefs Mark Bastille Day," *New York Times,* July 22, 1973.
11. *Craig Claiborne Journal,* July 15, 1973.
12. *Craig Claiborne Journal,* January 1, 1974.
13. Claiborne archive, Boston University.
14. Villas, James. "The Wave of the Future May Be Gravy." *New York Times,* August 12, 1973.
15. *New York Times,* May 31, 1973.
16. *New York Times,* June 1, 1973.
17. *New York Times,* July 20, 1973.
18. *New York Times,* August 20, 1973.
19. *Craig Claiborne Journal,* October 1, 1972.
20. *New York Times,* December 7, 1973.
21. *Feast,* p. 214.
22. *New York Times,* December 7, 1973.
23. *Feast,* pp. 214–215.

Chapter 13: La Nouvelle Cuisine

1. *New York Times,* January 20, 1974.
2. Hess, Karen, and John Hess. *The Taste of America,* p. 156.
3. All: Claiborne archive, Boston University.
4. *New York Times,* June 20, 1974.
5. *Craig Claiborne's Favorites from the New York Times,* p. 195.
6. *Craig Claiborne's Favorites from the New York Times,* p. 195.
7. Claiborne archive, Boston University.
8. http://www.kqed.org/w/theapprentice/movie.html.
9. *Feast,* p. 165.
10. Interview with Florence Aaron, February 20, 2010.
11. Interview with Florence Aaron, February 20, 2010.
12. *New York Times,* December 9, 1974.
13. *New York Times,* February 10, 1975.
14. *New York Times,* February 23, 1975.
15. *New York Times,* February 2, 1975.

16. *New York Times,* February 9, 1975.
17. *New York Times,* February 3, 1975.
18. *New York Times,* February 12, 1975.
19. *New York Times,* February 5, 1975.
20. *New York Times,* February 17, 1975.
21. *New York Times,* February 24, 1975.
22. *New York Times,* February 26, 1975.
23. Goodman, Mark. "Craig Claiborne Loves to Cook and Tell—The World." *People,* January 13, 1975.
24. *New York Times,* August 1, 1974.
25. *New York Times,* June 20, 1974.
26. Interview with Yanou Collart, January 6, 2011.
27. *New York Times,* August 22, 1974.
28. Robertson, Nan. *New York Times,* February 25, 1975.
29. *New York Times,* June 30, 1975.
30. Gringoire, Théodore, and Louis Saulnier. *Le Répertoire de la Cuisine,* pp. 93–109.
31. *Michelin France 1974,* p. 21.
32. http://www.gaultmillau.fr/history.jsp.
33. http://www.gaultmillau.fr/history.jsp.
34. *New York Times,* June 20, 1974.
35. http://www.gaultmillau.fr/history.jsp. Translation by the author.
36. Kifner, John. *New York Times,* September 5, 1975.
37. http://www.bocuse.fr/paul-bocuse.aspx.
38. Claiborne and Franey. *Classic French Cooking,* p. 109.
39. *New York Times,* June 10, 1976.
40. http://www.figandolive.com/rogerverge.php.
41. http://senga50.canalblog.com/archives/2009/10/09/15360421.html.
42. Chapel, Alain. *La Cuisine C'est Beaucoup Plus que des Recettes,* p. 130.
43. Chapel, Alain. *La Cuisine C'est Beaucoup Plus que des Recettes,* p. 327.
44. Greene, Gael. "Gael Among the Bries." *New York,* June 10, 1974.
45. Greene, Gael. "Eugénie les Bains: I Lost It at the Baths." *New York,* December 2, 1974.
46. Greene, Gael. "Eugénie les Bains: I Lost It at the Baths." *New York,* December 2, 1974.
47. *Craig Claiborne's Favorites from the New York Times,* p. xiii.
48. Sheraton, Mimi. *Eating My Words,* p. 126.

Chapter 14: The Feast

1. Goodman, Mark. "Craig Claiborne Loves to Cook and Tell—The World." *People,* January 13, 1975.
2. *New York Times,* April 1, 1979.
3. This and the whole story following: *Feast,* pp. 219–225.
4. Interview with Yanou Collart, January 6, 2010.
5. Roberts, Sam. *New York Times,* December 28, 2006.
6. All: *New York Times,* November 20, 1975.

7. *New York Times*, November 28, 1975.
8. *New York Times*, November 28, 1975.
9. *Feast*, p. 225.
10. http://www.alexprudhomme.com/his_work/speeches/tribute_to_julia/tribute.php.
11. Claiborne archive, Boston University.

Chapter 15: Pre-Emeritus

1. *New York Times*, May 21, 1971.
2. All: http://en.wikipedia.org/wiki/Raymond_Sokolov.
3. *New York Times*, January 18, 1974.
4. *New York Times*, September 6, 1959.
5. Sheraton, Mimi. *Eating My Words*, p. 88.
6. All: Sheraton, Mimi. *Eating My Words*, pp. 88–89.
7. Frankfurt, Harry G. *On Bullshit*, pp. 6 and 63.
8. Davis, Mitchell, "Who's Eating New York?: Craig Claiborne, The New York Times, and the Evolution of the Field of Gastronomy in America," p. 140.
9. *New York Times*, March 5, 1976.
10. Sheraton, Mimi. *Mimi Sheraton's The New York Times Guide to New York Restaurants*, 1982, p. x.
11. Sheraton, Mimi. *Eating My Words*, p. 90.
12. Binns, Brigit Légère. *The Palm Restaurant Cookbook*, p. 52.
13. Kamp, David. *The United States of Arugula*, p. 214.
14. Kamp, David. *The United States of Arugula*, pp. 213–214.
15. Sheraton, Mimi. *Eating My Words*, pp. 110–111.
16. Sheraton, Mimi. *Eating My Words*, p. 98.
17. Pers. comm., February 23, 2012.
18. Kamp, David. *The United States of Arugula*, p. 225.
19. Gelb, Arthur. *City Room*, pp. 616–617.
20. *New York Times*, November 10, 1976.
21. The 60-Minute Gourmet, *New York Times*, November 10, 1976.
22. Greene, Gael. "The Most Exciting Cooking in the World." *New York*, November 21, 1977.
23. *New York Times*, March 28, 1976.
24. *Feast*, p. 168.
25. Murrell, Peggy J. "Taste & Tell: Food Critics' Ratings Can Play Crucial Role in Restaurant Success." *Wall Street Journal*, November 2, 1978.
26. Claiborne archive, Boston University.
27. *New York Times*, June 12, 1976.
28. Rosenthal, Jacob. "The Four Thousand Dollar Dinner Controversy! The Wrong Reason . . ." *Taste*, winter-spring 1976.
29. Dorfman, Dan. "Dinner for Two: Only $5,004.20." *New York*, January 9, 1978.
30. Magida, Phylis. "The Man Who Tells N.Y. How to Eat." Chicago *Tribune*, June 26, 1978.
31. *New York Times*, September 29, 1976.

32. Commencement address, January 29, 1977. Reported in *Taste Journal*, the quarterly journal of the Culinary Institute of America, May 1977. Claiborne archive, CIA.
33. Claiborne archive, Boston University.
34. Claiborne archive, Boston University.
35. Sheraton, Mimi. *Eating My Words*, p. 123.
36. Translation by a French friend of the author.
37. All: Sheraton, Mimi. *Eating My Words*, pp. 123–125.
38. *People*. "Who's Killing the Great Chefs of France?" December 17, 1979.
39. Pépin, Jacques. *The Apprentice*, pp. 243–244.
40. McNamee, Thomas. *Alice Waters and Chez Panisse*, p. 111.
41. *New York Times*, June 3, 1981.
42. Grimes, William. *Appetite City*, p. 288.
43. *New York Times*, April 11, 1980.
44. *New York Times*, August 12, 1977.
45. *New York Times*, July 20, 1979.
46. *Mimi Sheraton's The New York Times Guide to New York Restaurants*, p. 202.
47. *Time*. "No Papers for New York." August 21, 1978.
48. Stetson, Damon. "The Times and News Resume Publication," *New York Times*, November 6, 1978.
49. All: Claiborne archive, Boston University.
50. *New York Times*, November 28, 1977.
51. The whole introduction occupies pp. 3–44.
52. Smilgis, Martha. "Saying No to Na (sodium) Gives Gourmet Craig Claiborne a New Look and a New Book." *People*, June 30, 1980.
53. *Cat on a Hot Tin Roof.*
54. *Feast*, p. 230.
55. Brisman et al. *New England Journal of Medicine*, August 31, 2006.
56. Smilgis, Martha. "Saying No to Na (sodium) Gives Gourmet Craig Claiborne a New Look and a New Book." *People*, June 30, 1980.
57. http://en.wikipedia.org/wiki/Cerebral_aneurysm.

Chapter 16: Love and Remembrance

1. *Craig Claiborne's Gourmet Diet*, pp. 3–4.
2. *Craig Claiborne's Gourmet Diet*, p. 8.
3. Interview with Ed Giobbi, November 19, 2009.
4. Interview with Vivian Bucher, October 1, 2011.
5. Pépin, Jacques. *The Apprentice*, pp. 256–257.
6. Interview with Elinor Giobbi, May 14, 2010.
7. Interview with Ed Giobbi, May 14, 2010.
8. Pépin, Jacques. *The Apprentice*, p. 257.
9. Interview with Florence Aaron, February 20, 2010.
10. Interview with Arthur Gelb, November 18, 2009.
11. All the above: *Orlando Sentinel*, January 6, 2005.
12. http://www.newsmeat.com/fec/bystate_detail.php?st=FL&last=DINNEEN&first=James.

13. Receipts from Villa St-Jean, Claiborne archive, Boston University.
14. Anderson, Scott P. "Craig Claiborne: An Elegant Epicure Talks about His Recipe for Success." *The Advocate,* January 6, 1983.
15. *New York Times,* April 22, 1981.
16. *New York Times,* May 21, 1980.
17. *New York Times,* April 28, 1980.
18. *New York Times,* April 9, 1980.
19. Schweid, Richard. *Catfish and the Delta,* p. 164.
20. Schweid, Richard. *Catfish and the Delta,* p. 8.
21. Fausset, Richard, and Richard Simon. "Mississippi Catfish Farmers Say Vietnam Is Sinking Their Business," *Los Angeles Times,* June 16, 1992.
22. *New York Times,* November 11, 1981.
23. *Feast,* p. 20.
24. Claiborne archive, Boston University.
25. Claiborne archive, Boston University.
26. Conway, Martin A., and Christopher W. Pleydell-Pearce. "The Construction of Autobiographical Memories in the Self-memory System." *Psychological Review,* vol. 107(2), April 2000, pp. 261–288.
27. Interview with Arthur Gelb, November 18, 2009.
28. Chapman, Georgeanna. *Craig Claiborne,* 2008.
29. Ferretti, Fred. "36 Chefs Go to East Hampton to Prepare Birthday Banquet," *New York Times,* September 5, 1982.
30. All this comes from Ferretti's *Times* article as well.
31. Carter, Sylvia. "A Celebrated Cook's Sometimes Spicy Confessions." *Newsday,* August 15, 1982.
32. Fremont-Smith, Eliot. "Sonstroke." *The Village Voice,* August 24, 1982.
33. Skow, John. "Memoirs of a Happy Man." *Time,* September 13, 1982.
34. Reed, Rex. "Books: Food, Glamour." *New York Times,* September 22, 1982.
35. Fussell, Betty Harper. "He Likes to Write and Likes to Cook." *New York Times Book Review,* October 10, 1982.
36. Claiborne archive, Boston University.
37. Hausen, Roslyn White. "Claiborne: A Country Boy at Heart." Stuart (Fla.) *News Accent,* April 7, 1982.
38. Anderson, Scott P. "Craig Claiborne: An Elegant Epicure Talks about His Recipe for Success." *The Advocate,* January 6, 1983.
39. Claiborne archive, Boston University.
40. Personal communication, January 23, 1982. Claiborne archive, Boston University. Quoted in Chapman, *Craig Claiborne,* 1988.
41. *Cooking with Craig Claiborne and Pierre Franey,* p. vii.
42. *Cooking with Craig Claiborne and Pierre Franey,* p. 296.
43. *Cooking with Craig Claiborne and Pierre Franey,* p. viii.
44. *New York Times,* May 18, 1983.
45. *New York Times,* May 30, 1983.
46. *New York Times,* December 18, 1983.
47. *New York Times,* December 7, 1986.
48. *New York Times,* January 4, 1987.
49. Kamp, David. *The United States of Arugula,* p. 289.

50. *Shorter Oxford English Dictionary.*
51. http://en.wikipedia.org/wiki/Tuinal.
52. National Institutes of Health (www.nlm.nih.gov).
53. Interview with Ed Giobbi, December 16, 2011.
54. National Institutes of Health.
55. *Craig Claiborne's Southern Cooking,* pp. xiii–xix.
56. *New York Times,* January 20, 1988.
57. Email to the author, September 17, 2011.

Chapter 17: Fate

1. Miller, Bryan. "12-Chef Farewell Meal for Claiborne," *New York Times,* May 20, 1988.
2. Various travel documents. Craig Claiborne archives, Boston University, and Culinary Institute of America.
3. Claiborne archive, CIA.
4. Courtesy of Craig Barnwell Skales.
5. Claiborne archive, CIA.
6. Claiborne archive, CIA.
7. Fabricant, Florence. "At a Gathering of Top Chefs, the Food Gets Star Billing," *New York Times,* September 5, 1990.
8. Fabricant, Florence. "At a Gathering of Top Chefs, the Food Gets Star Billing," *New York Times,* September 5, 1990.
9. *Craig Claiborne's Memorable Meals,* p. vii.
10. *Craig Claiborne's Memorable Meals,* p. ix.
11. Letter to Yanou Collart, June 17, 1992. Claiborne archive, CIA.
12. Claiborne archive, CIA.
13. Keegan, Peter O. "Waters, Chez Panisse Grab Top Beard Awards," *Nation's Restaurant News,* May 25, 1992.
14. Kracht, Alvin R. Letter to Craig Claiborne, February 21, 1992. Claiborne archive, CIA.
15. All: Craig Claiborne archive, CIA.
16. Craig Claiborne archive, CIA.
17. All the medical information regarding this incident comes from Beth Israel Hospital records in the Claiborne archive, CIA.
18. Interview with Ed Giobbi, November 19, 2009.
19. All the medical information comes from the records of Lenox Hill Hospital.
20. All of surgery report: Raja Skantharaja, M.D.
21. Signature on report is illegible.
22. Shapiro, Mortimer F., M.D, Lenox Hill Hospital, July 19, 1993.
23. Dillon, Evan H., M.D, Department of Radiology, Lenox Hill Hospital, July 27, 1993.
24. http://www.medicinenet.com/staph_infection/article.htm.
25. Rosenberg, Tina. "Better Hand-washing Through Technology." *New York Times,* April 25, 2011.

Chapter 18: Residuum

1. Transient Ischemic Attack Information Page, National Institute of Neurological Disorders and Stroke, National Institutes of Health, updated July 29, 2011.
2. Vermeer, et al. "Silent Brain Infarcts: A Systematic Review." *Lancet Neurology,* July 6, 2007.
3. Khawaja, Imran Shuja, et al. "Depression and Coronary Artery Disease." *Psychiatry,* January 2009.
4. Pozuelo, Leo, et al. "Depression and Heart Disease." *Cleveland Clinic Journal of Medicine,* January 2009.
5. Interview with Velma Cannon, September 24, 2011.
6. Prial, Frank J. "Pierre Franey, Whose Lifelong Love of Food Led to Career as Chef and Author, Dies at 75." *New York Times,* October 16, 1996.
7. Yazigi, Monique P. "Etiquette: Is It Back?" *New York Times,* September 22, 1996.
8. Interview with Elinor Giobbi, May 14, 2010.
9. Interview with Michael Tong, February 18, 2011.
10. Claiborne archive, Boston University.
11. Letter from Galef and Jacobs, attorneys, November 12, 1986. Claiborne archive, CIA.
12. Letter from Galef and Jacobs, attorneys, November 12, 1986. Claiborne archive, CIA.
13. Claiborne archive, CIA.
14. Claiborne archive, CIA.
15. *Craig Claiborne's Memorable Meals,* pp. vii–viii.
16. Reproduced in Greene, Gael, *Insatiable,* between pages 112 and 113.
17. Greene, Gael. *Insatiable,* pp. 153–154.
18. Interview with Elinor Giobbi, May 14, 2010.
19. Interview with Eugenia Bone, May 17, 2010.
20. Greene, Gael. "The First Foodie." *New York,* February 7, 2000.
21. Interviews with Joe Luppi, November 22, 2009, and October 1, 2011.
22. Interview with Velma Cannon, March 8, 2010.

Coda

1. Seligman, Craig. "Classic Italian." *New York Times,* October 3, 2008.
2. Hazan, Marcella. *Amarcord: Marcella Remembers,* p. 71.
3. Sietsema, Robert. "Everyone Eats . . . But That Doesn't Make You a Restaurant Critic." *Columbia Journalism Review,* January–February 2010.
4. *New York Times.* April 13, 1959.

BIBLIOGRAPHY

Binns, Brigit Légère. *The Palm Restaurant Cookbook: Recipes and Stories from the Classic American Steakhouse.* Philadelphia: Running Press Book Publishers, 2003.

Bourdain, Anthony. *Medium Raw: A Bloody Valentine to the World of Food and the People Who Cook.* New York: Ecco, 2010.

Bracken, Peg. *The I Hate to Cook Book.* New York: Harcourt, Brace & World, 1960.

Brenner, Leslie. *American Appetite: The Coming of Age of a National Cuisine.* New York: Perennial, 1999.

Britchky, Seymour. *The Restaurants of New York, 1978–1979 Edition.* New York: Random House, 1978.

———. *The Restaurants of New York, 1986 Edition.* New York: Simon & Schuster, 1985.

———. *The Restaurants of New York, 1990.* New York: Simon & Schuster, 1989.

Canaday, John. *The New York Times Guide to Dining Out in New York.* New York : Atheneum, 1975.

Chapel, Alain. *La Cuisine C'est Beaucoup Plus que des Recettes.* Paris: Éditions Robert Laffont, 1980.

Chapman, Georgeanna Milam. "Craig Claiborne: A Southern Made Man." Master's thesis, University of Mississippi, 2008.

Claiborne, Craig. *Au Gourmet Cookbook.* New York: Bloomingdale's, 1956.

———. *Cooking with Herbs and Spices.* New York: Harper & Row, 1970 (a revised and enlarged edition of *An Herb and Spice Cookbook,* Harper & Row, 1963).

———. *Craig Claiborne's Favorites from the New York Times.* New York: Times Books, 1975.

———. *Craig Claiborne's Favorites from the New York Times, Volume Two.* New York: Quadrangle / The New York Times Book Co., 1976.

———. *Craig Claiborne's Favorites from the New York Times, Volume Three.* New York: Times Books, 1977.

———. *Craig Claiborne's Favorites from the New York Times, Volume Four.* New York: Times Books, 1978.

———. *Craig Claiborne's Kitchen Primer.* New York: Alfred A. Knopf, 1969.

———. *Craig Claiborne's Memorable Meals: Menus, Memories, and Recipes from over 20 Years of Entertaining.* New York: E. P. Dutton, 1985.

———. *Craig Claiborne's The New York Times Food Encyclopedia.* New York: Times Books, 1985.

———. *Craig Claiborne's New York Times Video Cookbook.* New York: New York Times and Warner Home Video, 1984.

———. *Craig Claiborne's Southern Cooking.* New York: Crown, 1987.

———. *Elements of Etiquette: A Guide to Table Manners in an Imperfect World.* New York: William Morrow, 1992.

———. *A Feast Made for Laughter.* Garden City, N.Y.: Doubleday, 1982.

———. *An Herb and Spice Cookbook.* New York: Harper & Row, 1963.

———. *The New York Times Cookbook.* New York: Harper & Row, 1961.

———. *The New York Times Cookbook, Revised Edition.* New York: Harper & Row, 1990.

———. *The New York Times Guide to Dining Out in New York.* New York: Atheneum, 1964 (with numerous updated editions).

———. *The New York Times International Cookbook.* New York: Harper & Row, 1971.

———. *The New York Times Menu Cookbook.* New York: Harper & Row, 1966.

Claiborne, Craig, and Pierre Franey. *Cooking with Craig Claiborne and Pierre Franey.* New York: Fawcett Columbine, 1983.

———. *Craig Claiborne's Gourmet Diet.* New York: Times Books, 1980.

———. *The Master Cooking Course.* New York: Coward, McCann & Geoghegan, 1982.

———. *The Master Cooking Course* (video). Universal City, Calif.: MCA Home Video, 1985.

———. *The New New York Times Cookbook.* New York: Times Books, 1979.

———. *Veal Cookery.* New York: Harper & Row, 1978.

Claiborne, Craig, Pierre Franey, and the Editors of Time-Life Books. *Classic French Cooking.* Alexandria, Va.: Time-Life Books, 1970.

Claiborne, Craig, and Virginia Lee. *The Chinese Cookbook.* Philadelphia: J. B. Lippincott Co., 1972.

Clark, Robert. *James Beard: a Biography.* New York: Harper Collins, 1993.

Cobb, James C. *The Most Southern Place on Earth: The Mississippi Delta and Roots of Regional Identity.* New York: Oxford University Press, 1992.

Davis, Allison, Burleigh B. Gardner, and Mary R. Gardner. *Deep South: A Social Anthropological Study of Caste and Class.* Chicago: University of Chicago Press, 1965 (original publication 1941).

Davis, Mitchell. "Who's Eating New York?: Craig Claiborne, The New York Times, and the Evolution of the Field of Gastronomy in America." Chapter 4 of "A Taste for New York: Restaurant Reviews, Food Discourse, and the Field of Gastronomy in America." Ph.D. dissertation, Steinhardt School of Culture, Education, and Human Development, New York University, 2009.

Dollard, John. *Caste and Class in a Southern Town.* New Haven: Yale University Press, 1937.

Egerton, John. *Southern Food.* Chapel Hill: University of North Carolina Press, 1987.

Ephron, Nora. *Wallflower at the Orgy.* New York: Viking, 1970.

Fisher, M. F. K. *Consider the Oyster.* New York: North Point Press, 1988 (original publication 1941).

Fitch, Noel Riley. *Appetite for Life: the Biography of Julia Child.* New York: Doubleday, 1997.

Flammarion, Ernest, ed. *L'Art Culinaire Français.* Paris: Flammarion, 1950. (See English version under Winer.)

Fodor's New York City. New York: Fodor's Travel Publications, 1990.

Forbes Magazine's Restaurant Guide, Volume One. New York: Forbes Inc., 1971.

Franey, Pierre, with Richard Flaste and Bryan Miller. *A Chef's Tale: A Memoir of Food, France, and America.* New York: Alfred A. Knopf, 1994.

———. *The New York Times 60-minute Gourmet.* New York: Times Books, 1979.

Frankfurt, Harry G. *On Bullshit.* Princeton, N.J.: Princeton University Press, 2005.

Friedman, Andrew. *Knives at Dawn: America's Quest for Culinary Glory at the Legendary Bocuse d'Or Competition.* New York: Free Press, 2009.

Fussell, Betty. *Masters of American Cookery: M. F. K. Fisher, James Beard, Craig Claiborne, and Julia Child.* Lincoln: University of Nebraska Press, 1983.

Fussell, Paul. *Class: A Guide Through the American Status System.* New York: Summit Books, 1983.

Gabaccia, Donna R. *We Are What We Eat: Ethnic Food and the Making of Americans.* Cambridge, Mass.: Harvard University Press, 1998.

Gelb, Arthur. *City Room.* New York: G. P. Putnam's Sons, 2003.

Gindraux, Philippe. *L'Art et la Manière: L'École Hôtelière de Lausanne.* Lausanne: Éditions Payot Lausanne, 1993.

Girardet, Fredy, with Catherine Michel. *The Cuisine of Fredy Girardet.* New York: William Morrow, 1982.

Gladwell, Malcolm. *Outliers: The Story of Success.* New York: Little, Brown, 2008.

Greene, Gael. *Insatiable: Tales from a Life of Delicious Excess.* New York: Warner Books, 2006.

Grimes, William. *Appetite City: A Culinary History of New York.* New York: North Point Press, 2009.

Gringoire, Théodore, and Louis Saulnier. *Le Répertoire de la Cuisine.* Paris: Éditions Flammarion, 1986 (original publication 1914).

Hayes, Joanne Lamb, and Jean Anderson. *Grandma's Wartime Kitchen: World War II and the Way We Cooked.* New York: Saint Martin's Press, 2000.

Hazan, Marcella. *Amarcord: Marcella Remembers.* New York: Gotham Books, 2008.

———. *The Classic Italian Cook Book.* New York: Alfred A. Knopf, 1976.

Heldke, Lisa M. *Exotic Appetites: Ruminations of a Food Adventurer.* New York: Routledge, 2003.

Hess, Karen, and John Hess. *The Taste of America.* Urbana: University of Illinois Press, 2000 (original publication 1972).

Hesser, Amanda. *The Essential New York Times Cookbook: Classic Recipes for a New Century.* New York: W. W. Norton & Co., 2010.

Heywood, Margaret Weimer, and 56 Chefs. *The Red & White Stores' International Cookbook.* Buffalo: The Red & White Corporation, 1929.

Howard, John. *Men Like That: A Southern Queer History.* Chicago: University of Chicago Press, 1999.

Howard, John, ed. *Carryin' On in the Lesbian and Gay South.* New York: New York University Press, 1997.

Johnson, Hugh. *The World Atlas of Wine.* London: Mitchell Beazley Publishers Ltd., 1971, revised 1978.

Jones, Judith. *The Tenth Muse: My Life in Food.* New York: Alfred A. Knopf, 2007.

Kamp, David. *The United States of Arugula: How We Became a Gourmet Nation.* New York: Broadway Books, 2006.

Kennedy, Diana. *The Cuisines of Mexico.* With a foreword by Craig Claiborne. New York: Harper & Row, 1972.

Kuh, Patric. *The Last Days of Haute Cuisine: The Coming of Age of American Restaurants.* New York: Penguin, 2001.

Lazar, David, ed. *Conversations with M. F. K. Fisher.* Jackson and London: University Press of Mississippi, 1992.

Levenstein, Harvey. *Revolution at the Table.* Berkeley: University of California Press, 2003.

Lévi-Strauss, Claude. *The Origin of Table Manners.* London: Jonathan Cape, 1978.

Mariani, John, with Alex von Bidder. *The Four Seasons: A History of America's Premier Restaurant.* New York: Crown, 1994.

McLemore, Richard Aubrey, ed. *History of Mississippi,* in 2 vols. Jackson: University & College Press of Mississippi, 1973.

McNamee, Thomas. *Alice Waters and Chez Panisse: The Romantic, Impractical, Often Eccentric, Ultimately Brilliant Making of a Food Revolution.* New York: Penguin Press, 2007.

Meyer, Danny. *Setting the Table: The Transforming Power of Hospitality in Business.* New York: Harper Collins, 1986.

Michelin France 1961 ("guide rouge"). Paris: Pneu Michelin Services de Tourisme, 1961.

Michelin France 1974 ("guide rouge"). Paris: Pneu Michelin Services de Tourisme, 1974.

Miller, Bryan. *The New York Times Guide to Restaurants in New York City.* New York : Times Books, 1987.

———. *The New York Times Guide to Restaurants in New York City: Revised and Expanded.* New York: Times Books, 1988.

———. *The New York Times Guide to Restaurants in New York City 1991–1992.* New York: Times Books, 1991.

———. *The New York Times Guide to Restaurants in New York City 1993–1994.* New York: Times Books, 1992.

Morison, Samuel Eliot. *The Oxford History of the American People.* New York: Oxford University Press, 1965.

O'Neill, Molly, ed. *American Food Writing: An Anthology with Classic Recipes.* New York: Library of America, 2007.

Pépin, Jacques. *The Apprentice: My Life in the Kitchen.* New York: Houghton Mifflin, 2003.

Rabaudy, Nicolas de. *La Cuisine de Chez Allard.* Paris: Éditions Jean-Claude Lattès, 1982.

Reichl, Ruth, Eric Asimov, and William Grimes. *The New York Times Guide to Restaurants in New York City 2000.* New York: The New York Times, 2000.

Rechtschaffen, Joseph S., and Robert Carola. *Dr. Rechtschaffen's Diet for Lifetime Weight Control and Better Health.* New York: Random House, 1980.

Robinson, Jancis, ed. *The Oxford Companion to Wine,* 2nd edition. Oxford: Oxford University Press, 1999.

Rombauer, Irma S., and Marion Rombauer Becker. *The Joy of Cooking.* Indianapolis and New York: Bobbs-Merrill, 1953.

Root, Waverly, and Richard de Rochemont. *Eating in America: a History.* Hopewell, N.J.: Ecco Press, 1981.

Rosten, Leo. *The Joys of Yiddish.* New York: Pocket Books, 1968.

Schweid, Richard. *Catfish and the Delta: Confederate Fish Farming in the Mississippi Delta.* Berkeley: Ten Speed Press, 1992.

Shapiro, Laura. *Something from the Oven: Reinventing Dinner in 1950s America.* New York: Penguin Books, 2004.

Sheraton, Mimi. *Eating My Words: An Appetite for Life.* New York: William Morrow, 2004.

———. *Mimi Sheraton's The New York Times Guide to New York Restaurants.* New York: Times Books, 1982.

———. *Mimi Sheraton's Favorite New York Restaurants.* New York: Simon & Schuster, 1986.

Shilts, Randy. *Conduct Unbecoming: Gays and Lesbians in the U.S. Military.* New York: St. Martin's Press, 1993.

Sulloway, Frank. *Born to Rebel.* New York: Random House, 1996.

Tifft, Susan E., and Alex S. Jones. *The Trust: The Private and Powerful Family Behind the New York Times.* Boston: Little, Brown and Company, 1999.

Tuor, Conrad. *Wine and Food Handbook: Aide-Mémoire du Sommelier.* London: Hodder & Stoughton, 1977.

Tyree, Marion Cabell, ed. *Housekeeping in Old Virginia.* Louisville: John P. Morton and Company, 1879.

Villas, James. *Between Bites: Memoirs of a Hungry Hedonist.* Hoboken, N.J.: John Wiley, 2002.

Waldo, Myra. *The Diners' Club Cookbook: Great Recipes from Great Restaurants.* New York: Farrar, Straus and Cudahy, 1959.

Wechsberg, Joseph. *Dining at the Pavillon.* Boston: Little, Brown and Company, 1962.

Winer, Bart, ed. *The Art of French Cooking.* New York: Golden Press, 1962. (English-language version of Flammarion, *L'Art Culinaire Français,* q.v.)

Zabroski, Ann. *The Cheap and Cheaper Guide to Manhattan.* Englewood Cliffs, N.J.: Prentice-Hall, 1980.

SELECTED MAGAZINE AND
NEWSPAPER ARTICLES

Abbott, Jim. "Birthplace Evokes Strong Memories." *Greenwood* (Miss.) *Commonwealth,*
July 26, 1981.
Albelli, Alfred. "Soulé's Widow Sues on 1525 Estate Law." New York *Daily News,* August
3, 1967.
Anderson, Brett. "The Natural." (New Orleans) *Times-Picayune,* July, 2005.
Anderson, Scott P. "Craig Claiborne: An Elegant Epicure Talks About His Recipe for
Success." *The Advocate,* January 6, 1983.
Arnett, Alison and Sheryl Julian. "Craig Claiborne, 1921–2000; He Changed How We
Think about Food." *The Boston Globe,* January 26, 2000.
Anson, Robert Sam. "Craig Claiborne: The Typewriter Chef." *Metropolitan Home,* April
1984.
Avins, Jenny. "The Legacy of Craig Claiborne." *Saveur,* June 2009.
Barnwell, Marion. "Craig Claiborne: Reclaiming a Mississippi Delta Legend." *Delta,*
September–October 2009.
Barry, Mimi Neal. "The Cream of the Cooks," *Mississippi,* November/December 1987.
Baumgold, Julie, "Charlotte, Star Reporter." *New York,* October 6, 1969.
Bender, Marylin. "Elizabeth Howkins, Editor, Dies; Headed Times's Women's News."
New York Times, January 12, 1972.
———. "Where the Cuisine is Haute and the Atmosphere Haughty." *New York Times,*
December 24, 1968.
Beringer, Guy. "Brunch: A Plea." *Hunter's Weekly,* 1895, quoted in the Oxford English
Dictionary supplement of 1972.
Biggers, Jane. "New York Times Food Editor's Authority Remains Unchallenged; Even
by a Wild Duck." *Greenwood* (Miss.) *Commonwealth,* April 16, 1964.
Brisman J. L., J. K. Song., and D. W. Newell. "Cerebral aneurysms." *New England Journal
of Medicine,* August 31, 2006.
"Business: Ratings from Gourmets." *Time.* September 17, 1973.
Canaday, Margot. "We Colonials: Sodomy Laws in America." *The Nation,* September
3, 2008.
Cannon, Poppy. "The Seven Faces of Papa Soulé." *Town & Country,* March 1963.
Carruth, Eleanore. "Restaurateurs Need Some New Recipes for Survival." *Fortune,*
March 1972.

Carter, Sylvia. "A Celebrated Cook's Sometimes Spicy Confessions." *Newsday,* August 15, 1982.

Cattani, Richard J. "Food Critic Retires But Keeps Cooking." *Christian Science Monitor,* June 8, 1972.

Centers for Disease Control and Prevention. "Prevalence of overweight, obesity and extreme obesity among adults: United States, trends 1960–62 through 2005–2006." Atlanta: CDC Publications and Information Products, 2009.

Claiborne, Craig. Interviewed by Mary Goodbody. "A Cook for the Times." *Cook's Magazine,* May–June 1984, 14–15.

———. Commencement address at the Culinary Institute of America, Hyde Park, N.Y., January 29, 1977. Published in *Taste,* May 1977.

———. Commencement address at the Culinary Institute of America, Hyde Park, N.Y., January 20, 1984. Published in *Taste,* summer 1984.

———. "I Love to Cook." *Family Circle,* September 1969.

———. "Table Talk with Six French Chefs." *McCall's,* June 1966.

"Columnists: Dishing It Up in the Times." *Time.* October 29, 1965.

Conway, Martin A., and Christopher W. Pleydell-Pearce. "The Construction of Autobiographical Memories in the Self-memory System." *Psychological Review,* 2000, vol. 107, no. 2.

Courtine, Robert. "The Four Thousand Dollar Dinner Controversy! The Right Reason . . ." *Taste,* summer 1976.

"Craig Claiborne, Food Writer, Dies." *Greenwood* (Miss.) *Commonwealth.* January 27, 2000.

Crea, Joe. "Claiborne: No Regrets." *Florida Times-Union,* October 13, 1983.

———. "The Making of a Televised Cook." *Florida Times-Union,* November 25, 1985.

Davis, Mitchell. "Power Meal: Craig Claiborne's Last Supper for the *New York Times.*" *Gastronomica,* summer 2004.

Diebold, Ruth. "A Feast Made for Laughter." *Library Journal,* August 1982, 1453.

Dorfman, Dan. "Dinner for Two: Only $5,004.20." *New York,* January 9, 1978.

Doty, Robert. "Growth of Overt Homosexuality in City Provokes Wide Concern." *New York Times,* December 17, 1963.

Ephron, Nora. "Critics in the World of the Rising Soufflé." *New York,* September 30, 1968.

Erwin, Ray. "Reporter-epicure Knows How to Order." *Editor & Publisher,* December 24, 1966.

"Everyone's in the Kitchen." *Time.* November 25, 1966.

Fabricant, Florence. "La Caravelle, a French Legend, Is Closing After 43 Years." *New York Times,* May 12, 2004.

Fausset, Richard, and Richard Simon. "Mississippi Catfish Farmers Say Vietnam Is Sinking Their Business." *Los Angeles Times,* June 16, 1992.

Fiori, Pamela. "'If I Could Go Anywhere in the World to Live, I'd Settle in Tuscany': An Interview with Craig Claiborne." *Travel and Leisure,* January 1983.

Frankel, Haskal. "How To Take the Nonsense Out of Cooking: Julia Child, James Beard, and Craig Claiborne at Home with Recipes." *Redbook,* October 1970.

Fremont-Smith, Eliot. "Sonstroke." *The Village Voice,* August 24, 1982.

Geracimus, Ann. "The Restaurant Papers." *Lifestyle,* November 1972.

Goodman, Mark. "Craig Claiborne Loves to Cook and Tell—The World." *People,* January 13, 1975.

Greene, Gael. "Eugénie les Bains: I Lost It at the Baths." *New York,* December 2, 1974.

———. "The First Foodie." *New York,* February 7, 2000.

———. "Gael Among the Bries." *New York,* June 10, 1974.

———. "The Gourmet's Gourmet." *Look,* August 20, 1968.

———. "How Not To Be Humiliated In Snob Restaurants. *New York,* April 13, 1970.

———. "The Most Exciting Cooking in the World." *New York,* November 21, 1977.

———. "Papa Soulé Loves You." New York *Herald Tribune* Sunday magazine, June 13, 1965.

———. "Re-evaluating Manhattan's Top French Restaurants." *New York,* March 3, 1975.

———. "Remembering Craig Claiborne." *Insatiable Critic / Fork Play* (blog), January 10, 2011.

Griffith, Dotty. "Even THE Food Critic Has to Watch What He Eats." Dallas *Morning News,* June 26, 1980.

Grimes, William. "Alice Miller, Psychoanalyst, Dies at 87; Laid Human Problems to Parental Acts." *New York Times,* April 26, 2010.

Grogins, Marilyn. "The Claiborne Touch." (Stamford, Conn.) *Fairpress,* November 6, 1985.

Hausen, Roslyn White. "Claiborne: A Country Boy at Heart." Stuart (Fla.) *News Accent,* April 7, 1982.

Hess, Karen. "Recipe for a Cookbook: Scissors and Paste." *Harper's,* October 1975.

Hodges, Parker. "I Give Craig Claiborne an Enthusiastic Four Stars." *Moneysworth,* July 7, 1975.

Howard, Theresa. "Howard Johnson." *Nation's Restaurant News,* February 1996.

Karr, John F. "Come-Out Cookery." *Bay Area Reporter,* October 14, 1982.

Keegan, Peter O. "Waters, Chez Panisse Grab Top Beard Awards." *Nation's Restaurant News,* May 25, 1992.

Khawaja, Imran Shuja, Joseph J. Westermeyer, Prashant Gajwani, and Robert E. Feinstein. "Depression and Coronary Artery Disease: The Association, Mechanisms, and Therapeutic Implications." *Psychiatry* (Edgmont), January 2009.

Kleiman, Dena. "Allons Enfants! Chefs Mark Bastille Day." *New York Times,* July 22, 1973.

Knipff, Stephan C., Nadine Matatko, Hans Wilhelm, Marc Schlamann, Matthias Thielmann, Christian Lösch, Hans C. Diener, and Heinz Jakob. "Cognitive Outcomes Three Years After Coronary Artery Bypass Surgery: Relation to Diffusion-Weighted Magnetic Resonance Imaging." *Annals of Thoracic Surgery,* March 2008.

Krebs, Albin. "Michael Field, Food Writer, Dies: Once a Duo Pianist." *The New York Times,* March 24, 1971.

Kuhn, Eric. "Craig Claiborne: Knight in Shining Flatware." *Gastronome,* August 1988.

Life magazine. "A Most Magnificent Pique-Nique." August 25, 1965.

Linden, Pat. "An Afternoon with Craig Claiborne." *The Epicure,* Spring–Summer 1969.

Long Island Home. "Gourmet Retreat." 1967.

Long Island Living. "Christmas Dinner with Craig Claiborne." December 17, 1972.

Magida, Phylis. "The Man Who Tells N.Y. How to Eat." Chicago *Tribune.* June 26, 1978.

Manville, W. H. "That Anonymous Man in the Corner Can Make or Break This Restaurant." *The Saturday Evening Post,* December 14, 1968.

Martin, Douglas. "Howard Gotlieb, an Archivist With Persistence, Dies at 79." *New York Times,* December 5, 2005.

McFarland, Betty. "Craig Claiborne on Anything but Food." *The Miami Herald,* March 10, 1985.

Mendelson, Anne. "Glossy South." *Oxford American,* Spring 2005.

Mermelstein, Susan. "A Phantasmagoria of Fine Food." *The East Hampton Star,* September 9, 1982.

Miles, James C. "Capturing the Flavor of America." *Colonial Williamsburg Today,* Autumn 1983.

Mississippi State Alumnus Magazine. "Kathleen Craig Claiborne: Mississippi State Honors Beloved Housemother." 1961.

Murrell, Peggy J. "Taste & Tell: Food Critics' Ratings Can Play Crucial Role in Restaurant Success." *Wall Street Journal,* November 2, 1978.

Myers, B. R. "The Moral Crusade Against Foodies." *The Atlantic,* March 2011.

Nesbit, Martha Giddens. "Craig Claiborne, The New York Times." Savannah *Morning News*–Savannah *Evening Press,* November 17, 1979.

"No Papers for New York." *Time.* August 21, 1978.

Papamarkou, Alexander. "Golden Door Men's Week." *Town & Country,* January 1982.

Perlman, Dan. Interview with Craig Claiborne, unedited transcript. Recorded July 6, 1991. Broadcast in edited form on Outlet Radio Network, October 22, 2004.

Powell, Mary Alice. "He Didn't Invent Quiche, But He Introduced It." *The Blade* (Toledo, Ohio), February 27, 1983.

Pozuelo, Leo, G. Tesa, J. Zhang, M. Penn, K. Franco, and W. Jiang. "Depression and Heart Disease: What Do We Know, and Where Are We Headed?" *Cleveland Clinic Journal of Medicine,* January 2009.

Prial, Frank J. "What Was Eating James Beard?" *New York Times,* December 26, 1993.

Primavera, William J. "Travels with Craig Claiborne: Over the River and Through the Woods." *Taste,* May 1977.

Rader, Barbara. "Craig Claiborne Yearns for Country Cooking." *Newsday,* December 10, 1970.

Reed, Mary. "A Week of Eating, Visiting, Preaching." *The Jackson Sun* (Jackson, Tenn.), August 15, 1982.

"Reporting: Search Beyond Sadism." *Time.* August 16, 1968.

Richman, Phyllis. "Binge of the Beautiful People: Craig Claiborne's Pig-Out at the Hampton." *Washington Post,* September 6, 1982.

Rosenthal, Jacob. "The Four Thousand Dollar Dinner Controversy! The Wrong Reason . . ." *Taste,* winter-spring 1976.

Rubin, Marilyn McDevitt. "Claiborne: A Life in Food." *Pittsburgh Press,* September 12, 1982.

Seaver, Jeannette. "The Art of Cooking." *New York Times Book Review,* January 6, 1980.

Shaw, David. "Restaurant Critics Eat Their Words." *Los Angeles Times,* December 28, 1980.

Sietsema, Robert. "Everyone Eats . . . But That Doesn't Make You a Restaurant Critic." *Columbia Journalism Review,* January–February 2010.

Skow, John. "Memoirs of a Happy Man." *Time,* September 13, 1982.

Smilgis, Martha. "Saying No to Na (sodium) Gives Gourmet Craig Claiborne a New Look and a New Book." *People,* June 30, 1980.

Tomb, Geoffrey. "The Man Who Came to Lunch." Miami *Herald,* March 3, 1982.

Vermeer, S. E., W. T. Longstreth Jr., and P. J. Koudstaal. "Silent Brain Infarcts: a Systematic Review." *The Lancet Neurology,* July 6, 2007.

Villas, James. "The Wave of the Future May Be Gravy." *New York Times,* August 12, 1973.

"Waiter!" *Newsweek.* January 13, 1969.

Wallach, Amei. "Chefs Extraordinaire at **** Holiday Lunch." *Newsday,* July 6, 1971.

Wechsberg, Joseph. "The Ambassador in the Sanctuary." *The New Yorker,* March 28, 1953.

"Who's Killing the Great Chefs of France? Mimi Sheraton Proves They Can Dish it Out But Can't Take It." *People.* December 17, 1979.

Wilson, José. "Six Authorities Discuss Pre-dinner Drinking." *House & Garden,* October 1969.

Wolcott, Jennifer. "Voice of a Culinary Master." *Christian Science Monitor,* November 29, 2000.

Woodier, Olwen. "Craig's Kitchen." *US Air,* March 1983.

Writers' Digest. "Craig Claiborne: A Man for all Seasonings." April 1976.

Yaseen, Janet. "Craig! Craig Claiborne Won His Dream Job and Improved Our World." *Gastronome,* Autumn 1988.

Zimmerman, Diane. "The Great Restaurants: End of an Era?" New York *Daily News,* February 3, 1972.

Zuber, Amy. "Henri Soulé." *Nation's Restaurant News,* February 1996.

CREDITS

INDEX

Page numbers in *italics* refer to illustrations.

ABOUT THE AUTHOR

Thomas McNamee is the author of the *New York Times* bestseller *Alice Waters and Chez Panisse*. His essays, poems, and natural history writing have been published in *The New Yorker, Life, Audubon, Saveur*, the *New York Times*, and the *Washington Post*. He wrote the documentary film *Alexander Calder*, which was broadcast on the PBS American Masters series in June 1998 and received both a George W. Peabody Award and an Emmy. He lives in San Francisco.